D1475096

Best Practices for Technology-Enhanced Teaching and Learning

Best Practices for Technology-Enhanced Teaching and Learning

Connecting to Psychology and the Social Sciences

Edited by

Dana S. Dunn, Janie H. Wilson,
James E. Freeman, Jeffrey R. Stowell

OXFORD
UNIVERSITY PRESS

2011

OXFORD
UNIVERSITY PRESS

Oxford University Press, Inc., publishes works that further
Oxford University's objective of excellence
in research, scholarship, and education.

Oxford   New York
Auckland   Cape Town   Dar es Salaam   Hong Kong   Karachi
Kuala Lumpur   Madrid   Melbourne   Mexico City   Nairobi
New Delhi   Shanghai   Taipei   Toronto

With offices in
Argentina   Austria   Brazil   Chile   Czech Republic   France   Greece
Guatemala   Hungary   Italy   Japan   Poland   Portugal   Singapore
South Korea   Switzerland   Thailand   Turkey   Ukraine   Vietnam

Published by Oxford University Press, Inc.
198 Madison Avenue, New York, New York 10016

www.oup.com

Oxford is a registered trademark of Oxford University Press

Library of Congress Cataloging-in-Publication Data

Best practices for technology-enhanced teaching and learning :
connecting to psychology and the social sciences / edited by
Dana S. Dunn ... [et al.].
p. cm.
Includes index.
ISBN 978-0-19-973318-7   1. Internet in education. 2. Computer-assisted instruction.
3. Distance education. 4. Educational psychology. 5. Educational technology—Study and
teaching. 6. Science—Study and teaching. I. Dunn, Dana.
LB1051.B469 2011
371.33'44678—dc22
2010025249

9 8 7 6 5 4 3 2 1
Printed in the United States of America
on acid-free paper

For Bill Hill
Teacher, Leader, Friend

Foreword

When I was invited to write the foreword for this book, I was flattered but perplexed. Never having written a foreword before and not being especially prone to reading them, I wondered what, exactly, I had agreed to. My first action was to swivel in my desk chair and see what other people had written in forewords to other books on my shelves. The only one I found, by William Buskist in a previous book in this series (*Best Practices for Teaching Statistics and Research Methods in the Behavioral Sciences,* 2007), gave me an excellent model to follow, but I was uncomfortable with a single sample and did not have other examples at my fingertips. Or did I? What if I searched the Internet? A few words typed into the search engine and, as the French would say, *voilà*. Examples, definitions, and how-to-write-one advice. Ah technology! Some of us may be slow on the up-take, but we get there eventually.

If you see yourself in my example, thinking of technology only after trying a strategy that has worked for you in the past, this book is for you. And if you don't see yourself in my example, being either less or more technologically sophisticated than I, this book is still for you because it covers the gamut. Some chapters have the novice (technophobe, Luddite) in mind, gently urging dipping one's toes in the ocean of features available. Others have more adventurous and experienced users (technophiles, Geeks) in mind.

According to the Internet sources I consulted, it is not my job as foreword writer to point out which chapter is which–that's a job for the editors in their Introduction. But it is my job to urge you to sample at least some of the chapters. The book is not, after all, like a novel that must be read cover-to-cover to make sense of the plot. You might pick and choose from the Table of Contents based on the specific technological tools, such as presentation slides (AKA Microsoft PowerPoint®), "clickers," YouTube videos, course management systems (e.g., Blackboard Academic Suite™, Moodle™), interactive whiteboards, and virtual worlds (e.g., Second Life®); you can choose based on the type of course (hybrid, wholly on-line, wholly face-to-face) or task you face (e.g., advising, encouraging student interaction or collaboration, quizzing); or you can choose based on the authors, although I would be hard pressed not to just read the book from cover to cover if authorship were my criterion. Many of these authors are my dear colleagues. Some I have met at an earlier Best Practices conference. Others have corresponded concerning a manuscript they submitted to *Teaching of Psychology* or a resource they submitted to the Office of Teaching Resources in Psychology (OTRP). They may have served as reviewers for OTRP resources. We may have met over grading Advanced Placement tests or on the Executive Committee of the Society for the Teaching of Psychology (STP, which has sponsored this book). No matter the venue, I have come to respect their energy, their enthusiasm for the enterprise of teaching that we share, and most importantly, their expertise that they now share with you.

As I read their chapters, I was impressed by how down-to-earth these authors are. Their advice is practical. They anticipate what questions you'll have and offer answers; they anticipate your problems and offer strategies for problem-solving; they anticipate your reluctance to try something new and offer encouragement. So let me do the same: Should you read this book? Yes. It is often as important to know what does not appeal to you as to know what does, so reading about the pros and cons of the particular advances in technology these authors cover is useful information. How can you choose from the vast array of suggestions they offer? Figure out what element of your course is most in need of a fresh approach and start with chapters that address your immediate concerns. Is it worth trying to learn to use a new technology? Yes, in general, but perhaps No in a few instances, and authors of this marvelous volume tell you which is which through their empirical data and personal experiences. Both the faint of heart and the brave can wade into the technology ocean and not fear drowning, and all can learn something new from this volume. Enjoy!

Ruth L. Ault, Davidson College

Preface

The days of the mimeographed handout are over, and those of the marked up transparencies are numbered. Laptops, cell phones, and MP3 players abound. Technology is all around us and, as much as it is a cliché, it's quite true that it is always changing. Technology is also affecting how educators teach. How can teachers keep up with new and ever more recent advances? How should instructors use technology to improve teaching and learning in their classes? What technological tools are appropriate for different purposes? These and other pressing questions affect teachers in all kinds of educational settings along the secondary to post-secondary spectrum. At some point, even the most technologically-cautious instructor must take the leap and integrate some new technology into their teaching.

We developed this book to help teachers everywhere on the technology of teaching continuum—from simple to savvy to sophisticated—think about how current and emerging tools in our increasingly digital age can positively impact their students, whether close at hand or in virtual communities. Thus, this book discusses a variety of timely issues related to best practices for teaching well with technological enhancements, including:

- How teachers who eschew technology can learn to use it wisely
- Ways that technology can foster collaboration among students, as well as between students and faculty

- How technology in the classroom, including classroom response systems, can engage students so that they attend more closely to their own learning
- Teaching online, distance, and hybrid classes using course-management software
- How technology can advance a program's educational mission or aid in advising students
- Reviews of technological innovations that can be used at any level, from introductory to capstone courses
- How virtual worlds can be used as effective pedagogy
- Advantages and common pitfalls associated with using technology
- How to link traditional teaching to technological innovation
- Insights into future learning technologies

Who should read this book? Given technology's increasing sway over the educational landscape, it is not too far from the truth to say virtually any teacher, whether novice or established professional, would benefit from this book. Still, we believe that our main audience consists of college or university-level teachers and administrators, in the discipline of psychology or one of the related social sciences. That being said, faculty in the humanities and natural sciences, too, will find many helpful ideas, asides, and applications in this book that can be shaped or revised to suit different needs. Teachers in two-year or community-college settings will also find much grist for their teaching mills here. Finally, some high-school teachers who have opportunities to integrate technology into their classes or who want to use their current tools more effectively will appreciate the suggestions offered in this book. And even those who cheerfully refer to themselves as "Luddites" are apt to learn a thing or two herein.

We look forward to hearing from readers to see how they adopt or adapt the teaching materials, tools, and suggestions presented in this book in their own teaching efforts. In fact, we suspect that one of the exciting aspects of technologies in teaching is how they soon take on a life of their own in the classroom, not just as indispensable conveniences but as serious tools for enhancing what is taught and what is learned. Do keep us posted.

Acknowledgments

The development, implementation, and production of this book went very smoothly thanks to the efforts of our Oxford University Press colleagues. Our editor, Abby Gross, helped us to refine our vision for the project and to ensure that we could begin and finish on time. We are also grateful to our colleagues who organized and took part in the *Getting Connected* conference, including Bill Hill, Doug Bernstein, the Psychology faculty and CETL staff at Kennesaw State University, Janie Wilson, and the Psychology Department at Georgia Southern University.

We want to thank the peers who reviewed our project proposal and, through their constructive suggestions, helped us to develop our ideas further: David Daniel, Regan Gurung, and Tara Kuther.

As editors, each of us is grateful to those individuals who encouraged us in our work, including, of course, our hardworking authors. Dana is grateful to his family for their unstinting support and flexibility. Portions of this book were completed during his sabbatical leave from Moravian College in the spring of 2009. Janie is ever grateful to her supportive children. They always understand when she takes on just one more project. Jim is grateful for the love of his wife, children, their spouses, and grandchildren; however, even though only one of them knows anything about this project. Jeff is very appreciative of the support of his busy wife and children, and the collegiality and friendship of many members of the Society for the Teaching of Psychology (STP). And finally, the four of us are delighted to dedicate this book to our colleague and friend, Bill Hill, without whom our work and that of our authors herein would not have been possible. We are grateful, Bill. Thank you, indeed.

Dana S. Dunn, Bethlehem, PA
Janie H. Wilson, Statesboro, GA
James E. Freeman, Charlottesville, VA
Jeffrey R. Stowell, Charleston, IL

Contents

Technology: New Opportunities for Teaching

Contributors

Andrea H. Adams
Center for Instructional Technology
James Madison University
Harrisburg, VA

Kevin J. Apple
Department of Psychology
James Madison University
Harrisonburg, VA

Drew C. Appleby
Department of Psychology
Indiana University - Purdue
    University Indianapolis
Indianapolis, IN

Leslie Ashburn-Nardo
Department of Psychology
Indiana University - Purdue
    University Indianapolis
Indianapolis, IN

Ruth L. Ault
Department of Psychology
Davidson College
Davidson, NC

William N. Bailey
Psychology Department
Belmont University
Nashville, TN

Suzanne C. Baker
Department of Psychology
James Madison University
Harrisonburg, VA

Bernard C. Beins
Department of Psychology
Ithaca College
Ithaca, NY

Kim A. Case
Department of Psychology and
    Women's Studies
University of Houston-Clear Lake
Houston, TX

Anne M. Cleary
Department of Psychology
Colorado State University
Fort Collins, CO

Mandy Cleveland
Department of Counseling
    Psychology
Ball State University
Muncie, IN

David B. Daniel
Department of Psychology
James Madison University
Harrisonburg, VA

Michelle A. Drouin
Department of Psychology
Indiana University - Purdue
    University
Fort Wayne, IN

Dana S. Dunn
Department of Psychology
Moravian College
Bethlehem, PA

James E. Freeman
Department of Psychology
University of Virginia
Charlottesville, VA

Charles M. Harris
Department of Psychology
James Madison University
Harrisonburg, VA

Jeffrey L. Helms
Department of Psychology
Kennesaw State University
Kennesaw, GA

Beth Hentges
Department of Psychology
University of Houston-Clear Lake
Houston, TX

Kevin Hurysz
Woodward Academy
College Park, GA

Benjamin A. Jones
Department of Education
    and Training
New South Wales University
Australia

Ulas Kaplan
Department of Psychology
James Madison University
Harrisonburg, VA

Beth R. Kirsner
Department of Psychology
Kennesaw State University
Kennesaw, GA

Pam Marek
Department of Psychology
Kennesaw State University
Kennesaw, GA

Kathryn A. Morris
Department of Psychology
Butler University
Indianapolis, IN

Gary M. Muir
Department of Psychology
St. Olaf College
Northfield, MN

Robert J. Padgett
Department of Psychology
Butler University
Indianapolis, IN

Jorge Pérez
Computer Science and Information
    Systems Department
Kennesaw State University
Kennesaw, GA

Christopher K. Randall
Department of Psychology
Kennesaw State University
Kennesaw, GA

Monica Reis-Bergan
Department of Psychology
James Madison University
Harrisonburg, VA

Daniel T. Rogers
Department of Psychology
Kennesaw State University
Kennesaw, GA

Matthew B. Sacks
Department of Psychology
Touro College
South Miami Beach, FL

Grover Saunders
Center for Instructional Technology
James Madison University
Harrisonburg, VA

Jeffrey R. Stowell
Department of Psychology
Eastern Illinois University
Charleston, IL

Lauren A. Taglialatela
Department of Psychology
Kennesaw State University
Kennesaw, GA

Clayton L. Teem II
School of Social Sciences
Gainesville State College
Oakwood, GA

Laura B. Underwood
Department of Psychology
Kennesaw State University
Kennesaw, GA

Adrienne L. Williamson
Department of Psychology
Kennesaw State University
Kennesaw, GA

Janie H. Wilson
Department of Psychology
Georgia Southern University
Statesboro, GA

Lonnie R. Yandell
Psychology Department
Belmont University
Nashville, TN

Tracy E. Zinn
Department of Psychology
James Madison University
Harrisonburg, VA

Best Practices for Technology-Enhanced Teaching and Learning

1 Getting Connected

An Overview of Best Practices for Using Technology

to Improve Teaching and Learning in Psychology

Dana S. Dunn, Janie H. Wilson, James E. Freeman, and Jeffrey R. Stowell

The world of higher education has changed. Technology has introduced new ways of teaching and learning, redefining education in and out of the classroom. For example, computers are no longer novelties; they are not only as common as blackboards, they are much more portable. On many campuses, matriculating students come to college with cell phones, laptops, iPods, and more knowledge about recent technological advances than many of their professors. Of course, this is not a universal phenomenon, as some faculty members are technophiles who are used to incorporating the best and most helpful new technologies or advances on the Internet into their classes. But what about other faculty members, including those who do not follow technological changes with quite as much attention or enthusiasm? They are by no means technophobes, but they do have multiple responsibilities vying for their attention. How can they incorporate the most useful technological tools into their classes? What works well and what doesn't? What are the current "best practices" for teaching with technology?

We developed and edited this book with an eye to addressing just these sorts of issues. Our goal is to help all teachers, especially those who want to more effectively use technology in their teaching but are not certain which tools will best fit their needs and those of their students. The chapters in this book explore a variety of current themes in teaching with technology, including:

- Thinking deeply and strategically about the place of technology in teaching and learning
- Creating effective ways of communicating with students outside the classroom, including social networking sites and virtual worlds
- Using PowerPoint and interactive whiteboards efficiently and effectively
- Using Internet sites to explore issues of race and diversity, as well as implicit measures of attitudes
- Offering online academic advising resources
- Promoting student engagement by using technology, particularly classroom response systems ("clickers") for responding to questions and sharing points of view
- Teaching online and hybrid courses well
- Administering and managing courses using class management software (e.g., Blackboard);
- Using a host of Web-based sources for teaching, including Web sites, online surveys and quizzes, and YouTube videos
- Helping students to learn to collaborate with one another using online tools

At the risk of being immodest, we believe that virtually any teacher will acquire at least one new pedagogical idea from this book, such as increased awareness of new technology, more effective uses of existing technology, or new applications for current technology.

A Practical Focus on Getting Connected: What Works? How Well?

When we invited our authors to contribute to this book, we challenged them to consider how technology has changed their teaching for the better. We also encouraged them to discuss what aspects of technology have made their classrooms engaging places for their students. In other words, we hoped they would move beyond the sheer innovative nature of some technological classroom applications by focusing on what materials—whether software,

Web site, or hardware—really work well and can be integrated relatively seamlessly into established classes.

We are delighted to report that our authors delivered. Each chapter contains a review of one or more technological topics and tools that are classroom (local, distance, virtual) ready. In addition to explaining how authors came to rely on a particular technology or tool, we also asked them to place their work in a proper context by citing relevant research when it was available. Where appropriate to do so, authors also discussed the particular pros and cons of a given technology, as well as the shortcuts they discovered in implementing the technology into their courses. We encouraged our authors to be candid and critical writers, using their experience to truly inform readers who want to expand the role that technology currently plays in their classes.

We also asked authors to address assessment of technology. Introducing technology into the classroom requires time, money, and training. Although technology has the potential to benefit teaching and learning, instructors and students must see the potential benefits as outweighing the risks. Using technology for instruction does not necessarily translate into higher-quality learning. As teachers, educators, and even parents, how do we know that technology's ubiquity is a good thing for teaching and learning? Can causal connections be established between digital innovations and students' academic performance?

To this end, we invited our authors to seriously consider ways to assess the effectiveness of the technological tools and techniques they advocate for use, whether in or outside of the classroom. Assessment is now obligatory on most campuses, and there is a general recognition that clearly and publicly demonstrating student learning is an important part of the educational process (e.g., Dunn, McCarthy, Baker, Halonen, & Hill, 2007; Dunn, Mehrotra, & Halonen, 2004; Halpern, 2010). We believe that the most useful technologies are also those that are pedagogically sound. Thus, as you use technological ideas and applications from the chapters in this book, we invite you to consider and plan for how you will assess the impact of new teaching tools, especially where student learning is concerned.

As you will see, the orientation of many authors is firmly planted within the discipline of psychology, but with some minor planning and adjustments, each chapter can be readily applied to the other social sciences, the natural sciences, and even the humanities. The technological advances available in teaching and learning have the potential to improve education across all disciplines, and we hope you will accept this exciting challenge. The following overview of the book is organized by chapter, under three broad areas: issues and ideas, teaching in and outside of the classroom, and technology: new opportunities for teaching.

Teaching with Technology: Issues and Ideas

What does it mean to teach with technology? How can technology be integrated into an academic department or program's activities? This section of the book reviews issues concerning the role of technology in teaching, including if and when it should be used, as well as the ways in which technology is changing how faculty members teach their courses. Four chapters address these issues. A fifth chapter examines how to use PowerPoint, the ubiquitous slide software that has revolutionized how some people give talks, lead workshops, and, of course, lecture in the classroom. Given its prominence, influence, and impact as teaching software, we elected to include coverage of PowerPoint among the chapters dealing with the changes that technological advances have wrought in teaching.

Change is an important theme associated with technology, but some teachers wonder whether they should embrace it in their classroom practices. In Chapter 2, Dana S. Dunn (Moravian College), Janie H. Wilson (Georgia Southern University), and James E. Freeman (University of Virginia) discuss the costs and benefits of integrating new technologies into the classroom. The authors encourage teachers to consider how technology can improve their teaching as well as how students learn, while urging educators to add technological changes carefully and thoughtfully; there is no pressing need to integrate a particular tool into a course just because it happens to be available. The learning curve associated with operating any new device or piece of software should not be as steep as the benefits derived from it.

Technology is not a stranger in the classroom. Bernard C. Beins (Ithaca College) discusses how various types of technological tools evolved into regular use in the classrooms where psychology and other disciplines were taught. In our time, we tend to construe "technology" as referring to mechanical or digital methods, but the term can apply to all manner of devices and materials that enable teachers to expose their students to new ways of learning. In particular, Beins discusses the impact of technology on pedagogical advances in the classroom where, it seems, instructors have always tried to maximize student development. The ideal circumstance, of course, is when the technological innovation can be linked with beneficial teaching and learning principles.

Chapter 4 presents a good example of how technologies can be used to develop online curricula. Jeffrey L. Helms, Pam Marek, Christopher K. Randall, Daniel T. Rogers, Lauren A. Taglialatela, and Adrienne L. Williamson, all of Kennesaw State University, discuss how online courses can serve as a creative way to address the educational and lifestyle needs of students, many of whom are in the workforce or who have other responsibilities that keep them from attending traditional classes. These authors discuss how to develop online courses by formulating clear learning objectives, attending to students' preparation for the challenges of online learning, increasing student engagement, and examining how student learning can be effectively demonstrated.

A worry for many teachers who are accustomed to the traditional give-and-take of the classroom is the loss of face-to-face contact and communication, especially, though not exclusively, through online courses. A team of authors from James Madison University—Monica Reis-Bergan, Suzanne C. Baker, Kevin J. Apple, and Tracy E. Zinn—suggest that interaction with students is not lost when electronic venues are involved; indeed, they offer compelling evidence that connections and intellectual exchanges actually can be enhanced. The authors profile common technological tools for faculty–student communication (as well as student-to-student exchanges), including Facebook, instant messaging (or "IM-ing" in the parlance), and the new virtual world software known as Second Life. As readers will see, given that technology is second nature to the current generation of students, many avenues offered by technology may well increase the frequency and even quality of interactions between students and their teachers.

Finally, one area of connection for faculty and students is the presentation software known as PowerPoint, which has taken the classroom and much of higher education by storm. Its popularity varies depending upon whether one is the teacher-user or the recipient-student. David Daniel (James Madison University), who has studied the slide software extensively, provides cogent and often trenchant observations on why PowerPoint is both loved and hated. To paraphrase both Dr. Daniel and Shakespeare, the trouble with PowerPoint is largely within ourselves as designer-users because we neglect what we know about optimal learning and speaking. To wit, we corrupt our slides with too much information and then expect our students to decode dense slides instead of judiciously pointing to content while teaching what we know. The good news? As indicated by this chapter, there is hope for us and for PowerPoint if we follow Daniel's helpful guidelines.

Technology: Applications In and Outside the Classroom

Teaching is a broad term, one that does not include simply giving lectures or holding in-class discussions. This section of our book highlights other teacher and teaching-related activities that occur in the classroom and outside it, often employing the Internet in some way. Issues discussed in this section include course development and course management, advising issues, the use of in-class response systems, and a variety of Web-based and other interactive tools.

In Chapter 7, Charles M. Harris and Ulas Kaplan (James Madison University) offer strategies to create and maintain comprehensive hybrid courses. The authors set their chapter in the context of Vygotsky's social constructivism, pointing out that social interaction is an important aspect of learning and must be maintained in a hybrid course. After providing step-by-step instructions for constructing a hybrid course, including available technology, Harris and Kaplan approach goals of the hybrid course using Chickering and Gamson's seven principles of good practice in undergraduate education: (a) encourages faculty–student interaction, (b) encourages cooperation among students, (c) encourages active learning, (d) gives prompt feedback, (e) emphasizes time on task, (f) communicates high expectations, and (g) respects diverse talents and ways of learning. Each principle is examined in light of the particular challenges of the hybrid course.

How might technology enhance the process of undergraduate advising? In Chapter 8, Drew C. Appleby (Indiana University-Purdue University Indianapolis) provides the answer by sharing a systematic method of how advising materials on his Web site guide students through the advising process during their entire undergraduate career. The site has information how students can make a smooth transition from high school to college, how to get involved in undergraduate research, which classes to take for future careers or study, how to prepare for the GRE and graduate school, and more. Drew has prescribed these Web materials to help students acquire strategies and skills, along with a healthy dose of self-reflection, as they pursue their undergraduate degree.

Chapter 9, written by Gary M. Muir (St. Olaf College) and Anne M. Cleary (Colorado State University), offers a brief overview of traditional clicker (classroom response systems [CRSs]) use. Following classic uses, Muir and Cleary describe novel uses of CRS in behavioral-science courses: using student-generated data to (1) illustrate various statistics, (2) engage students in replications of known findings, and (3) engage students in the testing of hypotheses. When covering statistics, students become engaged in their own learning as they create data for central tendency, variability, and association. With clickers, student can also create data that replicate well-known studies, including the false memory phenomenon, levels of processing phenomenon, fundamental attribution error, "better than average" phenomenon, conformity, serial position effect, prisoner's dilemma, and the ultimatum game. Finally, the authors outline ways to use a CRS to conduct studies devised by students in which members of the class serve as participants. Throughout the chapter, Muir and Cleary provide specific examples to paint a clear picture of innovative CRS use.

Chances are that your university or college is already using a course-management system (CMS). If not, then Chapter 10 is critical reading for you. Michelle A. Drouin, of Indiana University-Purdue University Fort Wayne, reviews several of the most popular types of CMS software. For those who are already using a CMS, this chapter presents several tips for using a CMS effectively in the online classroom as well as in the face-to-face classroom.

In many classrooms, markerboards (or whiteboards) have replaced the old-fashioned blackboards because markerboards are cleaner compared to dusty blackboards. Now interactive whiteboards are replacing some of markerboards because teachers can interact and manipulate the images on the board. Chapter 11 explains how to create lively and interactive classroom presentations. Although interactive whiteboards can be expensive, Matthew B. Sacks (Touro College South) and Benjamin A. Jones (Department of Education and Technology) from Australia present a clever and inexpensive alternative using the Wii game console.

Social networking sites such as Facebook and MySpace can be used for more than just social drivel. In Chapter 12, Kim A. Case and Beth Hentges, of the University of Houston-Clear Lake, show how to enhance student interest and interaction using a social networking site. Using MySpace as a virtual classroom, students shared and educated each other. The authors also created Web-enhanced research labs to enhance communication among research assistants by combining a social networking site with a CMS (i.e., Blackboard).

In Chapter 13 Mandy Cleveland of Ball State University shows us how to incorporate YouTube videos into teaching. Because students choose to watch YouTube videos outside of course requirements (for fun), this video site has the potential to increase student engagement. Cleveland describes the history and features of YouTube and explains how it can be incorporated into classroom lecture, with many useful details for the new user. This chapter also describes the potential benefits and limitations of using YouTube in the classroom as well as helpful hints when integrating YouTube videos into your teaching repertoire.

Are the terms "blog," "wiki," "podcast," "screencast," and "graphic organizer" familiar to you? If not, then Chapter 14 will introduce you to some of these new vocabulary words in the Internet lexicon, which describe different technologies used in virtual communication. Of course, actions speak louder than words: besides reviewing a nascent vocabulary, the authors provide suggestions and guidance for learning to use, adapt, and apply a variety of online tools. In this chapter, Jorge Pérez (Kennesaw State University) and Kevin Hurysz (Woodward Academy) describe how teachers may effectively use these new tools in their classes, making the point that it will soon be difficult (if not impossible) to teach without using the Internet and the academic opportunities it provides.

Issues of prejudice are a likely topic in any course that discusses human interaction (i.e., English literature, history, sociology, political science). In Chapter 15, Kathryn A. Morris (Butler University), Leslie Ashburn-Nardo (Indiana University-Purdue University Indianapolis), and Robert J. Padgett (Butler University) describe two innovative Web-based tools that are used primarily to measure implicit racial bias but can also be used to measure similar bias based on gender, sexual orientation, and age, among others. The results are often surprising, and the discussion is generated from data the students collected from themselves.

Technology: New Opportunities for Teaching

The final section of the book examines the impact of technology for teaching and learning in new ways, and the opportunities that arise as a result. Online tools can be used to foster creativity and cooperation, as well as to promote active learning. Class time need not be lost giving traditional quizzes to assess reading and learning; instead, quizzes can be delivered in an online format. Finally, the promise of virtual worlds for teaching and even newer emerging technologies suggest that exciting and rewarding opportunities to improve pedagogy will continue to appear.

In Chapter 16, Kevin J. Apple, Monica Reis-Bergan, Andrea H. Adams, and Grover Saunders, all from James Madison University, share some tools that can be used for online student collaboration. Getting students to work with each other in or out of the classroom poses a challenge that can be overcome by using online collaboration tools. By avoiding the logistical problems of getting a group of busy students together at the same time and place, online tools such as Google Docs provide several advantages over other methods of document sharing. The authors attempt to tease out the conditions under which synchronous or asynchronous forms of collaboration work best, and conclude by sharing briefly other collaboration tools such as wikis, blogs, and social networking sites.

Beth Kirsner (Kennesaw State University), Clayton L. Teem II (Gainesville State College), and Laura B. Underwood (Kennesaw State University) discuss in Chapter 17 the advantages of using online polling. Not only are online polls conducted more efficiently electronically than on paper, but in the process students develop critical thinking skills and gain a greater under-standing of survey research as they write and revise survey items based on instructor and peer feedback. Online polls may also be helpful as ungraded pre-assessments of knowledge, as supplemental feedback to instructor evalu-ations, and as an online suggestion box to improve instruction. In a relatively short amount of time, students can use surveys to collect a large amount of data for a collaborative class project. The authors conclude with important guidelines, limitations, and considerations for implementing online surveys.

Chapter 18, written by Lonnie R. Yandell and William N. Bailey of Belmont University, highlights the value of using online quizzing to improve students' reading and retention of assigned material. Although students have access to expensive textbooks, they may not read them. To encourage students to read their textbooks before class, some instructors use in-class quizzing, which can increase student preparation and learning, but at the cost of class time that could be used for other things. The authors describe in detail how they used frequent, low-stakes online quizzing to increase the likelihood that students would complete the required readings before they discussed them in class, and to increase efficiency in the delivery and grading of quizzes.

The authors address potential problems with online quizzing and conclude by proposing that this technique will enhance students' reading habits, which will also be useful in other situations.

Suzanne C. Baker and Monica Reis-Bergan (James Madison University) offer an exciting look at Second Life (SL), a virtual-world online environment. According to the authors, SL can be used to enhance teaching and learning by creating connections between students as well as students and faculty. Users first create an avatar to represent them in the virtual world. Avatars interact with one another to socialize, form friendships, and collaborate on tasks. Also in the virtual world, users can create environments, such as a virtual campus that looks very much like a student's physical campus. Faculty might meet with students in the virtual campus for office hours, attend a lecture together, or just socialize to build rapport. One of the most tantalizing features of SL is the ability to infuse diversity into a course; for example, students can easily travel in the virtual world to foreign locations and interact with people of different cultures. Finally, Baker and Reis-Bergan offer practical considerations when using SL in teaching and learning.

In the final chapter, Jeffrey R. Stowell (Eastern Illinois University) gives us a peek into the future. Current technologies, such as clickers, cell phones, online video, and podcasts, will have new functions in teaching. Emerging technologies will be incorporated into teaching by those with vision and creativity. Examples include collaboration Webs, a personal Web that brings relevant information to you in a streamlined manner, mobile devices instead of bulky laptop computers, GPS mobile devices that allow you to interact with a virtual environment while moving through the physical world, and data mashups that integrate a large volume of data into a usable format. Finally, this chapter outlines the challenges associated with technology, including teacher resistance. Stowell asks us to examine where we fall on the technology continuum, ranging from Luddite to enthusiast, but he cautions that our choices should ultimately be based on becoming better teachers.

Technology and Teaching

As one of the authors herein reminds us, once upon a time chalk and pencils were suspect teaching tools that, with a little time, became accepted as common and essential parts of the classroom. Technology poses questions and challenges for at least some of the status-quo qualities of teaching;

change should be embraced and exploited if it truly helps our students learn. As teachers, too, we should consider how employing new technologies can help us rethink our own work in and outside the classroom. As you read the following chapters, we hope you will embrace technologies that can help you and your students become better thinkers, teachers, and learners. You will, no doubt, open your mind to a new world of teaching possibilities. We trust that you will be entertained and amazed to find the wealth of opportunities that technology provides if you dig deeply into these pages.

References

Dunn, D. S., McCarthy, M., Baker, S., Halonen, J. S., & Hill, G. W., IV. (2007). Quality benchmarks in undergraduate psychology programs. *American Psychologist, 62,* 650–670.

Dunn, D. S., Mehrotra, C., & Halonen, J. S. (Eds.) (2004). *Measuring up: Educational assessment challenges and practices for psychology.* Washington, DC: American Psychological Association.

Halpern, D. F. (Ed.). (2010). *Undergraduate education in psychology: A blueprint for the future of the discipline.* Washington, DC: American Psychological Association.

Teaching with Technology: Issues and Ideas

2 Approach or Avoidance?

Understanding Technology's Place in

Teaching and Learning

Dana S. Dunn, Janie H. Wilson, and James E. Freeman

Many teachers view technology as both a blessing and a curse. There can be great benefits ("approach"), but at what cost ("avoidance")? Regardless of teachers' reaction to technology, it is transforming higher education. Knowledge is being presented and taught in ways unthinkable even a few years ago. Almost weekly, a new term linking teaching with technology seems to appear. Older technologies—once novel and dramatic—are now taken for granted and seen as commonplace. Faculty members feel a push, if not outright pressure, to learn to use and adapt the latest tools for their courses. Departments and programs now see online or virtual classrooms as an important part of the array of services they offer students. Whether all these changes are good or bad is a matter of perspective; what is no longer debatable, however, is the degree to which technology has a part in higher education. Its presence and influence there cannot be denied (e.g., Laird & Kuh, 2005; Millis et al., 2010).

Our goal in this chapter is not necessarily to cast a cold eye on new technologies but to be appropriately skeptical about them. Just because technology enables a teacher to achieve a certain end in the classroom (or in an online venue), that does not mean that the instructor is duty-bound to adopt it. As classroom veterans, we prefer to ensure that the tools we use have a proper fit with our teaching goals, our intended learning outcomes, and most of all our students' needs. That being said, we believe that when technology is carefully and thoughtfully integrated into a course, it can make a superb contribution. Both teachers and students can benefit from technology's presence and its impact on how the course material is received and understood.

To achieve these ends, we seek balance in discussions regarding integrating technology into courses. We begin by discussing the potential benefits that technology provides within and beyond traditional classrooms. We then properly temper enthusiasm for technology by raising some caveats we believe educators should consider. Following arguments both pro and con (the approach–avoidance conflict of the decision), we offer suggestions regarding how teachers should go about deciding which technology to use, how much of it, and why. We then make the case that whenever new technologies are introduced, teachers should carefully assess the educational benefit of these tools where student learning is concerned. Educators need to do a cost–benefit analysis before deciding to adopt a new technology. We conclude the chapter by recommending that technology's role in any course should be periodically re-evaluated.

The Benefits of Using Technology for Teaching

When linked to teaching, the term "technology" refers to any educational technologies providing communication that is distinct from personal, face-to-face interaction (Bates & Poole, 2003). By this definition, technology can involve any of the following:

- Hardware (i.e., laptop or desktop computers, projectors, monitors)
- Software (i.e., word processing, presentation, statistical, and networks)
- Portable handheld devices (i.e., audio/video players, digital books, smart phones, and personal response systems)
- Web connections (i.e., online courses, course-management systems, social networks, RSS feeds, wikis, blogs, and podcasts)

In some ways, trying to identify all the available technology is fool-hardy; it is difficult to keep track of all innovations, as something new is introduced constantly. What educational technologies we know now is only the beginning. Even an incomplete catalog such as shown above, however, reveals the vast array of technology available for educational purposes.

How can technologies benefit teaching and learning? As we will show, when used appropriately, technology may foster:

- *Communication skills*—for reading, writing, listening, and speaking
- *Knowledge acquisition*—for searching for and locating information quickly and efficiently (e.g., online searches of a library catalog, databases, or the Internet itself)
- *Data-sharing skills*—sharing findings or results quickly and widely with interested others. Naturally, learning to exercise good judgment regarding what to share (or not) is important.
- *Critical thinking and problem solving*—enhancing skills involving numeracy, logic, and decision making. Users must learn to evaluate the information they acquire and share with others to be sure that it is reliable and valid.
- *Independence, self-direction, and goal orientation*—giving confidence to students to work independently (e.g., Smith, 1997). Most technologies allow the user to work alone, refining related skills along the way. Independence should be motivating and should not lead to disengagement.
- *Team or group work*—encouraging students to work cooperatively and to exchange information with one another (i.e., online communities). Group work and group projects can be accomplished synchronously or asynchronously in a virtual environment.
- *New social skills*—requiring students to learn to converse clearly and often concisely; yet by doing so, issues of ethics and personal responsibility are necessarily involved.
- *Creativity*—skill acquisition can be transferred from one domain to many others in new and creative ways
- *Openness to change*—if appreciated rather than feared or dreaded, technological developments and changes can teach valuable skills about the importance of learning to adapt quickly to new conditions

These general skills are all compelling reasons to view technology from the stance of "approach"—that is, something to be used and relied on for effectively educating students. We will review each one in some detail.

Communication Skills

Technology can be used to facilitate communication for teachers and students. Not so long ago, using chalk on a blackboard was the common medium used by teachers to illustrate and explain concepts in classrooms. Chalk and blackboards are all but gone on campuses today, replaced by markerboards that do not produce the dust that using chalk creates. Computers, invented about the same time as markerboards, are another reason for the move to a dustless technology. Computers, in turn, created the "electronic slide show." Presentation software, such as Microsoft's PowerPoint and Apple Computer's Keynote, is now ubiquitous in classrooms, in part because it allows teachers to easily display text, graphics, animations, and videos (e.g., Daniel, 2005; Huelsman, 2006). However, purchasing the software, computer, and projector is more expensive than buying markerboards. Also, teachers have to invest some time to learn to use the software that runs the system. Using new technology has a learning curve just like everything else. Teachers cannot expect to use most technologies effectively without reading the dreaded manual. Furthermore, lectures using presentation software do not necessarily make one a better teacher. For example, PowerPoint allows instructors to place essential course information in an easy-to-read, logical, and sequential series of slides that can be enhanced with color, graphics, animation, and sound. Yet Hardin (2007) found that although using PowerPoint increased the perceived teaching effectiveness of one instructor, it often reduced it for another.

Other tools that help teachers to communicate with their students include developing class Web pages or using course-management systems such as Blackboard where course material, such as syllabi, assignments, readings, and past exams, may be stored and retrieved electronically; using e-mail for getting information quickly to students; and creating podcasts for students to download lectures to computers or portable devices such as MP3 players (e.g., iPods), to be viewed outside of class time. Of these, class Web pages, course-management systems, and e-mail have become common in education. Podcasts have yet to be adopted widely, perhaps because creating them requires more technological savvy, not to mention the bravery involved in recording lectures that people other than our students may hear and see.

Students may also use technology to improve their ability to communicate. For example, e-mail is a common tool students and teachers use to communicate with each other when outside of the classroom (e.g., Hevern, 2006). Students who are too shy to ask questions in class may be more comfortable doing so via e-mail. Another method of communication similar to e-mail is the electronic discussion group, which allows communication among several participants. Compared with in-person discussions, an advantage of electronic discussions is that the contributions of each participant can be documented (Bryant, 2005). However, e-mail and discussion groups are both *asynchronous* forms of communication. Some time elapses, perhaps several minutes, between the time a message is sent and the time it is received. Chat rooms, instant messaging, and video conferencing provide *synchronous* communication: recipients receive the messages almost immediately. Of these, video conferencing most closely simulates a face-to-face discussion. Individuals are able to talk and see other people, who may be almost anywhere in the world. Another popular electronic medium with young people today is text messaging, but it is not yet widely used by students to communicate with teachers. And more recently, Facebook has emerged as a social networking medium that is popular with students and often faculty members as well. Although it is good that students are able to communicate with their teachers so easily, teachers can be overwhelmed if a large number of students send e-mails or other messages on a regular basis. Another downside to e-mail and text messages is that the quality of writing is often not very good. Abbreviations (i.e., imho for "In my humble opinion") are sometimes substituted for words or strings of words for the sake of expediency or style, posing interpretive problems, as do misspelled words and poorly constructed sentences.

For producing a better quality of writing appropriate for term papers or lab reports, word-processing programs are particularly useful because students (and anyone else, for that matter) can easily edit their prose. Writing is no longer as onerous as when it was done on typewriters. Word-processing software may even warn the student about potential spelling errors and suggest corrections to grammar. Teachers can choose to comment on or edit student writing electronically. However, not everyone would agree that reading papers on a computer screen is as easy as reading paper copies.

Unfortunately, as easy as word-processing programs make it for students to revise their writing, it makes it just as easy for them to copy writing that is not their own. Students may cut and paste material from other documents. At worst, a paper can be saved electronically and used over and over again, with a different student's name each time. For example, there have been several scandals on college campuses where students were caught buying papers off the Internet or using a paper written by a student who took the class earlier. These dishonest practices make it important for teachers to create writing assignments that require originality, rather than asking students to write about the same issues year after year.

Another recent innovation in communication in classrooms is the use of student response systems (also known as "clickers"; see Chapter 9). Students use a handheld device that enables them to respond to multiple-choice questions posed by the instructor. Student responses are received and recorded on the instructor's computer, and the instructor has the option of displaying a graph showing the results (Cleary, 2008; Morling, McAuliffe, Cohen, & DiLorenzo, 2008). Clickers are used to get students, even reticent ones, to participate in class because responses can be anonymous. Thus, clickers are a useful tool for students to communicate what they know or think about a given topic. Clickers are useful for increasing participation in class and possibly the honesty of the feedback (Stowell & Nelson, 2007), but as of yet the demonstrated gains in student learning have been minimal (Poirer & Feldman, 2007).

Knowledge Acquisition

Almost instant information is a possibility today. For many queries all it takes is typing a few words into an Internet search engine such as Google. Desktop computers are not required: on college campuses, laptop computers have become popular in part because of their portability and the wireless (WiFi) technology that allows these computers to have access to Internet services anywhere there is a "hot spot." Most campuses provide wireless services, as do many businesses, such as bookstores, coffee shops, and other popular places where students gather. Even more convenient than laptops are "smart" phones (e.g., iPhone, Blackberry, and other models) that make it possible to get information in places where WiFi services are unavailable but telephone networks (i.e., Edge, 3G) are. Teachers may take advantage of these Internet technologies by teaching students how to search libraries online (e.g., McCarthy & Pusateri, 2006). Teachers may also create online instruction and store it online (for examples, see MIT Open Courseware at http://ocw.mit. edu/OcwWeb/Brain-and-Cognitive-Sciences/9-00Fall-2004/LectureNotes/). However, caveat emptor! Generally there is no editorial review of the content found online; the quality of the information found on the Internet varies greatly. Students need to be taught how to cull the "wheat from the chaff" or how to evaluate the quality of the source (for suggestions on how to do so, see Dunn, 2008).

Team or Group Work

Students have the ability to collaborate with others in ways that only a few years ago were impossible. Student can "virtually" collaborate with individuals all over the world, or anywhere where there is Internet service. E-mail and text messaging are common communication tools, and Web cameras make it easy to see and talk to other people at the same time. It is also possible to share documents in such a way that groups can work on them. For example, Google Docs allows users to access and share documents online. To facilitate virtual teamwork, teachers may also create discussion groups within a class Web site.

Independence, Self-Direction, and Goal Orientation

Once basic skills are learned, some classroom-related technology is easy to use. Ease of use can give students the confidence to use technology to act independently of an instructor or classmates. For motivated students, for example, self-paced courses online can be a boon, enabling them to proceed when they wish and at a self-determined speed. Similarly, when the search parameters for a database are mastered, we have witnessed many students quickly elect to search for information on their own. With guidance from faculty members, students can gain confidence in using technology to pursue goals related to their major area of study, as well as future education or career plans.

New Social Skills

With a plethora of electronic tools for communicating and sharing (e.g., Facebook, MySpace, Twitter, iChat, text messages, YouTube, e-mail, blogs, discussion boards) new social skills are required. The ease and the quickness of electronic methods of communication, especially e-mail and text messages, increases the chance of someone saying something that he or she might not say to someone in a face-to-face encounter. Further, e-mail messages that were expected to be private may be later forwarded to countless others. Teachers too have to establish boundaries. Most do not expect students to call them at home, but some students may expect a prompt response to an "urgent" message sent late at night. Civility is another issue. Students need to learn the etiquette of electronic communication (Bryant, 2005). Statements intended as sarcasm may be misinterpreted, and the interpersonal distance of electronic communication may lead to inappropriate comments. We will need to teach our students that the rules of etiquette for electronic communication are different than those for oral communication.

Creativity

Technology is rarely used for just one purpose, and its producers cannot be certain how original uses will be applied in new and creative ways. Consider a simple example: PowerPoint probably began as a business-related application, but it quickly found its way into the college classroom as a lecture aid. The ubiquity of technology and software too has dramatically increased the role that audio and video play in the classroom. What began as entertainment is now often educational. Currently, students have moved from being consumers of videos on the Internet to producers of filmed vignettes, many humorous, some scandalous, but quite a few educational. As teachers, we are often amazed and delighted by students' cleverness when it comes to creating videos that document or explain course-related materials. In the past, students were forced to verbally describe events or rely on still images to illustrate points; now they can simply import video materials into their presentations, often with profound results.

Of course, teachers and students must judge when and whether a given application is creative in a positive sense, advancing knowledge about a topic. Our point is simply that some technologies provide students with the opportunity to develop novel ways to present, work with, think about, or apply course material. As new technologies emerge, student creativity will undoubtedly grow in new directions as well.

Openness to Change

The great lesson of technology is that nothing stays the same for very long. New developments and applications emerge quickly and often, encouraging, if not forcing, users to keep pace with them. This need to remain aware of new developments may provide students with a desire to be aware and open-minded when it comes to new technological developments. With luck, the lessons that such open-mindedness provides may be applicable to other arenas of student experience, including preparation for life beyond college. Being flexible, even comfortable, in the face of change is never a bad thing.

Other Classroom Benefits of Technology

Interesting or Engaging

By their very nature, new technologies are salient. They can capture student interest. When students become engaged with something new in class, they pay more attention, listen more closely, ask questions—in short, they display all the positive actions we hope that motivated learners will demonstrate.

Familiar

Where technological developments are concerned, our students sometimes know more than we do. They may, for example, already be familiar with a new technology that teachers introduce into their courses. This is no reason for teachers to chide themselves on presenting dated material, as it is unlikely all students will be familiar with any given advance. Rather, when some students are already familiar with a new technology being introduced, their recognition can actually make the class go easier. Indeed, sometimes students end up teaching one another.

Activity-Based Learning

The availability of technology often encourages teachers to find or construct activities to illustrate its use or application. Activity-based learning helps students to think about course material at a deeper level than listening to a lecture. Such opportunities for active learning enhance what students learn and retain from coursework (e.g., Davis, 1993; McKeachie & Svinicki, 2005).

Students Are Often Experts

We should not overlook the simple fact that technology has always been a large part of the daily lives of recent cohorts of students. They truly cannot imagine a life without various technologies. Why does this matter? Students are not only likely to be interested in new technologies, but may also be able to help instructors and student peers learn to use technology effectively (e.g., Sandholtz, Ringstaff, & Dwyer, 1997). Just as some of us rely on our students when the inevitable computer glitch arises, the same may hold true for still newer technologies. Granting someone expert status and acknowledging his or her assistance is never a bad thing.

Beyond the Classroom

Efficient

Justification for the use of technology need not always be based on whether its use improves teaching or learning. A new technology may simply make the process easier. Using presentation software may not necessarily produce better learning than using chalk and a blackboard, but it is an effective delivery system, especially for large audiences. Likewise, e-mail, for brief questions, can be more efficient than a student coming to office hours. Course material, syllabi, readings, assignments, and grades are now available whenever a student needs them.

Flexibility in Delivery

Traditional education settings and their delivery of services are no longer the only ways for teaching and learning to occur. Newer generations of students face different pressures and opportunities than those educated in the past.

Consequently, there is a distinct demand for more flexible delivery beyond the once-normative three weekly lecture meetings in a college classroom. The typical or average student is likely to be seeking more flexible learning activities (e.g., online courses) to accommodate full- or part-time employment. We should keep in mind that flexible learning offers flexible teaching. For example, more flexibility regarding teaching time and place can free faculty time for scholarly or administrative duties.

Cost-Effective

Technology can save on costs in big or small ways. Buzhardt and Semb (2005) reported that integrating online instruction in a college classroom saved labor costs. Online material need not be printed, which saves the school and the student money, not to mention an additional savings for the environment. Online material may be nothing more than short handouts for a class but could include an entire textbook. Online classrooms also save both the school and the student money in that the school does not have to maintain a room or a building, and the student does not have the expenses associated with commuting or living on or near the campus.

Caveats on Using Technology for Teaching

Technology is transforming what faculty and students do in course contexts. Some of the transformation may trigger unintended problems for both groups. Many of these potential problems will be outlined in the chapters of this book, which will allow an emphasis on specific technologies. However, one general problem is that students and faculty often become "addicted" to technology (Palloff & Pratt, 1999). We all have colleagues who are eager to employ the latest software, hardware, or application, regardless of whether or not it is useful in teaching. Instead of racing to use the newest technology for its own sake, we should consider the following issues when introducing innovation in or outside the classroom.

In-Class Issues

We need to examine technology in the context of our classroom strategies. The technology we use should enhance learning without taking too long (e.g., long YouTube videos that demonstrate simple concepts), distracting from the material (e.g., animated PowerPoint presentations with bells, whistles, and breaking glass), compromising rapport between teacher and students (e.g., any technology used in such a way that it attenuates the relational aspect of teaching), or simply breaking down. The focus in the classroom should be the people, not the technology; otherwise, there is no point to a class at all. In class, a teacher offers information to students or helps students offer information to each other, and technology should build on these goals. Indeed, in the virtual classroom, technology is the only way to make the "in-class" experience exist.

Beyond the Classroom

Students traditionally interact with their teachers in what researchers have called out-of-class communication (OCC) such as office hours. Since the dawn of education, students have accomplished OCC by physically traveling to the teacher's office. This type of interaction has been associated with better student attitudes toward learning (Clarke, Walker, & Keith, 2002), higher perceived teacher competence and caring (Myers, 2004), and more positive student evaluations of interpersonal relationships with teachers (Dobransky & Frymier, 2004).

Unfortunately, those of us who have taught for a number of years know that few students manage to arrange their schedules around the teacher's office hours. Technology allows us to remain in contact with students outside of the classroom, and the flexibility helps us reach substantially more of our students than could have been accomplished if we relied only on physical office visits. Our recommendation is to keep the physical office hours in place for students who want or require physical proximity during a meeting, and we should encourage students to come to our office given the positive outcomes associated with traditional OCC.

Deciding Whether and How Much to Rely on Technology

Teaching Philosophy

Our teaching philosophy addresses what we believe to be vital in teaching (see, for example, Korn, 2002). How do we accomplish teaching, and why is our approach important to us? For many teachers, keeping abreast of revolutions in teaching is crucial, and we cannot deny that technology is a revolution. Most of us are also dedicated to teaching students the latest developments that are relevant to them. Again, students must be proficient in technology to advance in today's world. Thus, at least part of our dedication to teaching should be to learn what is available in technology, apply what is useful, and share technology with our students.

Learning Curve

As we learn technology, we would like to believe that a steeper learning curve has a higher potential payoff. However, most of us know that this is not the case: some types of technology are just difficult to learn and offer little potential payoff. Unfortunately, by the time we realize how much trouble it is, we are already too invested in the technology to walk away. As an additional stressor, we tend to feel most comfortable only with technology that we use on a regular basis; if we only use it once a term (e.g., updating a Web page), we tend to forget the nuances we once knew. Finally, we might become proficient at some type of technology only to find that it has been updated (e.g., Microsoft Office) and has become nearly unrecognizable in a new version!

We are convinced that those who learn new technology on a regular basis and apply it to teaching are high in self-efficacy. These teachers know the learning curve may be steep, and they are comfortable with their ability to reach the asymptote. The rest of us need to remember to take notes on how a technology works and save the files to our desktop so they will be readily available when we need them. We also can rely on our colleagues or books such as this one to tell us the pleasures and pitfalls associated with specific technologies. In short, we can rely on each other as we navigate through learning in this new revolution.

Equipment Resources

We also rely on each other to develop a basic understanding of what equipment and software we need in order to use technologies of interest. You can find out what your school has to offer (e.g., a license for software that can be loaded onto your computer at no additional cost). Often, department chairs or deans are able to finance needed equipment, especially if you are willing to have the equipment placed in a central location so your colleagues can also use it. Of course, grants are always an option and can help pay for equipment and software tied to teaching and learning.

Types of Students

In the end, the most important factor may be the sorts of students you teach at your institution. Whether you use it in or outside the classroom, will they benefit from your use of technology in your teaching? We are accustomed to thinking of the current cohort of students as being especially technologically savvy—communicating electronically is second nature to them, as is surfing the Web for whatever information they might need. We believe that students' experiences and preferences should not be the deciding factor, however. Instead, we advocate that teachers take a long look at the academic skills that move students toward graduating.

Questions to Ask When Deciding Whether to Use Technology

Table 2.1 list some questions to ask yourself as you consider whether to use technology in one or more of your courses. As you review and answer these questions, keep in mind that these questions are a starting point; they should lead to other questions. Similarly, faculty members need to work within their local conditions, traditions, and resources; what works well at one institution may be a struggle or even a failure at another. Remember, too, that careful planning for a technologically enhanced or technologically based course can make all the difference (e.g., Lehman & Berg, 2007). Look—and plan—before you leap into wholeheartedly accepting any new technology. Methodical skepticism will serve you well.

A Necessity: Assessing Learning When Technology is Used

Information literacy and technology skills are important student learning outcomes that should be routinely assessed (e.g., Dunn, McCarthy, Baker, & Halonen, in press; Dunn, McCarthy, Baker, Halonen, & Hill, 2007). We believe that teachers need to assess the quality of learning that takes place once a new technology is introduced into a course. Some instructors may

Table 2.1

Questions to Answer When Considering the Use of Technology for Teaching and Learning

1. Who is the audience? Is the intended technology an appropriate method for serving this audience? Why or why not?

2. Why are you considering adopting the technology? Does it offer any teaching or learning advantages beyond what you already offer? Is a novel technology being chosen for novelty's sake?

3. How does the technology fit the learning outcomes identified for the course?

4. Does the technology complement, not compete with, the academic content of the course?

5. Will the technology advance, impede, or be relatively neutral where other educational goals (e.g., diversity) are concerned?

6. What are the costs and benefits of using the technology? Is it easy to use and reliable?

7. What skills do you and your students need to have in order to use the technology?

8. If you integrate the technology into the course, will any existing material need to be removed? Is there a learning curve for the instructor and students to become familiar with the technology? What is the estimated time frame?

9. Is technical/professional support available for maintaining and troubleshooting problems associated with the technology?

10. Is the technology appropriate for the course? Is the technology appropriate for the students?

11. Will students be able to evaluate the technology and alert the instructor quickly if problems using it arise?

12. How will you assess the technology effectiveness as a teaching and learning tool? Is there any evidence available regarding its effectiveness?

also want to evaluate how well students learn to use the new technology (e.g., demonstrating effective search strategies for a psychological database). Using new technologies requires a financial investment and one or more persons' time to implement. Also, there is no guarantee that a new technology will improve student learning. Consequently, it is important that new technologies be evaluated to determine whether the expense (time and money) is worth the cost. A common evaluation of teaching effectiveness is student evaluations. However, positive student evaluations may reflect nothing more than the demand characteristics created by the novelty of using the new technology. A proper evaluation should also include measures of student learning. For example, current students' exam performance can be compared with past students' performance.

A lesson about the importance of assessment can be learned from a non-technological example of a past innovative teaching method. The personalized system of instruction (PSI) threatened to revolutionize teaching in the early 1970s (for more information see Keller, 1968). It was popular on many college campuses for a several years before the flame of its popularity burned out. A search of the literature during the 1970s and 1980s reveals numerous citations related to this method of instruction, but since the 1990s there have been only a few (Eyre, 2007). It took a decade or more of research before it was decided that the method was not worth its cost, at least not with the technology available at the time. In light of PSI's history, we must be reasonably skeptical in regards to new technology, as well; not everything new will have staying power. Thus, as we embrace new technological tools for teaching, we must be prepared to jettison some of them later. Technology can just as easily make teaching and learning worse as make it better.

Re-Evaluating Technology's Role Across Time

Just because you decide to use a particular technology tool does not mean that you must use it for the foreseeable future. Instead, we advocate that teachers review whether a technological tool is continuing to substantively contribute to student learning. If so, then perhaps this valuable tool should be retained for the next iteration of the course. If not, then it should be dropped or at least appropriately reconfigured so that it meets your stated learning objectives and desired outcomes. Change takes work, and it can be quite painful to learn that the change did not enhance student outcomes or that it even harmed learning. It may be even more painful to discard months of hard work in the interest of helping students. However, we must be willing to learn, assess, and adjust throughout our teaching. We should approach technology with a positive attitude for what it has to offer, but we must be careful to avoid the pitfalls of glitz with no gain.

References

Bates, A. W., & Poole, G. (2003). *Effective teaching with technology in higher education: Foundations for success*. San Francisco: Jossey-Bass.

Bryant, B. K. (2005). Electronic discussion sections: A useful tool in teaching large university classes. *Teaching of Psychology, 32,* 271–275.

Buzhardt, J. & Semb, B. (2005). Integrating online instruction in a college classroom to improve cost effectiveness. *Teaching of Psychology, 32,* 63–66.

Clarke, R. K., Walker, M., & Keith, S. (2002). Experimentally assessing the student impacts of out-of-class communication: Office visits and the student experience. *Journal of College Student Development, 43,* 824–837.

Cleary, A. M. (2008). Using wireless response systems to replicate behavioral research findings in the classroom. *Teaching of Psychology, 35,* 42–44.

Daniel, D. B. (2005). How to ruin a perfectly good lecture. In B. Perlman, L. McCann, & W. Buskist (Eds.), *Voices of NITOP: Favorite talks from the National Institute on the Teaching of Psychology* (pp. 119–130). Washington, DC: American Psychological Society.

Davis, B. G. (1993). *Tools for teaching*. San Francisco: Jossey-Bass.

Dobransky, N. D., & Frymier, A. B. (2004). Developing teacher-student relationships through out-of-class communication. *Communication Quarterly, 52,* 211–223.

Dunn, D. S. (2008). *A short guide to writing about psychology* (2nd ed.). New York: Pearson Longman.

Dunn, D. S., McCarthy, M. A., Baker, S. C., & Halonen, J. S. (in press). *Using quality benchmarks for assessing and developing undergraduate programs*. San Francisco: Jossey-Bass.

Dunn, D. S., McCarthy, M., Baker, S., Halonen, J. S., & Hill, G. W., III. (2007). Quality benchmarks in undergraduate psychology programs. *American Psychologist, 62,* 650–670.

Eyre, H. I. (2007). Keller's Personalized System of Instruction: Was it a fleeting fancy or is there a revival on the horizon? *The Behavior Analyst Today,* Retrieved April 1, 2009, from http://findarticles.com/p/articles/mi_6884/is_3_8/ai_n28461022/

Hardin, E. E. (2007). Presentation software in the college classroom: Don't forget the instructor. *Teaching of Psychology, 34,* 53–57.

Hevern, V. W. (2006). Using the Internet effectively: Homepages and email. In W. Buskist & S. F. Davis (Eds.), *Handbook of the teaching of psychology* (pp. 99–106). Malden, MA: Blackwell.

Huelsman, T. J. (2006). Lessons learned using PowerPoint in the classroom. In W. Buskist & S. F. Davis (Eds.), *Handbook of the teaching of psychology* (pp. 94–98). Malden, MA: Blackwell.

Korn, J. H. (2002). Beyond tenure: The teaching portfolio for reflection and change. In S. F. Davis & W. Buskist (Eds.), *The teaching of psychology: Essays in honor of Wilbert J. McKeachie and Charles L. Brewer* (pp. 203–213). Mahwah, NJ: Erlbaum.

Laird, T. F., & Kuh, G. D. (2005). Student experiences with information technology and their relationship to other aspects of student engagement. *Research in Higher Education, 46,* 211–233.

Keller, F. S. (1968). "Good-bye Teacher..." *Journal of Applied Behaviour Analysis, 5,* 79–89.

Lehman, R. M., & Berg, R. A. (2007). *147 practical tips for synchronous and blended technology teaching and learning.* Madison, WI: Atwood Publishing.

McCarthy, M., & Pusateri, T. P. (2006). Teaching students to use electronic databases. In W. Buskist & S. F. Davis (Eds.), Handbook of the teaching of psychology (pp. 107–111). Malden, MA: Blackwell.

McKeachie, W. J., & Svinicki, M. (2005). *McKeachie's teaching tips: Strategies, research, and theory for college and university teachers* (12th ed.). Belmont, CA: Wadsworth.

Millis, K., Baker, S., Blakemore, J., Connington, F., Harper, Y., Hung, W-C., Kohn, A., & Stowell, J. (2010). Teaching and learning in a digital world. In Halpern (Ed.), *Undergraduate education in psychology: A blueprint for the future of the discipline.* (pp. 113–128) Washington, DC: American Psychological Association.

Morling, B., McAuliffe, M. Cohen, L., & DiLorenzo, T. M. (2008). Efficacy of personal responses systems ("clickers") in large, introductory psychology classes. *Teaching of Psychology, 35,* 45–50.

Myers, S. A. (2004). The relationship between perceived instructor credibility and college student in-class and out-of-class communication. *Communication Reports, 17,* 129–137.

Poirer, C. R. & Feldman, R. S. (2007). Promoting active learning using individual response technology in large introductory psychology classes. *Teaching of Psychology, 34,* 194–196.

Palloff, R. M., & Pratt, K. (1999). *Building learning communities in cyberspace: Effective strategies for the online classroom.* San Francisco: Jossey-Bass.

Sandholtz, J. H., Ringstaff, C., & Dwyer, D. C. (1997). *Teaching with technology: Creating student centered classrooms.* New York: Teachers College Press.

Smith, K. L. (1997). Preparing faculty for instructional technology: From education to development to creative independence. *Cause/Effect, 20*(3), 36–44, 48.

Stowell, J. R., & Nelson, J. M. (2007). Benefits of electronic audience response systems on student participation, learning, and emotion. *Teaching of Psychology, 34,* 253–258.

3 A Brief Stroll down Random Access Memory Lane

Implications for Teaching with Technology

Bernard C. Beins

Educators appear always to have been attracted to technology in one form or another. Among psychologists, for example, B. F. Skinner is well known for promoting the value of teaching machines in a variety of disciplines (Skinner, 1958, 1989), in addition to his general penchant for creating useful items, including the childhood device to remind him to hang up his pajamas (Fancher, 1979) and his air crib (Benjamin & Nielsen-Gammon, 1999). Teachers of psychology were also at the forefront in developing technology to help teachers across many disciplines (e.g., Pressey, 1926, 1927).

A century ago, college teachers desired apparatus for classroom demonstrations, advocated for forms of distance education (e.g., Whipple, 1910), recognized the desirability of active learning (e.g. Seashore, 1910), and urged the development of handbooks for teaching demonstrations (e.g., Sanford, 1910). These attitudes arose in the early years of the 20th century, and they have not moderated.

A perusal of available resources reveals that the wishes of the first generation of psychology teachers have come to fruition in ways that would undoubtedly amaze them. For instance, teaching aids of the type that Seashore (1910) and Whipple (1910) desired appear regularly in journals like *The Teaching Professor, Teaching of Psychology, Teaching Sociology*, and *Journal of College Biology Teaching*. The handbook for psychology teachers that

Sanford (1910) urged has appeared like a many-headed hydra, including five volumes of original activities by the American Psychological Association (APA) and at least nine published by Lawrence Erlbaum Associates with articles reprinted from *Teaching of Psychology*. In a broad sense, the technology of teaching has proliferated.

What Constitutes Technology?

It would be a mistake to include only mechanical and electronic devices in a discussion of technology. Teachers are in the business of transmitting information. Any means by which education is furthered (i.e., information is transmitted) is appropriate for inclusion in a discussion of the technology of pedagogy. As such, the movement from the scroll to the codex in the first few centuries of the common era represents a shift in technology that ultimately led to more effective dissemination of information. The independent invention of movable type provided the basis for widespread literacy, with wood and ceramic type by Bi Sheng in 11th-century China, metal type by the Goryeo Dynasty in 13th-century Korea, and Gutenberg's 15th-century invention. With movable type, books proliferated in the West, with as many as 20,000 different titles in Europe within a century and a half of Gutenberg's movable type (Bryson, 1991), and librarians no longer had to chain down books to keep them safe (Petroski, 1999).

Sometimes, information technology emerges and becomes standard or even indispensable, then disappears, like the library card catalog that was invented a little more than a century ago. As illustrated in Figure 3.1, the cards in the catalog provided information that alerted a savvy user to the general content of the item. Card catalogs still exist but are now exclusively electronic. Some libraries (e.g., Yale's Sterling Memorial Library) display their traditional card catalogs but do not update them. Another paper-based advance in information technology that benefitted students, even if pedagogy was not its primary intent, was *Psychological Abstracts*, which APA discontinued as of December 2006 after 80 years of publication (APA announces "retirement," 2006). It is easy to forget that new ways of offering ideas and materials constitute new forms of information technology, but new technology is exactly what it is.

After their introduction, innovations generally become standard, and everybody takes them for granted. As useful in retrospect as innovations may

```
362.7044
            362.7044 FLLS
            Hagans, Kathryn B.
            When your child has been molested : a
            parent's guide to healing and recovery
            / Kathryn B. Hagans ; Joyce Case.
            Lexington, MA : Lexington/D.C. Heath,
            c1988.
            159 p.
            0669179809 (alk. paper)        87-46364
            1. Sexually abused children--
            Psychology.  2. Child molesting--
            Investigation.  3. Sexually abused
            children--Family relationships.  4.
            Sexually abused children--Counseling
            of.  I. Case, Joyce.  II. Title.
            12/20/88

            3131614X              ●      Card 01 of 01 FG0309
                                       © 1960 BRODART
```

Figure 3.1 A card from a card catalog, a system formalized in 1876 in Charles Cutter's report *Rules for a Dictionary Catalog*. This card uses the Library of Congress designation rather than Cutter's system of using letters to indicate topics (e.g., BF standing for books about psychology).

be, there is often resistance on the part of teachers to new technology; such resistance is not new, as indicated in quotations collected by the late Stanley Bezuska at Boston College and reported by Thornburg (1992):

> Students today can't prepare bark to calculate their problems. They depend on their slates which are more expensive. What will they do when the slate is dropped and it breaks? They will be unable to write! (Teacher's Conference, 1703)
>
> Students today depend upon paper too much. They don't know how to write on slate without chalk dust all over themselves. They can't clean a slate properly. What will they do when they run out of paper? (Principal's Association, 1815)
>
> Students today depend too much upon ink. They don't know how to use a pen knife to sharpen a pencil. Pen and ink will never replace the pencil. (National Association of Teachers, 1907)
>
> Students today depend upon store-bought ink. They don't know how to make their own. When they run out of ink they will be unable to write words or ciphers until their next trip to the settlement. This is a sad commentary on modern education. (The Rural American Teacher, 1929) (pp. 58–59)

Ball point pens will be the ruin of education in our country.
Students use these devices and then throw them away.
The American virtues of thrift and frugality are being discarded.
Business and banks will never allow such expensive luxuries.
(Federal Teacher, 1950)

These quotations seem humorous and quaint from the current perspective. However, today's teachers have their own blind spots. For instance, Davis (2008) has commented that "the truth of the matter is that even professors find it easy to click on Wikipedia for quick definitions and sources of more information. We've all been spoiled and corrupted to some degree by Google and Wikipedia, though it hurts to admit it" (¶ 2).

Psychologists' Use of Technology in Pedagogy

Research has indicated that instructional technology is associated with better course performance by students and more favorable attitudes toward classes as indicated by judgments of course quality (Kulik, Kulik, & Cohen, 1980). Even with this positive result, though, there are caveats of relevance here. First, Kulik et al. noted that effect sizes associated with instructional technology are small (the mean Cohen's d = .28); in fact, the largest effects relate to Keller's Personalized System of Instruction (Cohen's d = .55), an approach that does not rely specifically on mechanized technology. Second, Kulik et al. noted that the effects of instructional technology on student achievement have been greatest in studies that did not control for instructor effects. They concluded that "it has often been said that the instructional technologies have been oversold, and this seems to be the case" (Kulik et al., 1980, p. 204).

One could argue that technology for teaching has been around as long as psychology, as a discipline, has been. For instance, William James established a laboratory at Harvard in 1875 (Harper, 1950) that was focused on demonstrations rather than research (Benjamin, 2007). And one of the prominent figures in the history of the teaching of psychology, Harry Kirke Wolfe, emphasized active learning with research instrumentation at the University of Nebraska in the next decade. In fact, he spent his own money to furnish the lab, spending $75.86. He hoped for reimbursement and submitted his receipts to the university, which caused consternation among the administration (Benjamin, 1991). In constant dollars, Wolfe's expenditure would equate to over $1,900 in 2008 (Sahr, 2009).

Using the broad sense of technology, I will outline some of the technological ventures in teaching that psychologists have made, although similar innovations are relevant to many disciplines. For example, Walton (1930) reported developing a mechanical device that allowed students to view a simulation of a small doll-like figure being classically conditioned, in some ways a mechanical relative of the computerized Sniffy the virtual rat (2005). Walton also devised a vertical maze to show how animals learn to find food at the end of the maze. (He did not use the term *reinforcement* as it was not in general use at that time.) Walton claimed effectiveness in conveying to students the points he wanted them to learn, even though only the rat was involved in active learning.

Another technology that instructors take for granted now but that has not always been in common use is the visual aid. The ubiquity of classrooms connected to the Internet and the ease and availability of PowerPoint presentations have rendered overhead transparencies outmoded. A decade or so ago, instructor's manuals (again, hearken back to Seashore, 1910) regularly came with a stack of transparencies that publishers deemed essential to make a book marketable. It is now hard to find an overhead transparency projector, but teachers still count on visual presentations in their classes.

At one point, such visual aids were sufficiently rare as to warrant a journal article about creating them. Andrews (1946) touted the advantages of filmstrips and glass slides to illustrate important points. He pointed out that for $6.50, one could procure slide-making equipment using etched glass plates; that sum would provide the materials for 25 slides that the instructors would have to make themselves. Converting $6.50 to 2008 dollars reveals that it would cost nearly $275 in today's dollars to buy materials to make those 25 slides (Sahr, 2009). Again, from the perspective of a teacher or a student in the 21st century, it is hard to fathom a classroom that did not involve extensive visual aids, but at one point glass slides were an advanced technology for teaching.

As instructors moved through the 20th century, they regularly developed pedagogical innovations. Pressey (1926, 1927) developed a typewriter-like teaching machine. Skinner (1958) later created his own brand of teaching machine based on principles of operant conditioning. Some of the modes of teaching that instructors used would undoubtedly seem archaic to current students and instructors. For instance, Gaskill (1933) broadcast a 20-minute radio lecture on psychology and athletics; one group of students listened in a radio studio while another listened over the radio in their homes, dormitories, or fraternity houses. The scores on a test 3 days later were higher for the radio group than for the studio group, a pattern that held true when the students switched locations for a subsequent lecture and test. The trend toward more learning with radio broadcasts was not limited to college classes or to psychology (Miles, 1940; Reid, 1940). The use of radio-based lectures appears not to have been uncommon (Miles, 1940), but no specific mention of it in the teaching of psychology appeared in the research literature after Gaskill's work.

A current descendent of Gaskill's radio broadcasts are podcasts, a series of digital audio files that a creator (i.e., a podcaster) can syndicate and make available for routine and automatic downloading by others. Gaskill and his contemporaries could not have conceived of podcasts in 1933, but his idea is prescient nonetheless. The current availability of podcasts (e.g., Chris Green's history of psychology podcasts at http://www.yorku.ca/christo/podcasts/) reflects a technology fundamentally different from Gaskill's, but the concept is similar.

With the spread of commercial television some two decades later, researchers provided useful information on the new medium, including guidance on how to structure one's television performance (e.g., McKeachie, 1952). Stromberg (1952) remarked on the power of televised classes broadcast remotely into people's homes to maintain student enrollment in a class compared to the then-used correspondence courses.

The finding of increased learning, or at least no worse performance, appears in periodic reports. For example, Husband (1954) taught a 10-week introductory-level class broadcast from Iowa State College. He reported that students who watched 20-minute televised lectures remotely or the same lecture followed by discussion in a classroom setting had better test scores than students actually present in the TV studio or students who received the material only in a standard classroom lecture. Not surprisingly, students who viewed the lecture and engaged in subsequent discussion scored better on a test of the material than those who only viewed the lecture. As Figure 3.2 makes apparent, the difference between television viewing and classroom presentation of the material was minimal. Husband reported no statistical tests, but the advantage of television *per se* seems slight at best.

Interestingly, Husband provided an estimate of the number of viewers who watched the lectures on television, which were sandwiched between

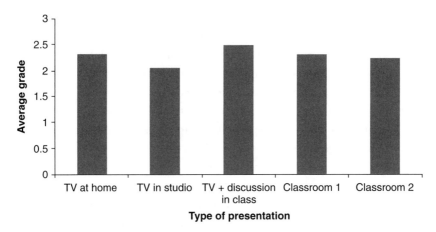

Figure 3.2. Average final grades in psychology classes (A = 4, B = 3, etc.) in Husband's (1954) examination of the efficacy of televised courses.

the game show *The Big Payoff* and the variety show *The Kate Smith Show*. Husband cited a figure of at least 60,000 viewers based on a survey. Stromberg (1952) reported that an estimated 70,000 viewers watched a different psychology course, suggesting that the populace was eager to use this new technology for learning.

After some time had passed, reports surfaced that television may not have been the panacea to learning that the initial reports had intimated (Coone & White, 1968). However, when tailored appropriately to the content of a given lesson, televised instruction could be effective (Dwyer, 1969). In the 1960s, it appears that the question of whether television was an effective medium for teaching became moot: psychologists simply continued to use it in their teaching. The reports on its use were descriptive of occasionally successful approaches.

Unfortunately, according to early commentary by Birney and McKeachie (1955), researchers continually failed to address the theoretical basis for their pedagogical research, and a critical evaluation of the empirical approach was also lacking. They suggested that the initial body of information had paved the way for stronger assessment of student learning with different pedagogical approaches, but they appear to have been more optimistic than was warranted. According to some current thinking, educators are still remiss in their failure to consider the combination of pedagogy, technology, and content knowledge in studies of innovation in teaching (Ferdig, 2006).

An unusual variant to the practice of broadcasting or telecasting lectures involved the teaching of psychology by telephone. The Michigan Bell Telephone Company approached Cutler, McKeachie, and McNeil (1958) about conducting a course by telephone. Student test performance via telephone and in a traditional classroom did not differ, and both sets of students showed gains in knowledge. The authors noted that teaching over the telephone was more satisfying than teaching on television because of the possibility of interaction among teacher and students. The reactions by students were positive because of the convenience associated with being at home. Nonetheless, there are no further reports of the use of the telephone in teaching.

Still, innovation continued. In the 1960s Skinner's teaching machines had their peak acceptance; programmed learning using paper and pencil also appeared. Interest was short-lived, though: *The Journal of Programmed Instruction*, for instance, lasted only a few years after its inception in 1962. Then, in the 1970s, handheld calculators became widespread, so that performing calculations "by hand" no longer meant actual manual calculations. Some instructors believe that such calculation gives students a better sense of the statistics; for example, my colleague Ann Lynn at Ithaca College still requires calculator use (Beins & Lynn, 2007). I have seen no empirical verification that students develop a better feel for a statistic through hand calculation, except for a nonsignificant tendency ($p = .08$) for traditionally taught students to show higher scores on free-response questions on a statistics test compared to those using SPSS (Gratz, Volpe, & Kind, 1993).

Interestingly, although computerized data analysis, often involving SPSS, is the norm now for most statistics classes (Fredrich, Buday, & Kerr, 2000), statistics textbooks in psychology still appear to present computational formulas that rely on hand calculation rather than on the more meaningful theoretical formulas (Guttmanova, Shields, & Caruso, 2005). Computational formulas were helpful in reducing tedium and computational error when students (and researchers) analyzed data truly by hand; in fact, at least one book provided nothing but computational formulas to aid one's data analysis (Bruning & Kintz, 1968, 1977). But such formulas have outlived their usefulness in any practical way. In fact, a regression toward the past may be occurring wherein statistics textbooks are focusing on the theoretical formulas, ignoring computational formulas (Chris Spatz, personal communication, May 1, 2009).

Subsequently, personal computers were visible on the horizon in the late 1970s, and they rapidly gained attention because of their pedagogical potential (e.g., Brothen, 1984). Today's classrooms invariably feature computers that are likely to allow Internet access, providing flexibility in their use that would astound Calkins (1910), Sanford (1910), Seashore (1910), and Whipple (1910). What does current research indicate about the efficacy of computer-based pedagogy? If articles appearing in *Teaching of Psychology* provide useful information, the current technology may lead to the same small treatment effects that Kulik et al. (1980) noted in previous instructional technologies.

For example, Daniel and Broida (2004) studied the use of the course-management approach of WebCT. They initially discovered that students performed at a higher level on exams when the students had taken in-class practice quizzes compared to students who had no practice quizzes or who had taken them on WebCT. However, there was no advantage of WebCT over having no practice quizzes. By adding a timed component to the online tests, however, scores on in-class quizzes and on WebCT quizzes were comparable.

One of the latest technologies to have captured the fancy of instructors is the so-called clickers (personal response systems [PRS]; see Chapter 9). Research into the enhancement in learning of PRS suggests that clickers may motivate teachers, but the impact they have on increased student learning or motivation seems inconsistent. Poirer and Feldman (2007) discovered a small effect (Cohen's d = .17), but they reported that half the class did not improve their test scores with the new system. Morling, McAuliffe, Cohen, and DiLorenzo (2008) found that clickers were associated with better student test scores on only two of four tests in a class they monitored, with an effect size of η^2 = .006; furthermore, students reported no greater engagement with PRS than without. Other research has shown no difference in learning with PRS but greater student participation (Stowell & Nelson, 2007).

Thus, the record of efficacy of pedagogical innovation is questionable. The meta-analysis by Kulik et al. (1980) involving 312 studies has shown an enhancement in student learning with the use of teaching technology including computer-based instruction, programmed learning, audio-based instruction, and visually based instruction, but the effects tend to be small at best. Furthermore, one might argue that many of the salutary effects of such innovation could be due to the revolutionary zeal of the teacher. Such a conclusion does not obviate the advantage of innovation, but the positive effect on student learning may be as much associated with the teacher as with the technology.

What Do Teachers Want to Accomplish?

A comparison of the use of computers in teaching, as reflected in *Teaching of Psychology* articles, illustrates the constancy of teachers' goals. It is apparent from Table 3.1 that the broad goals of computer use in teaching have not changed in the new millennium when compared with the first 15 years of the journal. Of the broad categories reported, the only addition involves fostering critical thinking, which seems to be a prime goal in education.

There is no shortage of sources to guide readers in evaluating information critically, including focus on psychological topics (e.g., Smith, 2002), evaluating sources when writing (Beins & Beins, 2008), and general, practical strategies for solving problems (Rehner, 1994). The proliferation of these sources reflects the importance that teachers attach to such thought.

As noted in the quotation cited early in this chapter, there has been resistance to one particular technology-based resource: Wikipedia. Is this resistance based on sound critical thinking? The online encyclopedia has been the target of multifaceted criticisms (e.g., McHenry, 2004). Furthermore, some colleges have forbidden students from citing Wikipedia in their papers (Jaschik, 2007). However, the extent of its failings is an empirical question, one that *Nature* magazine addressed. For all of the resistance in the academy

Table 3.1

Illustration of Computer-Focus Use Reported in Teaching of Psychology in 1974–1988 and 2000–2008

Time Period	
1974–1988	2001–2008
Generating data	Generating data
Simulations	Simulations
Administering tests	Administering tests
Delivering course content	Delivering course content
Presenting online study questions	Presenting online study questions
Searching online databases	Fostering critical thinking

to Wikipedia, it seems to be as accurate as *Encyclopedia Britannica* in its coverage of scientific topics (Giles, 2005). In fact, Wikipedia can be more useful than some material that doctoral-level psychologists have written.

For example, Figure 3.3 shows the representation of research on stereotype threat (Steele & Aronson, 1995). A perusal of introductory psychology books in widespread use revealed that this graph or one essentially identical to it is pervasive. Unfortunately, textbooks fail to include some very important qualifying information that Wikipedia does include in its figure caption: "An experiment on college students in 1995 showed the impact of stereotype threat by asking students to fill out a form, indicating their race, before taking the test. The scores in this graph have been adjusted by SAT" (Stereotype threat, n.d.). This adjustment is critical to understanding the research on stereotype threat. In fact, when I notified Joshua Aronson, one of the original researchers on stereotype threat, that I wanted to use the graph from his article, he specifically pointed out that I should make note of the adjustment according to SAT scores because of its importance in understanding the phenomenon (Joshua Aronson, personal communication, March 4, 2009).

The logic of prohibiting citation of Wikipedia is troublesome if one allows students to use a published book (e.g., an introductory psychology textbook) on the grounds that it is accurate but not a source like Wikipedia because it is, putatively, not accurate. In some cases, the problematic source is more accurate than a preferred source.

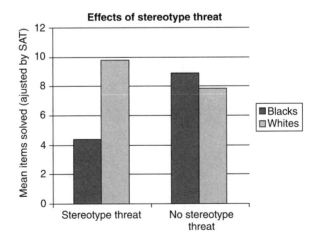

Figure 3.3. Results of stereotype threat research (Steele & Aronson, 1995) as presented in Wikipedia. Original figure copyright American Psychological Association.

Some critics have also commented that the writing style in Wikipedia is poor and often basically unreadable (Orlowski, 2005). If this were a serious limitation to the use of a source, teachers would probably ban journal articles, whose prose is often quite turgid and tangled. Current writers do not constitute the first generation of psychologists with less-than-admirable writing skill. In fact, the original APA style guide noted that "the writer who is incompetent in spelling, grammar, or syntax should seek help" (Instructions in regard, 1929, p. 58), suggesting that poor writing may not have been all that rare decades ago. Somewhat later, an editorial assistant at APA listed writing problems of psychologists of that era, noting that in writing, a psychologist "bends all his efforts to the paradoxical search for the most colorless expressions, the least pointed, and the most roundabout" (Bruner, 1942, p. 53), all the while resorting to "tortured circumlocutions of the passive voice" (p. 55).

This digression is intended to show that some of the criticisms of Wikipedia are not peculiar to the online encyclopedia. Rather, the problems (such as they might be) of Wikipedia exist because human beings, with the foibles that all people display, created and maintain it.

The critical point is that technology has provided access to vast amounts of information of unknown quality, whether that information be in a traditional book or in a wiki. The issue to which teachers should attend is not whether information is part of a wiki as opposed to a traditionally edited source: students are using Wikipedia and will continue to do so. Rather, teachers should help students learn to evaluate critically the information they encounter, not to dismiss potentially useful sources out of hand because of the nature of the source. In the end, the goal of teachers is likely to be simply to foster the willingness and ability of students to engage in critical thought about information they encounter.

It would be impossible in this chapter to capture all elements involved in critical thought, but some issues are obvious. One of these issues is whether a source is credible. Is it authoritative, objective, accurate, and current? An example involving these characteristics on the Internet is the belief held by many that if an Internet address ends in .org, it is credible, certainly more so than an address ending in .com. This acceptance of .org sites as being credible makes little sense because anybody, credible or not, can create a Web site with such an extension. The Web site MartinLutherKing.org is run by a neo-Nazi organization that presents what many would consider an unbalanced presentation of information about Martin Luther King. On the other hand, the site StanleyMilgram.com contains highly credible and authoritative information about Stanley Milgram and his research. It would be better for students to learn to evaluate the content of the site than to make decisions based on the extension of the Web address.

Likewise, information may be accurate and authoritative, but not objective. In fact, pharmaceutical companies sometimes create unbranded Web sites that present accurate information that directs a reader to its product. A writer and information researcher familiar with the modes of conveying information about treatments for psychological problems on the Internet has noted that "It's usually more about what they don't say than what they do" (Simon F. Beins, March 13, 2009, personal communication). This point leads to an important element of critical thinking: that there is a reason that people convey the information they do and that their perspective will color the message they present.

Receivers of information are also a factor in the equation. When students learn about evaluating information, they also need to know about weak and strong critical thinking. Most people are likely to evaluate information critically when they disagree with its content, looking for holes in an argument; this is weak critical thinking. The tendency is less pronounced to look for holes in a point that one believes. Seeking flaws in information consistent with one's worldview requires strong critical thinking.

Similarly, students need to learn that just because one finds two sides of an issue represented on the Internet or in the popular media, it does not mean that an actual controversy exists and that both sides present credible ideas. For instance, information debunking phrenology is easy to find on the Internet. On the other hand, a particular Web site for phrenology could lead a reader to conclude that this pseudoscience has some merit when the author writes that "extensive experimental verification of the Phrenological localisations have proven their practical value. The Phrenological analysis of personality remains of incomparable value to assess the character" (The Future of Phrenology, ¶9, Retrieved April 3, 2009, from http://www.phrenology.org/). This bald assertion might convince people who are untutored in the use of data to inform their conclusions. Teachers are the ideal people to guide students toward data in drawing conclusions.

Because human behavior and learning deal with complex constructs operating within even more complex organisms (i.e., people), answers to behavioral questions are always incomplete and evolving. A major goal of teaching is enhancement of critical thinking so students recognize this complexity and learn to appreciate it. Contemporary issues of teaching with technological innovation make issues of critical thinking vitally important. But technology is only a tool, and tools are essentially neutral. Teachers need to foster the development of critical thinking regarding the uses of these and any other pedagogical tools to which they have access.

In the end, teachers need to remember that learning is hard work. Consequently, educators should welcome new, potentially effective technologies that will enhance student performance and apply those technologies using psychological principles associated with effective learning.

Fortunately, research has provided knowledge about learning and motivation that educators can apply to the classroom. Teachers have access to a wealth of information that can lead to effective pedagogical approaches and to greater student achievement. Similarly, the pace of technological innovation has generated new tools for disseminating information that creative teachers can adapt for the classroom and for distance learning. There are many reasons to believe that educators will continue to incorporate new technology into their teaching as it emerges and no reasons to think otherwise. The combination of psychological knowledge, technological innovation, and the teacher's zeal provides the capacity for modes of learning undreamed of when Whipple (1910) recommended the creation of teaching conferences and compilations of classroom activities and demonstrations.

References

Andrews, T. G. (1946). Demonstrations for the introductory psychology course. *American Psychologist, 1*, 312–323. doi:10.1037/h0056589

APA announces "retirement," 2006. Retrieved from http://www.apa.org/publications/releases/psycabstracts.html

Beins, B. C., & Beins, A. M. (2008). *Effective writing in psychology: Papers, posters, and presentations.* Malden, MA: Blackwell.

Beins, B. C., & Lynn, A. (2007). Integrating computer applications in statistics and research methods. In D. S. Dunn, R. A. Smith, & B. C. Beins (Eds.), *Best practices for teaching statistics and research methods in the behavioral sciences* (pp. 203–219). Mahwah, NJ: Lawrence Erlbaum Associates.

Benjamin, L. T., Jr. (1991). *Harry Kirke Wolfe: Pioneer in psychology.* Lincoln, NE: University of Nebraska Press.

Benjamin, L. T., Jr. (2007). *A brief history of modern psychology.* Boston: Blackwell.

Benjamin, L. T., Jr., & Nielsen-Gammon, E. (1999). B. F. Skinner and psychotechnology: The case of the heir conditioner. *Review of General Psychology, 3*, 155–167.

Birney, R., & McKeachie, W. (1955). The teaching of psychology: A survey of research since 1942 *Psychological Bulletin, 52,* 51–68.

Brothen, T. (1984). Three computer-assisted laboratory exercises for introductory psychology. *Teaching of Psychology, 11,* 105–107.

Bruner, K. F. (1942). Of psychological writing: Being some valedictory remarks on style. *Journal of Abnormal and Social Psychology, 37,* 51–70.

Bruning, J. L., & Kintz, B. L. (1968). *Computational handbook of statistics.* Glenview, IL: Scott, Foresman.

Bruning, J. L., & Kintz, B. L. (1977). *Computational handbook of statistics* (2nd ed.). Glenview, IL: Scott, Foresman.

Bryson, B. (1991). *The mother tongue: English and how it got that way.* New York: Harper Perennial.

Calkins, M. W. (1910). The teaching of elementary psychology in colleges supposed to have no laboratory. *Psychological Monographs, 12*(4, Whole 51), 41–53.

Coone, J. G., & White, W. F. (1968). Role of the classroom instructor in a televised introductory psychology course. *Psychological Reports, 23,* 43–47.

Cutler, R. L., McKeachie, W. J., & McNeil, E. B. (1958). Teaching psychology by telephone. *American Psychologist, 13,* 551–552. doi:10.1037/h0043096

Daniel, D. B., & Broida, J. (2004). Using web-based quizzing to improve exam performance: Lessons learned. *Teaching of Psychology, 31,* 207–208. doi:10.1207/s15328023top3103_6

Davis, R. (2008). Survey: College students love Wikipedia (profs not so happy). Retrieved March 24, 2009 from http://www.powerset.com/blog/articles/2008/09/03/survey-college-students-love-wikipedia-profs-not-so-happy

Dwyer, F. M., Jr. (1969). An analysis of the instructional effectiveness of visual illustrations presented via television. *Journal of Psychology: Interdisciplinary and Applied, 72,* 61–64.

Fancher, R. E. (1979). *Pioneers of psychology* (3rd ed.). New York: W. W. Norton.

Ferdig, R. E. (2006). Assessing technologies for teaching and learning: Understanding the importance of technological pedagogical. *British Journal of Educational Technology, 37,*749–760. doi: 10.1111/j.1467-8535.2006.00559.x

Fredrich, J., Buday, E., & Kerr, D. (2000). Statistical training in psychology: A national survey and commentary on undergraduate programs. *Teaching of Psychology, 27,* 248–257.

Gaskill, H. V. (1933). Broadcasting versus lecturing in psychology; preliminary investigation. *Journal of Applied Psychology, 17,* 317–319.

Giles, J. (2005). Internet encyclopaedias go head to head. *Nature, 438,* 900–901. doi: 10.1038/438900a

Gratz, Z. S., Volpe, G. D., & Kind, B. M. (1993). *Attitudes and achievement in introductory statistics classes: Traditional versus computer-supported instruction* (Report No. JH940166). Ellenville, NY: Teaching of Psychology: Ideas and innovations: Proceedings of the 7th Annual Conference on Undergraduate Teaching of Psychology, March 24–26. (ERIC Document Reproduction Service No. ED365405)

Guttmanova, K., Shields, A. L., & Caruso, J. C. (2005). Promoting conceptual understanding of statistics: Definitional versus computational formula. *Teaching of Psychology, 32*, 251–253.

Harper, R. S. (1950). The first psychological laboratory. *Isis, 41*, 158–161.

Husband, R. W. (1954). Television versus classroom for learning general psychology. *American Psychologist, 9*, 181–183.

Instructions in regard to preparation of manuscript (1929). *The Psychological Bulletin, 26*, 57–63.

Jaschik, S. (2007, January 26). A stand against Wikipedia. *Inside Higher Ed*. Retrieved March 30, 2009, from http://www.insidehighered.com/news/2007/01/26/wiki

Kulik, C. C., Kulik, J. A., & Cohen, P. A. (1980). Instructional technology and college teaching. *Teaching of Psychology, 7*, 199–205.

McHenry, R. (2004, November 15). The faith-based encyclopedia. *TCS Daily*. Retrieved March 30, 2009, from http://www.tcsdaily.com/article.aspx?id=111504A

McKeachie, W. J. (1952). Teaching psychology on television. *American Psychologist, 7*, 503–506.

Miles, J. R. (1940). Radio and elementary science teaching. *Journal of Applied Psychology, 24*, 714–720.

Morling, B., McAuliffe, M., Cohen, L., & DiLorenzo, T. M. (2008). Efficacy of personal response systems ("clickers") in large, introductory psychology classes. *Teaching of Psychology, 35*, 45–50.

Orlowski, A. (2005, October 18). Wikipedia founder admits to serious quality problems: Yes it's garbage, but it's delivered so much faster! *The Register*. Retrieved March 30, 2009 from http://www.theregister.co.uk/2005/10/18/wikipedia_quality_problem/page2.html

Petroski, H. (1999). *The book on the bookshelf*. New York: Knopf.

Poirer, C. R., & Feldman, R. S. (2007). Promoting active learning using individual response technology in large introductory psychology classes. *Teaching of Psychology, 34*, 194–196.

Pressey, S. L. (1926). A simple apparatus which gives tests and scores—and teaches. *School & Society, 23*, 373–376.

Pressey, S. L., (1927). A machine for automatic teaching of drill material. *School & Society, 25*, 549–552.

Rehner, J. (1994). *Practical strategies for critical thinking*. Boston: Houghton-Mifflin.

Reid, S. (1940). Reading, writing, and radio: a study of five school broadcasts in literature. *Journal of Applied Psychology, 24*, 703–713.

Sahr, R. C. (2009). Inflation conversion factors for years 1774 to estimated 2019. Retrieved March 13, 2009, from http://oregonstate.edu/cla/polisci/faculty-research/sahr/infcf17742008.pdf

Sanford, E. C. (1910). The teaching of elementary psychology in colleges and universities with laboratories. *Psychological Monographs, 12*(4, Whole 51), 54–71.

Seashore, C. E. (1910). General report on the teaching of the elementary course in psychology: Recommendations. *Psychological Monographs, 12*(4, Whole 51), 80–91.

Skinner, B. F. (1958). Teaching machines. *Science, 128*, 969–977.

Skinner, B. F. (1989). Teaching machines. *Science, 243*, 1535.

Sniffy the virtual rat, 2005; retrieved March 12, 2009 from http://www.wadsworth.com/psychology_d/special_features/sniffy.html

Smith, R. A. (2002). *Challenging your preconceptions: Thinking critically about psychology*. Belmont, CA: Wadsworth.

Steele C. M, & Aronson J. (1995). Stereotype threat and the intellectual test performance of African Americans. *Journal of Personality and Social Psychology, 69*, 797–811. doi: 10.1037/0022-3514.69.5.797

Stereotype threat (n.d.). Retrieved March 24, 2009, from http://en.wikipedia.org/wiki/Stereotype_threat

Stowell, J. R., & Nelson, J. M. (2007). Benefits of electronic audience response systems on student participation, learning, and emotion. *Teaching of Psychology, 34*, 253–258.

Stromberg, E. L. (1952). College credit for television home study. *American Psychologist. 7*, 507–509.

Thornburg, D. D. (1992). *Edutrends 2010: Restructuring, technology, and the future of education*. Starsong Publications.

Walton, A. (1930). Demonstrational and experimental devices. *American Journal of Psychology, 42*, 109–114.

Whipple, G. M. (1910). The teaching of psychology in normal schools. *Psychological Monographs, 12*(4, Whole 51), 2–40.

4 Developing an Online Curriculum in Psychology

Practical Advice from a Departmental Initiative

Jeffrey L. Helms, Pam Marek, Christopher K. Randall, Daniel T. Rogers, Lauren A. Taglialatela, and Adrienne L. Williamson

When student enrollments exceed existing instructional facilities, institutions must employ creative methods for managing enrollment growth without turning away prospective students. The strategic plans of both the University System of Georgia Board of Regents and the Kennesaw State University (KSU) administration now emphasize managing enrollment growth, in part, via distributed learning. In response, the KSU Center for Excellence in Teaching and Learning (CETL) recently organized a series of workshops that provided faculty with stipends, training, technology, and opportunities to research and share effective practices in online teaching and student learning. In 2008, the university selected the Psychology Department to participate in this inaugural program.

To expand our online course offerings while concentrating somewhat limited support resources, this initiative began as a collaborative effort of a number of support groups at KSU. These groups, collectively known as the KSU eLearning Collaborative, provided technical and instructional design support to faculty participants during the summer program and subsequently worked with faculty throughout the course development process. Participants, a mix of experienced and novice online instructors, met regularly over the course of 8 weeks. Each faculty member developed an online class during the subsequent academic year. As part of the program, participants collaborated on the development of a common structure, consistent organization, and flexible resources for use across a variety of online classes in the curriculum. To date, this program resulted in the transition of seven classes to an online delivery format, enabled us to enhance our existing hybrid/blended classes, and encouraged faculty to begin developing several additional online classes.

Buoyed by the success of the online course development initiative, our primary goal in this chapter is to provide both departments and individuals with practical advice for incorporating effective practices in online course development and instruction. We also believe the collaborative development of online courses and materials promotes the consistency and quality of online courses and instruction across the curriculum and, thus, merits consideration. This chapter is organized into five sections covering the critical course components for providing quality instruction and promoting student success in the online classroom: developing and presenting learning objectives, student preparedness and orientation to online learning, increasing engagement through technology, managing online discussions, and assessment of student learning.

Developing and Presenting Learning Objectives: Increasing Clarity and Transparency to Impel Student Action

The utility of learning objectives in education is not a new discussion (see Bloom, 1956; Mager, 1962, 1975). In fact, that conversation began long before online education was possible, and it certainly predates the growing reliance on distributed learning. Despite the changing landscape of modern education, such traditional values applied in the online environment can guide student expectations, inform instructional techniques, and provide scaffolding for other course components (Shank, 2005). However, an online course is not just material from a face-to-face class dropped capriciously into an Internet framework. Instructors must be mindful that traditional ways of organizing and presenting information may not be as effective in online courses (Carr-Chellman & Duchastel, 2000; Koszalka & Ganesan, 2004; Sims, Dobbs, & Hand, 2002). In their qualitative research, Menchaca and Bekele (2008) indicate that clarity of goals and course organization are two of the "major course factors" (p. 249) related to success in online learning. Below we have outlined some best practices for how to construct, organize, and present learning objectives in an online learning environment to increase clarity and provide transparency to encourage student action through the course.

Clarity

In an online environment, which is arguably less rich in conversational exchanges than in face-to-face classes, it is of paramount importance to communicate learning expectations to students in a clear and measurable way (Grant & Thornton, 2007; Newlin & Wang, 2002). Instructors should write the course learning objectives in action language and from the students' perspective (what *they* will do, not what *the instructor* will do; Cantor, 2008; Mager, 1962). Also, to provide students with continued direction throughout the academic term, instructors should buttress broad course objectives with module (or unit/chapter) objectives to focus students' attention on the particular expectations for each portion of the course. Educators use the term *alignment* to refer to the degree to which these course and module objectives overlap and work to direct student learning (see Webb, 1997). Alignment of course objectives (and other course components) in Internet-supported learning environments is linked with student success measures, including learning outcomes, critical thinking, and metacognition, as well as student and faculty satisfaction (Bekele, 2008, as cited in Menchaca & Bekele, 2008).

Below are course- and module-level objectives from an online Learning and Behavior course. In the examples below, please note the following:

1. Each objective contains measurable and accomplishment-oriented terms in italics to highlight to students the expected behavioral outcome. Although many are available, two useful compendiums of action verbs that may be effectively incorporated into learning objectives are available at http://www.ispe.org/galleries/publications-files/ SuggestedVerbsForLearningObjectives.pdf, and at http://www.edpsycinteractive.org/topics/cogsys/bloom.html
2. Each objective provides a non-exhaustive list of topics to underscore the relation between the module-level objectives (what the student is doing now; sub-goal) and the course-level objectives (what the student is doing across an academic term; end goal).

3. Course- and module-level objectives share a common format and vernacular.

Example: Course Learning Objective: Learning and Behavior

At the end of this course, you should be able to *identify*, *define*, and *explain* theories and concepts related to learning and behavior using appropriate terminology. [Topics include, but are not limited to, historical antecedents, classical conditioning, operant conditioning, social learning, biological dispositions, and language learning.]

Example: Module Objective: Classical Conditioning Module

At the end of this module, you should be able to *identify*, *define*, and *explain* behavioral phenomena and the underlying mechanisms from a classical conditioning perspective using appropriate terminology. [Topics include, but are not limited to, reflexes, contiguity, habituation/sensitization, basic terms of classical conditioning, acquisition, extinction, overshadowing, blocking, latent inhibition, Rescorla-Wagner Theory (1972), and practical applications to phobias and taste aversion.]

Transparency

In distance learning, instructors do not have the luxury of being able to remind students verbally about such things as "What we're doing today" or "How this material is related to the overall course." Therefore, instructors should publicize and direct students' attention to course- and module-level learning objectives repeatedly. Specifically, we suggest that instructors do the following:

1. Provide the course objectives in the course syllabus, which is easily accessible from the homepage of the course Web site.
2. Indicate to students that these objectives represent the declarative knowledge (i.e., factual knowledge/information), critical thinking skills, and procedural knowledge (i.e., the skills) that graduates from this course should possess ("When you complete this class, these are the things you should be able to do").
3. Indicate on the syllabus that these course objectives serve as the "end goals" of the course, and that these goals are

supported by more specific sub-goals for each module (or unit/chapter) ("Accomplishing the module-level objectives will help you to accomplish the course-level objectives").

4. State that every module has a set of objectives and that these objectives appear at the beginning of each learning module ("When you click on each module, the first thing you will see is a list of objectives for that particular module").

5. Construct the online modules such that the entry page of each module is a document prominently displaying both module objectives and the associated course objectives to reinforce the relation between course-level and module-level objectives ("When you click on each module, you will also see the broader course-level objectives that are supported by what you will do in that particular module").

Action

Educators (e.g., Gordon, 2009) consider students as agents of action, working to construct their knowledge rather than passively absorbing it. The extent to which students assume responsibility for their learning and construction of knowledge is perhaps greater in the online environment than in the traditional classroom because of the level of autonomous, self-paced work required. As detailed elsewhere in this chapter, student engagement is a significant factor in determining success or failure in an online course. Quite simply, if students do not know what skills and content their instructors expect them to learn, then they will not know what to do or how to allocate their instructional time. Therefore, providing clear expectations via specific, measurable learning objectives, as outlined above, may encourage students to be active agents in their education.

Student Preparedness and Orientation to Online Learning

Setting the stage and tone for the online course is critical to student success. If the stage and tone are not set sufficiently, students are likely to flounder, creating frustration for both the instructor and the students. In fact, we view orientation to the "nuts and bolts" of taking an online course as the foundation for success. Orienting students (especially online novices) on the first day or two of a course via specific directions may increase retention, progression, and successful completion of the course. The result is an online delivery method that accentuates the virtual classroom experience and learning.

To start the orientation process, we encourage a pre-orientation step, especially for students new to the online educational experience. The pre-orientation step occurs the first day that the course is available to students (or even before this time if possible) and includes a self-assessment of their readiness for taking an online course. The self-assessment that we find particularly helpful is the Readiness for Education at a Distance Indicator (READI-SmarterMeasure; SmarterServices, 2010). Through a quiz-like delivery, students evaluate their readiness for online learning by assessing such aspects as their experience with technology, access to the software and hardware generally required for online courses, and personal study habits. Students access READI-SmarterMeasure at http://goml.readi.info/.

Once students self-assess and self-select for an online course, the orientation process really begins, accomplished via a series of documents that we provide for each course. The series of documents that pave the orientation process for students include:

1. *Course road map.* This "read me first" document directs students to what to do first, second, third, and so on. The map also includes associated symbols and icons used in the course (e.g., to view the grade book, students click on a particular icon).

2. *Technology requirements for the course.* Although READI includes what is generally required for online courses, this file specifies the type of hardware and software required for the particular course. Most of the associated software products (e.g., Adobe Reader) we use in our courses are available online for free.

3. *Assistance for technology problems.* Sometimes software programs do not work the way they should. To help students, we list university resources available via e-mail, telephone, and in-person. We avoid online (non-university) resources because they are often unreliable and expensive.

4. *Academic and general student support services.* This item provides a list of resources along with descriptions and contact

information that may be useful to the students. Some of these include writing labs, a counseling center, and disabled student support services.

5. *General instructor policies.* Specific policies may vary considerably between instructors. However, consistent policies focus on late work and/or missed deadlines, academic integrity, and netiquette. In terms of netiquette, we find that Shea's "The Core Rules of Netiquette" (http://www.albion.com/netiquette/corerules.html; 1990-2005) meets our needs.

6. *Course documents.* These documents include the course syllabus, schedule, readings, and grading rubrics.

7. *Student resources.* This file provides links to graduate school and career preparation resources that are particularly useful to our majors, including a link to our department's student information series (*PsycSeries*; http://www.kennesaw.edu/psychology/psycseries.shtml).

Of course, providing these documents and information does not mean that students will actually read them. As a result, we actively engage students in the course in ways reminiscent of what we do in face-to-face courses. For example, some of us give students (minimal) extra credit on the first assignment for finding errors in these introductory documents that we may have missed when originally developing them. This type of "scavenger hunt" prompts them to pay more attention to these resources and to the details found therein. Also, familiarity may encourage students to revisit these pages throughout the course. The extra credit also costs the instructor little in terms of grade inflation and improves the course documents for the next semester. Incorporating a test on the resources also may help students. A short quiz that forces students to locate and read the orientation materials can help limit confusion later in the course (e.g., "Where are the grading rubrics for this assignment?").

Orientation to the course encompasses familiarization with the documents, course structure, students, and professor. In particular, we believe that encouraging students to become acquainted with their classmates and the professor at the beginning of the course via the discussion boards may serve to increase interaction later in the course (e.g., graded discussions). Arguably, the best example of requiring engagement is course discussions, which we review in a subsequent section of this chapter. However, the use of an "Introduction" discussion post by which the professor and the students introduce themselves to one another deserves special mention here. This activity appears to increase the development of community that is important in online learning. In addition, we maintain engagement in our online courses by providing two other opportunities:

1. *Ask the Professor.* This discussion area allows students to post course-related questions. This encourages open dialogue between the professor and students. In fact, it is common for students to assist their peers in locating answers to posted questions before we even respond.
2. *Cyber Café.* This discussion area allows students to post non–course-related material. For example, students often post opportunities for career-related job experience and campus activities (e.g., Psi Chi or Psychology Club meeting announcements).

Regardless of the specifics that vary among our courses, these tools to orient and engage students in the online experience assist each of us in successfully navigating the online environment for our students and for ourselves.

Increasing Engagement through Technology

The development of new technologies allows for continued improvement in online course design and delivery. Advances in technology enable distance-learning courses to evolve from simply transmitting information to fostering learning. Technology can enhance learning in a variety of ways, including promoting student interactivity with the instructor as well as the content, engaging the student, and encouraging active learning. In this section, we will focus on several ways instructors can leverage technology to motivate students and positively influence student learning.

It is important to create a sense of connection between the instructor and students, but this may be more difficult to develop in online courses because there usually is no face-to-face interaction. The foundation of this relationship begins with the introduction, and a video is an option for making the introduction more personable. An introductory video allows instructors to show a bit of their personalities, and it helps students put a face and voice with the words they read on screen. Reminding students that they are communicating with a real person on the other end of the computer can help them feel more comfortable and promote interaction from the beginning of the course (Jones, Naugle, & Kolloff, 2008). Fortunately, web cameras are relatively inexpensive and come with many laptops and desktop monitors. Also, software designed to help individuals create videos often comes bundled with web cameras.

In addition to creating a connection between the instructor and students, it is also important to help students interact with the material. To achieve this goal, instructors can use narrated PowerPoint slides to add an auditory component to the visual presentation of material. Narrated PowerPoint slides are easy to produce within the PowerPoint program itself or by importing slides into a software program such as Adobe's Captivate (http://www.adobe.com/products/captivate/) or TechSmith's Camtasia Studio (http://www.techsmith.com/camtasia.asp).

Narrated PowerPoint slides allow instructors to explain a complex concept as they would in a face-to-face class. In a traditional lecture, instructors often verbally elaborate key points and images on slides by providing examples and anecdotes. Using the same slides without elaboration in an online course limits the information students receive. Although it is possible to elaborate and include examples in a text format, adding narration to the slides makes it easier for students to understand the material (Walker, 2006). Using a software program such as Captivate allows instructors to highlight important sections of the slide while they talk about them, so students can visually focus on the slide while they are listening to an explanation of the concept. Also, presenting information in more than one sensory modality provides opportunities for multiple retrieval cues.

Narrated PowerPoint is also beneficial for instructors. It is often quicker for the instructor to explain the concept verbally than it is to type a detailed explanation. Moreover, if multiple courses include the same concept, it is possible to use the same set of narrated PowerPoint slides across courses. Such flexibility increases the number of students who benefit from the materials while minimizing the work involved in producing these materials.

Captivate also enables instructors to make PowerPoint slides interactive by incorporating textboxes where students can enter answers to questions. Captivate compares the students' answers to the correct answers and provides immediate feedback to the students. Instructors can program the feedback to provide the correct answer or offer a hint and give students an opportunity to try again. Thus, as they progress through the slides, students can assess their level of learning. This type of formative assessment can help students determine whether they need to review previous slides before proceeding to new material. Also, as students learn to solve statistical equations, they can enter their answers in the interactive textboxes and receive feedback at every step. This feedback is particularly useful for correcting simple math errors in complex equations.

Another technology that can enhance the level of interaction in an online course is screen capture or screencast software, which records everything that occurs on a computer screen in real time (e.g., Wink, http://www. debugmode.com/wink/). By connecting a microphone, instructors can also record audio at the same time or add a narrative later. This technology can guide students through course components at the beginning of a course. Such practice in navigation might be particularly helpful for students who may not be computer savvy or experienced online students.

With screen capture software, instructors can also create demonstrations and simulations to help students learn to use computer programs, such as statistical software packages, that are important for class. Instructors can record their computer steps while using the software. When students play the video, they see the mouse movements and text descriptions detailing buttons clicked to carry out the procedure. Simulations may incorporate prompts and feedback that guide students' practice of the recorded steps.

These are just a few of the ways that technology can enhance learning in online courses as well as in face-to-face classes. Because incorporation of emerging technologies may seem a bit overwhelming to faculty who are new to teaching online, we recommend that faculty members start small and add new modules and/or technologies over time. We recognize that some instructors may resist teaching online because of the perceived steep learning curve that they associate with technology. However, we do not believe that such a learning curve is a prohibitive factor for the technologies mentioned in this section; many of these technologies are both easy for instructors to use and user-friendly for students.

Managing Online Discussions: Fostering Engagement and Learning

Discussions are vital to the learning process in any course. The exchange of ideas among students and the instructor supports the mastery of new information and skills. In traditional, face-to-face courses, opportunities for discussion abound in a variety of formats and settings. Many of these options are restricted in online courses. In our experience, such limitations actually serve to elevate the importance of discussion for fostering and assessing student learning. In this section, we will discuss effective practices for incorporating and assessing discussions in online classes.

Instructors often incorporate discussions into online courses with varied success. Creating discussion opportunities, and even requiring students to participate, does not guarantee that productive interactions will occur. Based on our experience with discussions in our online courses, we recommend the following four action steps:

1. Identify the objectives of the discussion.
2. Select discussion formats that support these objectives.
3. Anticipate common problems that can occur.
4. Select techniques that will both reduce these problems and support your objectives.

All discussions have two overarching goals: engagement and learning. In other words, these interactions should lead students to connect with their instructor and classmates as well as the course content, assignments, and activities. The discussions should promote interactions that enhance the absorption, retention, and application of new knowledge and skills. Recognizing these goals, we develop specific objectives to identify the type of engagement and learning that we desire for the discussion. There is general support for the utility of online discussions in fostering student engagement and learning. Online discussions build class rapport (Clawson, Deen, & Oxley, 2002; Tiene, 2000), enhance mastery of content (Ertmer et al., 2007; Hoadley, 2000), foster critical thinking (Guiller, Durndell, & Ross, 2008; Yang & Ahn, 2007), and promote overall course success (Swan et al., 2000).

Online discussions occur in a variety of formats, with synchronous and asynchronous being a common dichotomy. Synchronous discussions involve simultaneous interaction between contributors (e.g., chat rooms, live classrooms, virtual offices). Asynchronous discussions occur with contributors engaging each other through consecutive messages or postings (e.g., e-mail, threaded discussions, blogs). Some social messaging technology, such as micro-blogging (e.g., Twitter), occupies a middle ground by using asynchronous discussion that is condensed in both content and time frame. In addition to these basic structural differences, instructors can design discussions with a variety of parameters. For example, interactions can be led by the instructor or students, focused on content or product, and be class-wide or restricted to small groups. Most course-management systems contain options for creating various types of synchronous and asynchronous discussions and modifying basic parameters, such as the length of contributions, who can view them, and whether authors can make revisions. In addition, a variety of free software applications is available for hosting and managing these interactions.

Despite their potential contributions to student learning and engagement, there are three common problems that plague online discussions and that have at times frustrated our efforts to incorporate them into our courses. First, some students make contributions to discussions that have limited significance and meaning. Often this stems from low motivation, lack of engagement with the task, procrastination, or poor critical thinking skills. A second common problem involves disruptive communication styles that lead to personalized, inappropriate, or tangential contributions. A third problem frequently encountered involves management of the volume of material that students contribute. Some discussion formats require careful tracking and organization of contributions in order for students to participate fully and for instructors to assess learning and participation.

We have used several strategies both to combat these common problems and to improve the effectiveness of discussions in our online courses. Keep in mind that creating effective online discussions is contingent upon variables unique to your particular course. However, the following general strategies can be helpful to most courses' discussion components:

1. *Make navigation of the discussion easy and intuitive* (Kear, 2001; Murphy & Coleman, 2004; Xie, DeBacker, & Ferguson, 2006). Create as few barriers as possible for students to contribute.

2. *Make some posts compulsory and time restricted* (Jeong, 2004; Khan, 2005; Xie et al., 2006). Not all contributions need strict structure, but having some that do promotes engagement.

3. *Provide clear protocols, including exemplars* (Gilbert & Dabbagh, 2005; Spatariu, Hartley, Schraw, Bendixen, & Quinn, 2007). Provide students with detailed instructions they can follow and concrete examples of quality contributions.

4. *Provide clear, simple grading rubrics* (Gilbert & Dabbagh, 2005; Spatariu et al., 2007). Inform students about the components you value and the ways in which you will assess the quality of their contributions.

5. *Be actively engaged and provide feedback, but avoid prominence* (Hewitt, 2005; Jung, Choi, Lim, & Leem, 2002; Mazzolinin & Maddison, 2007). Play a visible role in the discussion, but be wary of how your presence influences student engagement.

6. *Build a sense of community that tolerates open debate* (Cheung, Hew, & Ng, 2008; Masters & Oberprieler, 2004). Establish the expectation that you will welcome any contribution, even controversial ones.

7. *Create topics that are relevant to students' course needs* (Dennen, 2005; Guzdial & Turns, 2000). Design ways for students to simultaneously contribute and make progress on other assignments. For example, a discussion topic could require students to share their topic idea for an upcoming paper and offer feedback regarding their peers' topics.

8. *Compel engagement of others' ideas* (Kanuka, Rourke, & Laflamme, 2007). Having students think critically about the ideas of peers can foster interactions that are self-sustaining.

9. *Include collaborative learning and social interaction components* (Jung et al., 2002). Requiring students to work together and allowing for a degree of social and interpersonal communication outside of a specific task fosters a sense of community.

10. *Use unique topics across the course to maintain intrinsic motivation* (Dennen, 2005; Hewitt, 2005; Xie et al., 2006). Varied topics and methods of discussion promote students' interest in sharing their ideas with peers.

Obviously, asynchronous online discussions provide only one opportunity for instructors to assess student engagement and learning in an online course. We now turn our attention to other ways to incorporate varied and distributed assessments in the online environment.

Assessment of Student Learning

As is the case for classroom-based courses, assessment of online student learning involves the development of measures that relate directly to course and module learning objectives. Indeed, educational principles espousing the importance of a variety of formative and summative assessment techniques transcend the distinction between classroom and online learning environments. In addition, the problem of academic dishonesty plagues both classroom and online instructors (Olt, 2002) although it is perhaps of greater concern in online education because of the absence of face-to-face monitoring (Benson, 2003).

Online instructors have a variety of measurement tools available, such as quizzes and exams; written reports; contributions to discussions, wikis, and blogs; and portfolios (see Reeves, 2000). The tools we use depend on the course objectives; for example, we measure attainment of objectives relating to evaluation and analysis through open-ended responses rather than multiple-choice items. Ideally, our instruments measure both higher-order thinking skills, such as analysis and evaluation, as incorporated in Bloom's Taxonomy (1956), and knowledge. Course level guides the balance of higher-order skills and content knowledge that we evaluate. Some educators advocate extensive use of authentic assessment (e.g., Frederick, 2002) that involves students in iterative problem-solving tasks to simulate application of concepts outside the classroom, but as we transition courses from face-to-face to online environments, quizzes and examinations remain a common form of evaluation.

Most learning management systems offer opportunities for instructors to create or import test banks of questions, with each question linked to a specific learning objective. We group questions into objective-related sets and direct the testing program to select questions randomly from each set for each student's exam. Thus, although the specific questions displayed likely vary for each student, the selected items consistently span the same range of objectives. In addition, instructors may allow students to retake a quiz, in effect creating a formative assessment opportunity. Aviles (2001) has documented that students consider formative quizzes to be the most preferred advantage of mastery learning. We set time limits for online tests to reduce students' ability to check their textbooks for answers to questions. We use many conceptual and application questions so that simply knowing (or looking up) a definition will seldom result in a correct answer (also see Olt, 2002). After the closing date of each quiz, we provide students with feedback about correct and incorrect answers, thus allowing the students to review material they did not know prior to a major examination. Klecker (2007) has argued that feedback is an important component of any effective learning environment because it can motivate students to correct misconceptions or can serve as a reward for good work.

Written assignments serve as an additional evaluation tool. Beyond extending students' knowledge base, we design assignments in which students apply course material to their personal experience. For example, in an online introductory psychology course, students prepare brief papers (see Marek, Christopher, Koenig, & Reinhart, 2005) to explore topics related to stress and health and topics related to hunger and obesity. For each assignment, students gather material from four Internet sites, complete a scale to measure a relevant construct (e.g., personal stress, body shape), and prepare a three- to five-page paper incorporating factual information, personal examples, and personal opinions. To clarify expectations for all written assignments, we provide students with grading rubrics, highlight important precautions for avoiding plagiarism, and inform students of the penalties for plagiarism. We use Turnitin (http://turnitin.com) to expedite the process of checking for plagiarism that may occur. Depending on course objectives and instructional philosophies, we sometimes include individual writing, collaborative writing, or both in our online courses. Tools such as Google Docs (http://docs.google.com) enable multiple individuals to work simultaneously on a single document and may be particularly useful for collaboration in online courses.

Given burgeoning online enrollments, particularly for 2-year institutions (Allen & Seaman, 2007), and considering that assessment has been conceptualized as "the engine that drives student course activity" (Swan et al., 2000, p. 45), we encourage instructors to investigate the potential use of other interactive tools that might be appropriate for assessment beyond those discussed in this section. Clearly, there is a learning curve for both instructors and students when they initially become involved in online learning environments. As familiarity with basic online assessment techniques increases, instructors may gradually expand their technological and pedagogical toolboxes, as appropriate for course objectives, to scaffold and assess student learning in the ever-changing realm of technology.

Concluding Remarks

Transitioning from the traditional classroom to online teaching and learning requires significant effort for faculty course developers. The KSU online course development initiative presents one model for easing that transition. Specifically, our university chose to focus limited support resources on a collaborative departmental effort to produce several online classes. By participating in this initiative, faculty participants developed instructional materials that promoted consistency and quality across our emerging online curriculum. We focused on areas that we considered critical for encouraging student success in the online classroom: developing and presenting learning objectives, student preparedness and orientation to online learning, increasing engagement through technology, managing online discussions, and assessing student learning. In summary, we are encouraged by our successes to date and hope that our collaborative model and suggestions for course development will assist faculty across disciplines in efficiently preparing the curriculum for online delivery.

References

Allen, I., E., & Seaman, J. (2007). Online nation: Five years of growth in online learning. *Sloan Consortium*. Executive summary downloaded June 23, 2010, from http://www.sloan-c.org/sites/default/files/pages/online_nation.pdf

Aviles, C. B. (2001). *A study of mastery learning versus non-mastery learning instruction in an undergraduate social work policy class*. (Research Report). Resources in Education, 36. (ERIC Document Reproduction Service No. ED449413)

Benson, A. D. (2003). Assessing participant learning in online environments. *New Directions for Adult & Continuing Education, 100*, 69–78.

Bloom, B. S. (1956). *Taxonomy of educational objectives: The classification of educational goals. Handbook 1: The cognitive domain*. New York: Longman.

Cantor, J. (2008). *Delivering instruction to adult learners* (3rd ed.). Toronto: Wall & Emerson.

Carr-Chellman, A., & Duchastel, P. (2000). The ideal online course. *British Journal of Educational Technology, 31*(3), 229–241.

Cheung, W. S., Hew, K. F., & Ng, C. S. L. (2008). Toward an understanding of why students contribute in asynchronous online discussions. *Journal of Educational Computing Research, 38*, 29–50.

Clawson, R., Deen, R., & Oxley, M. (2002). Online discussions across three universities: Student participation and pedagogy. *Political Science & Politics, 35*, 713–718.

Dennen, V. P. (2005). From message posting to learning dialogues: Factors affecting learner participation in asynchronous discussion. *Distance Education, 26*, 127–148.

Ertmer, P. A., Richardson, J. C., Belland, B., Camin, D., Connolly, P., Coulthard, G., et al. (2007). Using peer feedback to enhance the quality of student online postings: An exploratory study. *Journal of Computer-Mediated Communication, 12,* 78–99.

Frederick, P. (2002). The need for alternative authentic assessments in online learning environments. *Journal of Instruction Delivery Systems, 16,* 17–20.

Gilbert, P. K., & Dabbagh, N. (2005). How to structure online discussions for meaningful discourse: A case study. *British Journal of Educational Technology, 36,* 5–18.

Gordon, M. (2009). Toward a pragmatic discourse of constructivism: Reflections on lessons from practice. *Educational Studies, 4,* 39–58.

Grant, M. R., & Thornton, H. R. (2007). Best practices in undergraduate adult-centered online learning: Mechanisms for course design and delivery. *Journal of Online Learning and Teaching, 4*(4), 346–356.

Guiller, J., Durndell, A., & Ross, A. (2008). Peer interaction and critical thinking: Face-to-face or online discussion? *Learning and Instruction, 18,* 187–200.

Guzdial, M., & Turns, J. (2000). Effective discussion through a computer-mediated anchored forum. *The Journal of Learning Sciences, 9,* 437–469.

Hewitt, J. (2005). Toward an understanding of how threads die in asynchronous computer conferences. *The Journal of the Learning Sciences, 14,* 567–589.

Hoadley, C. M. (2000). Teaching science through online, peer discussions: SpeakEasy in the Knowledge Integration Environment. *International Journal of Science Education, 22,* 839–857.

Jeong, A. (2004). The combined effects of response time and message content on growth patterns of discussion threads in computer-supported collaborative argumentation. *Journal of Distance Education, 19,* 36–53.

Jones, P., Naugle, K., & Kolloff, M. (2008, April). Teacher presence: Using introductory videos in online and hybrid Courses. *Learning Solutions e-Magazine.* Retrieved on August 20, 2010, from http://www.learningsolutionsmag.com/articles/107/teacher-presence-using-introductory-videos-in-online-and-hybrid-courses

Jung, L., Choi, S., Lim, C., & Leem, J. (2002). Effects of different types of interaction on learning achievement, satisfaction and participation in Web-based instruction. *Innovations in Education & Teaching International, 39,* 53–162.

Kanuka, H., Rourke, L., & Laflamme, E. (2007). The influence of instructional methods on the quality of online discussion. *British Journal of Educational Technology, 38,* 260–271.

Kear, K. (2001). Following the thread in computer conferences. *Computers and Education, 37,* 81–99.

Kennesaw State University Department of Psychology. (2008). *PsycSeries.* Retrieved March 24, 2009, from http://www.kennesaw.edu/psychology/psycseries.shtml.

Khan, S. (2005). Listservs in the college science classroom: Evaluating participation and "richness" in computer-mediated discourse. *Journal of Technology and Teacher Education, 13,* 325–351.

Klecker, B. M. (2007). The impact of formative feedback on student learning in an online classroom. *Journal of Instructional Psychology, 34,* 161–165.

Koszalka, T. A., & Ganesan, R. (2004). Designing online courses: A taxonomy to guide strategic use of features available in course management systems (CMS) in distance education. *Distance Education, 25*(2), 243–256.

Mager, R. (1962). *Preparing instructional objectives* (1st ed.). Belmont, CA: Fearon Publishers.

Mager, R. (1975). *Preparing instructional objectives* (2nd ed.). Belmont, CA: Fearon-Pitman Publishers.

Marek, P., Christopher, A. N., Koenig, C. S., & Reinhart, D. F. (2005). Writing exercises for introductory psychology. *Teaching of Psychology, 32,* 243–245.

Masters, K., & Oberprieler, G. (2004). Encouraging equitable online participation through curriculum articulation. *Computers and Education, 42,* 319–332.

Mazzolini, M., & Maddison, S. (2007). When to jump in: The role of the instructor in online discussion forums. *Computers and Education, 49,* 193–213.

Menchaca, M. P., & Bekele, T. A. (2008). Learner and instructor identified success factors in distance education. *Distance Education, 29*(3), 231–252.

Murphy, E., & Coleman, E. (2004). Graduate students' experiences of challenges in online asynchronous discussions. *Canadian Journal of Learning and Technology, 30*(2). Retrieved on February 1, 2009, from http://www.cjlt.ca/index.php/cjlt/article/view/128/122

Newlin, M., & Wang, A. (2002). Integrating technology and pedagogy: Web instruction and seven principles of undergraduate education. *Teaching of Psychology, 29,* 325–330.

Olt, M. R. (2002). Ethics and distance education: Strategies for minimizing academic dishonesty in online assessment. *Online Journal of Distance Learning Administration, 5*(3). (EJ657819). Retrieved from http://www.westga.edu/~distance/ojdla/fall53/olt53.pdf

Reeves, T. C. (2000). Alternative assessment approaches for online learning environments in higher education. *Journal of Educational Computing Research, 23,* 101–111.

Rescorla, R. A., & Wagner, A. R. (1972). A theory of Pavlovian conditioning: Variations in the effectiveness of reinforcement and nonreinforcement. In A. H. Black and W. F. Prokasy (eds.), *Classical conditioning II: Current research and theory.* New York: Appleton-Century-Crofts.

Shank, P. (2005). Writing learning objectives that help you teach and students learn (Part 1). *Online Classroom, 5*(11), 4–7.

Shea, V. (1990-2005). *The core rules of netiquette.* Retrieved March 24, 2009, from http://www.albion.com/netiquette/corerules.html

Sims, R., Dobbs, G., & Hand, T. (2002). Enhancing quality in online learning: Scaffolding planning and design through proactive evaluation. *Distance Education, 23*(2), 135–148.

SmarterServices. (2010). *Readiness for education at a distance indicator.* Retrieved on June 23, 2010, from http://goml.readi.info/

Spatariu, A., Hartley, K., Schraw, G., Bendixen, L. D., & Quinn, L. F. (2007). The influence of the discussion leader procedure on the quality of arguments in online discussions. *Journal of Educational Computing Research, 37,* 83–103.

Swan, K., Shea, P., Fredericksen, E., Pickett, A., Pelz, W., & Maher, G. (2000). Building knowledge building communities: Consistency, contact, and communication in the virtual classroom. *Journal of Educational Computing Research, 23,* 359–383.

Tiene, D. (2000). Online discussions: A survey of advantages and disadvantages compared to face-to-face discussions. *Journal of Educational Multimedia & Hypermedia, 9,* 371–384.

Walker, L. (2006). Narrated PowerPoint as a self-learning resource. *The International Journal of Learning, 13,* 1–6.

Webb, N. L. (1997, April 1). Criteria for Alignment of Expectations and Assessments in Mathematics and Science Education. Research Monograph No. 6. (ERIC Document Reproduction Service No. ED414305). Retrieved June 16, 2009, from ERIC database.

Xie, K., DeBacker, T. K., & Ferguson, C. (2006). Extending the traditional classroom through online discussion: The role of student motivation. *Journal of Educational Computing Research, 34,* 67–89.

Yang, Y.-C., & Ahn, S-H. (2007). The effects of synchronous online discussion on the improvement of critical thinking skills. *The Korean Journal of Thinking and Problem Solving, 17,* 41–50.

5 Faculty–Student Communication

Beyond Face to Face

Monica Reis-Bergan, Suzanne C. Baker, Kevin J. Apple, and Tracy E. Zinn

The three traditional roles of the faculty member are teaching, research, and service, with varying emphasis by institution type and mission. The growing impact of technology influences all three of these roles. Research manuscripts are no longer typed with a typewriter and mailed to editors; instead, documents are now submitted electronically. Service committees conduct work through e-mail, discussion boards, and Web-based survey instruments. Teaching has been transformed by the availability and use of instructional technologies. In fact, many classrooms are equipped with computers, projectors, and a wide variety of software. However, despite the changing landscape of technology, the teacher remains the center of the learning experience.

In general, the more teachers interact with students, the better the outcomes in term of effort put forth by students, overall student development, and student satisfaction (Astin, 1993; Kuh & Hu, 2001). Buskist, Sikorski, Buckley, and Saville (2002) highlighted 28 qualities and behaviors of master teachers, many of which focused on creating a foundation for building relationships with students. Similarly, McKeachie (1978) described six roles of teachers: the expert, the formal authority, the ego ideal, the socializing agent, the facilitator, and the person. The latter three of these roles relate specifically to faculty–student interpersonal communication. McKeachie (1978) described the "socializing agent" as a gatekeeper connecting deserving students to other communities of intellectuals. The teacher and student are linked together in a socialization process specific to the discipline or profession the teacher represents. As the "facilitator," the teacher helps students not only learn the material but also overcome obstacles in the process of learning. The facilitator should also help students formulate and pursue their own goals. Finally, the teacher is a person. Through this role, teachers open up and reveal aspects of their lives beyond the classroom, and in turn encourage students to share appropriate and relevant personal information. The basic premise of this role is to convey how academic issues are related to "everyday life." Knowing the reasons why a teacher has selected a particular area or knowledge of a teacher's academic challenges may encourage students to consider their own interests and personal needs (McKeachie, 1978).

Faculty roles, and the way students and faculty communicate and interact, have clearly changed with the advent of technologies developed since McKeachie (1978) discussed this framework. Before the use of the Internet, the teacher was the primary source of information. Grades, advising reports, and student records were paper-based. If a student wanted information about performance in a class or advising information, the student could call on the telephone or set up an office appointment with the faculty member. One way to think about this experience is to consider the impact of technology on the music industry. In 1978, the year McKeachie published his book, the faculty member was similar to a 12-inch vinyl long-playing record. Manufacturers packaged the songs together in the form of an album, and a record player was needed. The student visiting the office of the 1978 professor was likely to listen to the entire album and get the full experience of whatever the faculty member wanted to share. In the current generation, our music is "unbundled" and available from a variety of sources. Likewise, students can access many types of academic information from a variety of sources. Online course-management systems, such as Blackboard and WebCT, reduce the need to consult with faculty about grades. Online electronic advising portfolios also reduce the need for meeting with students face to face to discuss progression through the curriculum (see Appleby, Chapter 8). This "unbundled" academic information creates unique challenges for faculty following McKeachie's advice (1978) to connect interpersonally with students.

Using Technology to Connect with Students

This chapter highlights three technologies: social networking sites, instant messaging, and virtual worlds. All three technologies provide opportunities for faculty and students to interact on topics relevant to the educational experience (for related discussions of these technologies, see also Chapters 11, 15, and 20). We discuss ways these avenues can approximate face-to-face interaction, with the general belief that face-to-face interaction is the gold standard for education. For example, Armstrong and Reis-Bergan (2005) reported that students' frequency of contact with professors in person was positively associated with higher academic motivation and personal development. However, frequency of e-mail contact was not significantly related to these variables. Contrary to the indication that in-person contact is most beneficial, students indicated that they e-mailed faculty more often than meeting with them in person: 79% reported e-mailing faculty three or more times, whereas only 48% reported meeting with faculty in person three or more times. Thus, although electronic communication is preferred by students, this method does not offer the same benefits as face-to-face interaction. Perhaps we can capitalize on student preferences for electronic communication but find ways to enhance student outcomes. In this chapter, we will examine faculty–student interactions using three electronic methods: Facebook, Instant Messaging, and Second Life.

Facebook

Facebook is a social networking Web site. Numerous social networking sites exist, including MySpace, Xanga, and others. The majority of our students at James Madison University use Facebook, so our experiences focus on this particular site. Facebook users create personal Web sites called Facebook profiles that can contain a wide variety of personal information, such as demographics, pictures, friends, group affiliations, and personal messages. The essential element that makes Facebook more than just a personal Web site is the connection between users. The user's basic information, name, and selected photo are available to all users of Facebook. However, users can send a message to other users asking if he or she would agree to be Facebook friends. If this request is accepted, the "friend" is then listed in the other person's profile in the form of a hyperlink. Friends can view personal information on each other's profile pages that is often blocked for non-friends and can post messages on each other's walls. Although originally designed to be available only to college and university students, Facebook currently has open enrollment and boasts more than 200 million active users as of May 2009 (http://www.facebook.com/press/info.php?statistics). It is difficult to find accurate counts of the number of students in a given institution using Facebook. However, in an undergraduate sample assessed by Kolek and Saunders (2008), more than 82% of the general sample had a Facebook account; more specifically, 95% of first-year students had an account. Activity on social-networking sites is high: 63% of respondents reported spending at least some time on social networking sites each day, with 57% of respondents reporting signing on to a social networking site more than once per day (Subrahmanyam, Reich, Waechter, & Espinoza, 2008).

Student–Faculty Interaction in Facebook

Facebook presents the opportunity for faculty to disclose information to students and engage in discussions. The authors use Facebook in a variety of ways. The second author invited students in an online comparative psychology class to join a class Facebook group for extra credit. The purpose of the group was to provide students with the opportunity to interact with one another and with the instructor outside the confines of the "formal" class discussions (which took place on the class Blackboard site). The opportunity for informal social interaction may be especially important for students in an online class who never have the opportunity to meet face to face. Students in the Facebook group were allowed to post any items, comments, or information they wanted to share with the group. Of the 34 students in the class, 28 joined the group. Postings were primarily course-related photos, videos, and Web links. Because this was a comparative psychology course, many students posted wildlife photos they had taken or funny videos of animals. The instructor occasionally posted non-class-related material (e.g., requests for restaurant recommendations in town), but few students responded to these wall postings.

The third author used Facebook to create an advising group. Advisees received an invitation to join each semester. The rationale for joining the group is described as "just another way for us to interact." Approximately 15% of the advisees became members of the group. Advising tips and useful Web links are available to members of the group.

Advantages associated with adopting Facebook to interact with students include sharing information and creating rapport. The Facebook profile allows students to see the teacher as a person. Faculty may post personal information that allows for connections with students. Mazer, Murphy, and Simonds (2007) conducted an experimental study examining the effects of teacher personal information posted on a Facebook profile on students' class expectations. The researchers manipulated the amount of disclosure in a teacher's Facebook profile: "high-disclosure" profiles had a variety of personal photographs, personal biographical information, and social posts on the Facebook wall. Students viewing the high-disclosure profile reported higher anticipated motivation, more positive attitudes about the instructor (i.e., affective learning), and more positive impressions of the classroom climate than students viewing the low-disclosure teacher profile.

Rapport is one of the 28 qualities of master teachers and a quality that is particularly important to students (Buskist et al., 2002). It is likely that by providing some personal information, faculty can better develop rapport with students. Furthermore, it has been our experience that interacting on Facebook increases our ability to link names and faces, another factor that increases student perceptions of rapport.

Additional advantages include convenience to the student. Compared to a teacher's personal Web site housed on the university server, students may be more likely to access the teacher's profile on Facebook because many students are already using Facebook for personal use. It is also convenient for students to check recent posts and keep in touch with the instructor. Another advantage is that unlike visiting faculty during office hours, Facebook can be accessed at any time. Easy access allows students to read postings at their leisure, quite possibly at 2 a.m., and faculty to respond at their preferred time.

There are also disadvantages to connections with students in Facebook. Although similar to the work involved in managing any type of personal Web site (e.g., posting information, pictures), Facebook itself continues to evolve. New features are continually added, and other features are modified or discontinued. Users must invest time to stay current with the technology. Another disadvantage is the somewhat uncomfortable process involved in "friending." Like a middle-school dance, the process of initiating and accepting friends has numerous pitfalls. The authors have different opinions on requesting friend status from students. Some only accept friend requests initiated by students, whereas others actively seek out students by searching for them on Facebook, and ask to become "friends." After the friend process is completed, the tricky nature of friend maintenance is also potentially problematic. Connecting with former students is rewarding. However, being Facebook friends with a student who is disgruntled with some aspect of the experience can be awkward. One way faculty can avoid mixing professional "friends" and personal "friends" is to set up different "friend" lists. For instance, if you are using Facebook as a tool for one of your classes, you can set up a list for that class such that only members of that list see selected information. On a Facebook page, a user can select "create a new list" and add certain "friends" to that list. After creating the list, the user can specify what types of content "friends" on that list can see. For example, one author allows "friends" from her family list to see all content, whereas members of her student list can see only selected content. By doing so, she can share personal information in the form of notes and pictures with her family to which students do not need to be privy.

Mazer et al. (2007) found variability in students' attitudes toward faculty use of Facebook. Thirty-seven percent of the participants in their study felt that faculty use of Facebook was somewhat inappropriate or very inappropriate, and 41% felt that it was somewhat or very appropriate. The remaining students were undecided. It is possible that as more faculty members use Facebook, student attitudes will become more positive. However, given students' mixed opinions of faculty use of Facebook, it seems wise for faculty to show discretion about actively seeking out students as Facebook friends.

Social network sites, like Facebook, provide a service to their users. These sites offer a convenient way to keep in contact with people they already know and to meet new people. Facebook is also a technological tool that can be used to enhance student–faculty relationships as well as alumni–faculty relationships. Although potential problems may arise, we would argue that even traditional office visits between faculty and students can be less than ideal. In both mediums, the faculty member must behave in a highly professional manner while offering information and building rapport.

Instant Messaging

Instant messaging (IM) systems allow two users to communicate privately in a manner that is near-synchronous. The concept of instant messaging has been around since the 1970s in the form of the Unix "talk" command that allowed instant messages to other Unix operating system users. Although current systems differ, most contain the following features: a "pop-up" mechanism to display incoming information, contact or "buddy" lists, a feature that notifies the user if another user is logged into the application, the ability to create a status message, the ability to send files, a feature set of emoticons (symbols that can convey emotions; e.g., "☺"), and integration with mobile devices. Some of the most popular instant messaging platforms include AOL Instant Messenger (AIM), Google Chat (GCHAT), ICQ, Skype, Windows Live Messenger (WLM), Apple iChat, and Yahoo! Messenger. Facebook also has a chat platform so that "friends" can have synchronous communication.

Most students come to college with years of instant-messaging experience. In a survey of adolescents, Boneva, Quinn, Kraut, Kiesler, and Shklovski (2006) reported that 83% had used instant messaging, and 72% used it at least 1 or 2 days per week. We should note that measurement of instant messaging is complex. Students are often logged into the instant-messaging programs even when they are not at their computers. Students also tend to multitask while logged into instant-messaging programs (Baron, 2004; Quan-Haase, 2008). Some students may log in to see who else is logged in but chose to appear as "offline." The consensus is that a large number of students use this medium for communication, but reliable data on frequency and duration of use are lacking (Quan-Haase, 2008).

Student–Faculty Interaction Using Instant Messaging

Instant messaging enhances the ability of faculty members to be accessible to students during their office hours. Students can "visit" office hours even if they are off campus. Likewise, a faculty member can have online office hours if he or she is not available to meet on campus. For example, a faculty member could have instant-messaging office hours while recovering from surgery. The "pop-up" nature of instant messaging allows the faculty member to do other tasks while being accessible to students during a specific time.

Instant messaging surpasses e-mail in speed of response. More similar to the experience of face-to-face interaction, the student can ask a question, and the faculty member can ask a series of clarifying questions in response to the question. The near-synchronous nature of instant messaging provides the opportunity for dialogue about an issue. Hickerson and Giglio (2009) maintained a log of the types of instant-messaging topics discussed between students and faculty in an introductory-level communication course. The most frequent reason for the message was specific to the course requirements (80%). Other types of discussion topics included general class information (14%), academic advising (4%), and socializing (2%). Using instant messaging was entirely optional; even so, nearly two thirds of the students used instant messaging at some point in the semester to communicate with their teacher.

Two primary advantages for faculty to incorporate instant messaging into their repertoire of communication with students relate to perceptions of accessibility and approachableness. Both of these qualities are evident in master teachers and are rated as important by students and faculty (Buskist et al., 2002). Instant messaging can provide accessible routes of communication for students constrained by location, and we believe that instant messaging makes it easier for students to ask questions and talk about course issues. Because of instant messaging, students may see faculty who use this tool as more approachable. In support of this belief, results of a student questionnaire completed at the end of a semester indicated that 80% of students either agreed or strongly agreed that instant messaging increased the number of interactions with the instructor (Hickerson & Giglio, 2009). Moreover, 67% agreed or strongly agreed that instant messaging improved the quality of the interaction with the instructor (Hickerson & Giglio, 2009).

The use of instant messaging, as with any technology, also comes with disadvantages. We strongly recommend that faculty using instant messaging set up clear guidelines of when they are available. Instant messaging should not equal 24-hour accessibility. It is quite possible that the concerned student will have a question about the assignment at 3 a.m. The student can certainly instant message the faculty member, but the instant message will not have any advantage over e-mail in this particular situation. The message will be stored, and the faculty member can respond later, just as with e-mail. Another disadvantage of instant messaging for faculty might be the name attached to the student's instant messaging account. Students create user names when they initially set up their account, and typically they are not thinking that they will be sharing this name with their future college professors. This requires the extra step of identifying the user in the instant-messaging process; *Luvkittens* must tell the faculty member her actual name when she IMs her professor.

Some argue that instant-messaging technology encourages students to rely on this type of communication instead of face-to-face interactions with faculty. The concern is that students will use instant messaging when the topic or issue should be addressed face to face; however, this concern may be unfounded. Hickerson and Giglio (2009) compared similar courses with and without access to instant messaging and found the number of office visits and e-mails were similar for classes with instant messaging and classes without instant messaging. Therefore, they concluded that instant messaging supplements typical forms of faculty–student interaction. The second concern is about the nature of topics discussed in instant messages, with the belief that some students will make inappropriate comments on instant messaging. Unfortunately, inappropriate commenting is more of a student issue than a technology issue. Students who ask inappropriate questions on instant messaging may also be likely to ask an instructor that same question in the dairy aisle of the grocery store. It is up to the faculty member to establish appropriate guidelines for the use of any type of communication.

Second Life

As a third method of electronic communication, Second Life (www.secondlife.com) is an online virtual world. A user of Second Life (SL) creates an "avatar," a character that represents him or her in the virtual world. Avatars can travel throughout the virtual world, visiting virtual locations and interacting with other avatars currently online. At the time of this writing, hundreds of colleges and universities have a presence in SL. Many of these institutions have elaborate virtual campus sites in SL at which they hold classes, meetings, and informal gatherings (see Baker & Reis-Bergan, Chapter 19). For example, the James Madison University SL campus hosts recreations of several buildings on the "real-life" JMU campus, as well as prominent features on campus such as the Arboretum. Faculty members in multiple departments use the campus site for class meetings, class projects, and small-group meetings.

Faculty–Student Interaction and Second Life

Similar to instant messaging, SL can increase accessibility for interaction during office hours. Particularly in the case of an online course, SL office hours create a visual presence to represent the instructor and may enhance the relationship between instructor and students. Especially in a realistic SL setting like the James Madison University campus, the similarities between face-to-face interaction and SL interaction are striking until the avatar flies away at the end of the interaction.

SL provides faculty the opportunity to get to know students as people and vice versa. Similar to Facebook, students and faculty can interact about common interests and hobbies. In SL, it is possible for students and faculty to visit virtual museums or attend virtual concerts together. Of course, it is possible for students and faculty to get together in the "real world" to participate in these activities, but with SL these types of interactions can take place without faculty or students leaving their desks. Getting together with a student for a virtual cup of coffee in SL requires no transportation, no dealing with traffic or parking issues, and no weather concerns. In short, SL makes this type of informal interaction easier.

For students in an online class who may be completing the course at a location some distance from the instructor, SL provides a convenient venue for meeting. For example, in a course on health psychology, students were provided the extra-credit opportunity to visit "Health Info Island" on SL with the instructor. This virtual field trip enhanced the relationships between students and faculty and served as a beginning for numerous conversations about SL and other topics.

A potential limiting factor in the use of SL relates to computer accessibility. The nature of the SL program requires a fast Internet connection and a computer with good graphics capability (see system requirements on the SL home page, www.secondlife.com). It is frustrating for students to interact in this medium when the connection is slow and their communication has a significant time lag. The problem can be particularly frustrating when the student is going through the training required to navigate his or her avatar. Unlike the other communication methods discussed in this chapter, most students are not familiar with SL, and the learning curve is steep. Finally, SL is not accessible to students under 18 years of age, which may restrict some first-year college students from participating.

From both the students' and instructors' perspectives, an interesting aspect of social interaction in SL has to do with the appearance of the avatars. Research indicates that many SL users create avatars that resemble their actual physical selves (Messinger et al., 2008). In fact, some of our students report feeling uncomfortable talking to avatars that do not resemble the person's actual appearance; however, this is less of an issue in online classes who are not aware of the appearance of their peers. In a class of 60 students, the first author had two students who selected animal avatars. Discussing the upcoming exam with a penguin was unusual but not distracting enough to discontinue using the program.

Conclusion

Chickering and Gamson (1987) outlined seven principles for good practice in undergraduate education. Number one on their list was that good practice encourages student–faculty contact. More recently, Chickering and Ehrmann (1996) saw emerging technology as beneficial in this process. Indeed, we agree that technology can provide more opportunities for communication, and current technologies improve overall communication by making student–faculty interactions more convenient.

The metaphor of technology as a carpenter's tool is accurate and useful. If you have poor-quality lumber, it really makes no difference in the final product if you use a hammer or a nail gun. Likewise, poor teaching will not become good teaching simply because an instructor uses the bells and whistles of technology. If your desire is to improve as a teacher, reviewing the 28 qualities and behaviors of master teachers is a good start (Buskist et al., 2002). Many of these behaviors can be accomplished with and without technology. As noted in our chapter, in some situations, technology makes communicating easier for the faculty member, the student, or both. Table 5.1 summarizes questions relevant to consider when thinking about using the three technologies discussed in the chapter. In our view, instructors should focus on the final goal—enhancing student–faculty communication—and choose the tools that work best for them and for their students.

Table 5.1

Comparison of Communication Technologies

	Social Networking (e.g., Facebook)	Instant Messaging	Online Virtual Worlds (e.g., Second Life)
Are majority of students using the technology?	• Yes	• Yes	• Varies
Does this require extra work to keep current/updated?	• Yes	• No	• No
How steep is the learning curve?	• Short	• Very short	• Variable
Can I do this away from the office?	• Yes	• Yes	• Yes
Is the program free?	• Yes	• Yes	• Yes

References

Armstrong, C. S, & Reis-Bergan, M. (2005). *The benefits of mentoring relationships between professors and students.* Unpublished manuscript, James Madison University.

Astin, A.W. (1993). What matters in college? Four critical years revisited. *The Jossey-Bass higher and adult education series* (p. 482). San Francisco.

Baron, N. S. (2004). See you online: gender issues in college student use of instant messaging. *Journal of Languages and Social Psychology* (23)4, pp. 397–423.

Boneva, B. S., Quinn, A., Kraut, R. E., Kiesler, S., & Shklovski, I. (2006). Teenage communication in the instant messaging era. In R. E. Kraut, N. Bryan, & S. Kielser (Eds.), *Computers, phones, and the Internet: Domesticating information technology,* (pp. 201–218). Oxford: Oxford University Press.

Buskist, W., Sikorski, J., Buckley, T., & Saville, B. K. (2002). Elements of master teaching. In S. F. Davis & W. Buskist (Eds.), *The teaching of psychology: Essays in honor of Wilbert J. McKeachie and Charles L. Brewer* (pp. 27–39). Mahwah, NJ: Erlbaum.

Chickering, A. W., & Gamson, Z. F. (1987). Seven principles for good practice in undergraduate education. *Wingspread Journal.* (9)2. Retrieved on May 14, 2009 from http://catedraunesco.es/modeloeducativoupm/documentos/2.pdf

Chickering, A., & Ehrmann, S. C. (1996). Implementing the seven principles: technology lever. *AAHE Bulletin,* pp. 3–6. Retrieved May 14, 2009 from http://www.clt.astate.edu/clthome/Implementing%20the%20Seven%20Principles,%20Ehrmann%20and%20Chickering.pdf

Hickerson, C., A., & Giglio, M. (2009). Instant messaging between students and faculty: a tool for increasing student-faculty interaction. *International Journal on E-Learning* 8(1), 71–88.

Kolek, E. A., & Saunders, D. (2008). Online disclosure: an empirical examination of the undergraduate facebook profiles. *NASPA Journal,* (45)1.

Kuh, G. D., & Hu, S. (2001). The effects of student-faculty interaction in the 1990's. *Review of Higher Education,* (24)3, 309–332.

Mazer, J. P., Murphy, E. R., & Simonds, C. J. (2007). I'll see you on "Facebook": the effects of computer-mediated teacher self-disclosure on student motivation affective learning, and classroom climate. *Communication Education,* (56)1, 1–17. doi: 10.1080/03634520601009710

McKeachie, W. (1978). *Teaching tips: A guidebook for the beginning college teacher* (7th ed.). Lexington: Health and Company.

Messinger, P. R., Ge, X., Stroulia, E., Lyons, K., Smirnov, K., & Bone, M. (2008). On the relationship between my avatar and myself. *Journal of Virtual Worlds Research,* 1(2), 1–17.

Quan-Haase, A. (2008). Instant messaging on campus: use and integration in university student's everyday communication. *The Information Society,* 24, 105–115. doi: 10.1080/0197224071883955

Subrahmanyam, K., Reich, S. M., Waechter, N., & Espinoza, G. (2008). Online and offline social networks: Use of social networking sites by emerging adults. *Journal of Applied Developmental Psychology, 29,* 420–433.

6 Practical PowerPoint

Promising Principles for Developing Individual Practice

David B. Daniel

The lights are dimmed or completely turned off. A brightly lit screen in the front center of the room draws attention to a PowerPoint slide. Somewhere from the peripheral darkness emerges the lone voice of a teacher, often in monotone, and often reading the words verbatim from the text-heavy slide on the screen. As the students scramble to transcribe the slide's content, they secretly hope that the voice would quiet down so that they can concentrate on writing their notes. This very common description of a college classroom projects a clear message: the PowerPoint slides are the most important feature in the room.

PowerPoint has been demonized as an essentially evil tool (Tufte, 2003) that "turns clear-thinking adults into addle-headed boobs" (Shwom & Keller, 2003, p. 3). Such sentiments are to be expected with anything new but should not be dismissed out-of-hand as the ravings of simplistic Luddites. Plato related that Socrates strenuously objected to the advent of the written word as a form of teaching for very similar reasons. The written word, he proclaimed, could not possibly adapt itself to the learner or encourage active consideration. The student would possess the vocabulary of knowing without true knowledge (Hackforth, 1972). Sound familiar?

When overheads became an alternative to the chalkboard, many of us remember intense criticism and fear that the new technology would rely upon undependable devices with uncertain outcomes. I still remember the look of panic and the flop-sweat-strewn brow on one of my teachers who dropped her overhead transparencies and picked them up out of order. The result? Class was cancelled. The same teacher became indignant when the bulb burned out later that semester. Again, class was cancelled. I still hear of classes cancelled when the PowerPoint projector or class computer does not work as planned. It is as though the knowledge to be taught resides in the technology rather than the teacher. Perhaps Socrates was on to something.

PowerPoint is ubiquitous in the university classroom. Thus, I assume that most readers of this chapter either use it or have seen enough of it to have opinions about presentation software. Studies about its use have been available for several years. Yet, the number of bad PowerPoint presentations in the classroom seems to be growing exponentially. There are many studies on "good" practices that enjoy a consensus in the literature, but the availability of that information doesn't seem to be making a broad impact on classroom practice. Perhaps this is because the literature has focused on the tool, again intimating that the program is more important than the user. It is time to shift focus from the tool to the users and their interaction with it. Technological tools such as PowerPoint are only as effective or ineffective as a teacher designs them to be. This chapter's goal is to provoke reflection about learning goals and the strategic use of technology to facilitate them. I will address the use of technology from the perspective of the practitioner, relying on the literature as well as personal observations regarding what we teachers are doing when we bring a tool like PowerPoint into our classroom. Simply put, PowerPoint should not overshadow teaching and learning as the most important features of a classroom.

What is PowerPoint?

Before committing to a new technology, it is important to discriminate what a given technology was created to do, how it affects the person using it, and the potential effects on the people being subjected to it. With these issues in mind, users can then adapt the technology toward their goals, style, and context. At its core, PowerPoint is a flexible tool designed for presenting information to colleagues, primarily developed for use in business settings, not the classroom.

The primary criticisms of PowerPoint are that its default settings encourage simplistic thinking while burying related points within a linear structure of bullets and simplistic presentation style (Tufte, 2003: see Ludwig, Daniel, Froman, & Mathie, 2004, for a summary of Tufte's primary criticisms). The program also allows the user to easily change slide backgrounds and add graphics (including simple charts, graphs, and tables) and multimedia content such as movies, Web links, and some Flash animations. The ease with which one can add pictures and other multimedia content is one of the primary classroom benefits of PowerPoint as well as one of its main sources of distraction (Bartsch & Cobern, 2003; Daniel, 2005a).

Keep in mind that PowerPoint was designed as a presentation tool for peers to present information to each other, and it is honestly marketed as "Presentation Software," not "Teaching Software," "Lecture Software," or "Learning Software." I would argue that presenting to colleagues and teaching to students are quite different endeavors. One can assume, often correctly, higher levels of prior knowledge, interest, and skill in colleagues as compared to students. Presenting information to peers does not necessarily require the amount of scaffolding, flexibility, or pacing that teaching requires. In fact, because it is rather linear, text-heavy at default, easy to get lost in, and replete with optional distractions, it takes significant effort to adapt PowerPoint to serve as a teaching tool (Daniel, 2005b). Teachers must integrate their experience, training, and learning objectives together with knowledge of this medium to develop appropriate teaching practices and to adapt the program toward achieving their learning objectives.

PowerPoint is a Tool

The literature on multimedia and PowerPoint use is, in many ways, quite encouraging. When used properly, PowerPoint can be a very effective classroom tool. As noted earlier, PowerPoint offers the ability to add dynamic graphics, including pictures, video, charts, and, in some cases, animations that visually represent concepts and terms. It also allows one to link out to Web sites, other files, other presentations, or different points within the same presentation. There is a consensus in the literature that proper use of computer-based multimedia can improve learning and retention of material (see Bagui, 1998; Fletcher, 2003; Kozma, 1991; Mayer, 2001). In general, the ability to use dynamic visual elements in conjunction with a quality narrative is primarily responsible for the positive effects of PowerPoint.

The literature can offer general guidelines, but tips to guide specific practices are not easily derived from these studies. For example, there are a number of reviews of the related literature (see Bartsch & Cobern, 2003; Craig & Amernic, 2006; Ludwig et al., 2004; Mayer, 2001, for just a few examples). However, it is rarely possible to distinguish *good* use of PowerPoint as opposed to simply *the* use of PowerPoint in order to guide classroom practice. Despite the clearly interactive nature of the PowerPoint presentation, for example, few researchers report the content or use of their slides in sufficient detail to allow replication. This is an important point for those of us who have to create presentations, as the content, flow, and construction of the slides significantly influence their effect. One would expect, for example, a different learning outcome from slides consisting of dense paragraphs as opposed to slides using pictures with short bullets. Also, the effects of PowerPoint may be mitigated by the type and difficulty of the material being taught. In fact, when the difficulty of the to-be-learned material is accounted for, no consistent effect for PowerPoint is evident (Szabo & Hastings, 2000).

Importantly, the skill and qualities of the teacher also influence the effectiveness of PowerPoint. For example, Hardin (2007) performed a provocative study illustrating the potential strength of teacher-by-technology interactions. Hardin examined learning outcomes and student preferences across three instructors before and after using PowerPoint in their classes. Interestingly, she found differential effects of PowerPoint depending on the teacher, indicating that the instructor is a powerful variable to consider in the context of evaluating instructional technology. Of the three instructors, one instructor was rated highest regardless of whether PowerPoint was used; another instructor's scores were improved with the use of PowerPoint; and the remaining instructor's scores were negatively affected by the use of Power-Point. Thus, differential effects of PowerPoint use were mediated by teacher characteristics, a variable seldom controlled for in this literature. It is essential to remember that classroom teaching is inherently a dynamic interaction between a number of variables: it is more complex than simple main effects. In the best of all scenarios, the use of PowerPoint in a particular classroom will depend on a number of variables thus far unexamined in dynamic combination by the literature (see Daniel & Poole, 2009).

The practice of teaching in context is therefore personally empirical. Although the literature can offer some broad guidelines for use (and misuse) in specific areas, teachers must work out how to integrate and benefit from the use of new pedagogical tools through reflective experimentation in the context in which they teach. I would like to encourage teachers to reflect on their practice and strategically utilize the best tools in the best ways to demonstrably affect learning in the context of their own practice and context.

Promising Principles

As the preceding section implies, a good teacher is not going to adequately derive effective adaptations of pedagogical tools directly from the literature. Implementation in the context of one's learning outcomes and personal practice must be carefully and systematically developed. Thus, I eschew the temptation to recommend "Best Practices" from the literature or even from my own practice. However, there are some emerging "Promising Principles" (Worrell et al., 2009) to guide the development of personal practice. These principles seem to have a strong basis in theory, research, and practice across a variety of settings but must be integrated in your teaching. Let's begin with three general principles to guide classroom implementation: (1) PowerPoint is primarily a visual medium, (2) Multimedia aids dual processing, and (3) Busy or crowded slides increase cognitive load.

PowerPoint is a Visual Medium

The first point, that PowerPoint is a visual medium, sounds obvious. Yet if you look at the propensity of teachers to place words (that are also spoken) on slides, one may wonder if this point is clear to practitioners. While the judicious use of words or short bullets to signal transitions and topics may be a good idea to help students organize their note-taking, especially in introductory-level survey courses, complete sentences and paragraphs that duplicate the primary narrative content are not recommended and are not beneficial to learning. The primary question to ask oneself when developing a PowerPoint presentation to support learning is: "What do the students need to *see* in order to better learn the content?" The most effective use of PowerPoint is to display content that is primarily graphic in nature to emphasize the narration, offering mutually reinforcing narrative and visual content.

Dual Processing

When presenting complementary visual and verbal materials simultaneously, teachers take advantage of a well-known finding in the cognitive literature and one of the main values of using PowerPoint: dual processing (Clark & Paivio, 1991; Najjar, 1996; Paivio, 1986). Because of this ability to process visual and verbal information through different channels, narration with complementary pictures is remembered at higher rates than either picture or narration alone. Please note, however, that the picture and narration have to be overtly and obviously complementary to facilitate dual processing. Slides containing pictures that do not accentuate the lecture content (as many teachers include for "entertainment" value) are not as helpful to students as slides imbedding related pictures, or even slides containing no picture at all (Bartsch & Cobern, 2003; see also Mayer, Griffith, Jurkowitz, & Rothman, 2008). Further, pictures that must be extensively explained in order to make the link with the narrative are typically less effective than more obviously related pictures. Because such detours do not lead to effective learning outcomes, random clip art, off-subject cartoons, or movies that are "cool" but not obviously related to the content are more appropriately termed "seductive details" (Harp & Maslich 2005; Mayer, Griffith, Jurkowitz, & Rothman, 2008) than pedagogical aids.

Cognitive Load

A pet peeve of students and PowerPoint skeptics alike is that many PowerPoint presentations seem overflowing with text, random pictures, strange noises, and busy backgrounds. Some presentations are so densely packed with information that it becomes a challenge to process even a portion of the information. In fact, using such crowded and busy slides, especially when presented quickly and/or in abundance, overloads the students' cognitive resources and leads to much lower retention (Mayer, Heiser, & Lonn, 2001; Mayer, Moreno, Boire, & Vagge, 1999). Thus, the concept of cognitive load becomes an important consideration when developing a presentation. The teacher must provide information at an accessible level and pace to encourage thinking without overloading the students' resources. Too much information (TMI) too quickly overwhelms the system and encourages much shallower levels of processing (Craik & Lockhart, 1972).

Taken in conjunction, these three principles can help guide the teacher toward developing truly effective slides: (1) Represent your narrative with clear and complementary visuals, (2) Use minimal text, and (3) Deliver your presentation at a reasonable pace.

Don't Be a Slide Guide: Avoid TMI

With regard to classroom teaching, perhaps one of the greatest liabilities of PowerPoint is how much and how quickly information can be shown. Every argument in the literature, practice, or common sense should lead us to minimize the amount of written text on a slide and in a slide presentation in general. Yet TMI is the biggest complaint about PowerPoint. As is evident from the concept of cognitive overload, dense text presented relatively briskly often overwhelms the learner, encouraging lower retention (possibly due to shallower processing) or a sense of futility, while relegating the role of teacher to that of a "slide guide."

Consider a comparison with the chalkboard. While some teachers may speak quickly, the problem of TMI did not exist to such an extent when teachers relied on the chalkboard. Both the chalkboard and PowerPoint encourage students to transcribe text; however, the amount of text the student is confronted with at any given time is much greater in a typical PowerPoint presentation than when using a chalkboard. In fact, it is not uncommon to find that the number of words on one or two PowerPoint slides exceeds the total number of words written on the chalkboard for an entire class period! Writing on the chalkboard was also typically done in real time. Consequently, students were able to take notes at a much more reasonable pace than when presented with multiple slides of dense text written prior to class. Lastly, the board was typically used during the lecture to emphasize, not compete with or deliver, the narrative content, as is often done in PowerPoint. This comparison with the chalkboard can help inform the amount of information and pacing of a PowerPoint lecture. One should pace the amount of information and the speed of delivery to correspond with processing the information at the appropriate level in real time.

Instructional Egocentrism: Keep Your Lecture Notes to Yourself

Why do teachers tend to put so much text on their PowerPoint slides? Do you remember the jokes about the professor who brought the same set of yellowed lecture notes to class year after year? It was a standard derision aimed at lecturers back in the day, but you don't hear that one much any more. In fact, it is becoming increasingly rare for professors who use PowerPoint to bring out any notes, other than their slides. Are teachers getting smarter? No, it is a potentially unproductive practice used by PowerPoint enthusiasts: showing students their personal lecture notes. It is this practice, perhaps more than any other, that is responsible for the dense paragraphs, long lists, and jargon-laden bullet points on many slides in the college classroom. PowerPoint is commonly used as a public teleprompter for the teacher's benefit rather than to support student learning. Let me be very clear: the projector presents the slides on a big screen to the entire class. This should be a hint that the slides are meant for the students more than for the teacher.

In addition to the perplexing habit of sharing one's lecture notes with the students, the practice of developing one's lecture within the PowerPoint program from the very beginning is problematic. Opening up the program prior to creating a basic lecture outline greatly increases the likelihood that the default settings of PowerPoint may have a strong, often negative, influence on how the lecture develops. PowerPoint, arguably a tool to help *students* master the material, has become for many a lecture-development and memory aid for the teacher. While possibly facilitative to the instructor, neither of these teacher-centric strategies is focused on the use of PowerPoint's strengths to affect *student* learning.

Have a Plan

The source of most PowerPoint criticisms is predominantly a consequence of using the program in the absence of a pre-existing lecture outline, class plan, or overt learning objectives. I strongly encourage each instructor to develop his or her lecture plan and content before developing the slideshow to support it. Only after you have determined what visual support would help students best learn the concepts should you open up the program, placing only those things in the slideshow that strategically and *visually* support your learning objectives (sound files, when appropriate, are also an option). This visual and student-focused presentation, in conjunction with your personal lecture notes, can then be used to deliver an effective lecture.

I cannot emphasize the value, and even necessity, of content mastery in this process. A teacher who has a thorough understanding of the content and its relationship to other concepts encourages the depth, flexibility, and creativity to cultivate multiple representations and methods of delivery. Content mastery is a prerequisite to the development of mature instructional strategies and truly facilitative PowerPoint. A teacher who is not very familiar with the material has many challenges, especially when it comes to cultivating options for delivering the content. I have argued quite strongly that good teachers first develop a vision for their class and use PowerPoint to provide visual support. Content mastery makes this process much richer and more productive.

While the lecture plan should optimally be developed prior to opening up the PowerPoint program, I understand that many have come to rely upon the program to write their lectures. In fact, many who find it difficult to develop a lecture argue that the program helps them to develop a structure. In this case, I would like to suggest that you develop two presentations: one for you and the other for the students. Develop your lecture within the program as fully as you would like, then save and print it. These are your lecture notes. Then open it up and delete the slides that do not add visual support to your narrative. This is the presentation that you show your students.

Lastly, there is a function within PowerPoint called "Presenter View" for PCs or "Presenter Tools" for Mac users (see http://office.microsoft.com/en-us/powerpoint/HA010565471033.aspx). This option allows the presenter to see the slides and their notes while the students can see only the slides projected on the screen. In addition, it displays the coming slides and time to help pace the lecture.

This little-known function is a great way to keep your notes to yourself, anticipate the next slide, and set it up before switching to it. You can even skip to non-consecutive slides if the class has a question that may require review or force you to deviate from the prescripted order. One way to use Presenter View effectively when developing your lecture is to open the program and write your lecture in the "notes" section first, rather than on the slides themselves. After the narrative content is written in the notes section, you can add complementary visual elements to the corresponding slides. When presenting to the class, you will have the notes that support your narration on your computer screen, but the classroom's screen will depict only the slides that visually reinforce the narrative.

Be the Master of Your Domain: Create Your Own Vision, Create Your Own Slides

It seems to be more and more common for teachers to use publisher-provided PowerPoint slide as their primary source of lecture content, often without adapting the provided presentations to their own style and learning objectives (publisher-provided PowerPoint presentations are typically outlines of the chapter). In this instance, the book and its organization are dictating content, while the PowerPoint program is dictating format and structure. Without modification, the instructor seems to be simply a delivery system for

Figure 6.1. Presenter View. PowerPoint has a built-in feature that allows the presenter to see notes and other content while the audience can see only the slide. This allows teachers to keep lecture notes private and to use PowerPoint more effectively.

the publisher's content, providing little added value. With modification, however, adapting the publisher-provided content (some of which is excellent) to your learning plan is a great way to discover appropriate artwork, video, and other visual elements to realize your vision.

Especially in introductory-level survey courses, there is considerable overlap between text-based material and course content. However, the teacher has an opportunity, if not an obligation, to present the material in a more dynamic fashion, adding depth, examples, and opportunities to intellectually interact with the concepts. The ability to engage the learner in this dynamic fashion is difficult to replicate in a textbook. Similarly, the use of PowerPoint allows a teacher to present the visual elements related to the concepts, including strong multimedia content, in a fashion difficult to replicate by narration. Each medium has advantages and disadvantages over the other. Used together and with a complementary strategy, however, we have a dynamic learning environment that reciprocally reinforces and extends the content of each medium. Thus, while the publisher-provided material can be used as a resource, the organization, flow, and content of the presentation is the sole responsibility of the teacher.

With regard to PowerPoint, it is similarly important that the teacher master some of the basic functions and develop a philosophy of use for the program in order to conceptualize where the program can be of help, and how. Table 6.1 lists a dozen basic suggestions to guide presentation development as a start.

Say It, Don't Display It: Narration Works Better than Reading Text Back to the Class

Perhaps as a consequence of the instructor's overreliance on PowerPoint as a substitute for proper lecture notes, it is not at all uncommon to see teachers reading from the slides, often turning their backs completely to the students (how rude!). I had a colleague with slides filled to the brim with paragraphs of text, one after another, for the entire class. He would click on a slide and begin reading his points while the students ignored him in their desperate attempt to write down everything before he went to the next slide. His recitation was actually a source of distraction, and more than one student expressed the sincere hope that he would shut up so they could focus on the important stuff: writing down everything on the PowerPoint slide. If, as this colleague argued, this practice is acceptable because "Everything they need to know is on the slides," teachers must reconsider their reason for even being in the room.

It isn't uncommon to hear presenters defending the use of redundant text and narration by claiming that the text on the screen is for "visual learners" and reading the text aloud is for "auditory learners." This is a fairly easy argument to dispel, even without challenging the concept of learning styles (see Kavale & Forness, 1987; Stahl, 1999, for sample critiques of the concept). After a word enters the system, it is basically processed similarly whether it is heard or read. In fact, from the brain's perspective, reading adds an extra challenge to the processing of words (Wolf & Ashby, 2006). Rather than reinforcing each other, then, reading directly from slides puts the instructor and the slides in direct competition for resources and encourages excess demands on the student while inhibiting the potential for true dual processing. As discussed in the section on dual encoding, the advantage of visual information

Table 6.1

Suggestions for Presentation Development

First Things First	Develop your lecture plan and learning goals well in advance of opening the program. Informed by your class vision, PowerPoint becomes a tool for increasing the richness of the student experience.
Optimize the Context	Try to arrange the room and lighting to optimize the space. Strongly consider the use of a presentation remote and a structure that encourages you to move away from the technology and toward the student (literally as well as metaphorically).
Keep it Simple	A busy slide is a difficult slide to learn from. Avoid weird transitions and silly sounds. Use solid-colored backgrounds with highly contrasting (though not shocking) letters. Relatedly, make sure that your font size and style and line spacing make the slide easy to read even from the back of the room. Like using less text, the goal here is to make the content easy to process more deeply and to focus the learner on the important content.
Use Visuals Strategically	Choose your graphics to take advantage of dual encoding and to complement your narrative. Pictures (and movies) that complement narrative content help improve retention and understanding. On the other hand, unrelated or distracting pictures detour the student from the primary objectives.
Use Your Big Boy/Girl Voice	Develop your narrative and minimize text on the screen. Not only will this improve retention, but it will also place you firmly in the role of teacher, increase participation, and liberate you from overreliance on the technology.
Don't Be a Slide Guide	Don't use the PowerPoint displayed to the students as your source of comprehensive lecture notes. Simply clicking from one slide to the next, reciting the text on each, does not take advantage of the medium and reduces your effectiveness as a teacher. Keep your notes out of the students' sight, address the students rather than the screen, and signal in every way possible that you know the material better than does PowerPoint.
Time Your Presentation to Your Narration	To maximize the benefits of dual processing, timing is very important. Present the picture with, or just slightly after, the narrative content. If you are using a complex chart or graph, consider unveiling it one piece at a time to encourage understanding and not overload the students with information. Don't forget to allow time for the students to take it in and connect the pieces (guided by your narration). In the case of movies and animations, take a tip from Jay Leno: Always set up the clip with a brief statement about what to look for and why it is relevant. This will encourage students to make the link back to the material.

Table 6.1
Suggestions for Presentation Development (Continued)

Make it Yours	Even if you are using publisher-provided slides as a start, alter them to fit your style, pace, and priorities, in addition to adding visual support for your personal examples and explanations. You may want to delete certain topics to make room for more explanation, reduce the number of words, change the pace of the presentation by making the points (often several long bullets that fill the screen) appear one at a time, etc. After you decide what you want to happen in class that day, make the PowerPoint conform to your vision.
Don't Forget That This is Live	A common mistake is to develop a set of slides that we rush through, trying to finish before class is over. This trains students to minimize questions and inhibits many teachers from in-depth explanations and spontaneity. Create a leisurely, though enthusiastic, pace. If you notice that students seem to be focusing too much on the last slide when you want more interaction, simply hit the "b" or "w" key on your computer. This fades the screen to black (or white), signaling that something more important is going on in the room! When you are ready, hit the key again and you are back in your presentation.
Don't Over-commit	Not all technology is good for every learning objective. Don't hesitate to move in and out of PowerPoint on a daily basis or even within the same class period, as your goals dictate.
Experiment	Key to my arguments above is the simple idea that teaching is personally empirical. Try new ways to present the information and evaluate their effectiveness. Avoid the ruts. Many new and ingenious uses of PowerPoint are emerging every week. For examples, one of this book's editors explained how she was using PowerPoint to create "hot spots" where one can click on a part of a slide and the presentation will jump to a designated spot. Instructors can create such spots in their presentations to jump to sections of the presentation if certain questions are asked. Or, the instructor can use the same function to create assignments for students where they click on, for example, a part of the brain and an explanation of its function appears. There are infinite possibilities when such technology is paired with vision.
It's About Learning	It is ironic that this point needs to be emphasized in a book about teaching, but far too often PowerPoint has become a tool for the instructor to cue recall rather than a tool to help students encode and process. Whatever you show your students should be strategically developed to encourage learning. Looking cool, adding distractions, or making easy lecture notes should be very secondary goals. If it doesn't increase learning, it is no longer a pedagogical tool.

and text is best achieved by pairing pictures, not redundant words, with related text.

We see even bigger benefits, however, when the relevant pictures are paired with complementary narration rather than text on a screen. Mayer (2001) has developed a few related principles that may be instructive. Similar to a dual-encoding perspective, the *redundancy principle* states that presentations involving both words and related pictures are retained at higher rates. It further states that words should be presented in either written or verbal form, but not both. Relatedly, the *modality principle* states that people learn better in multimedia formats when the narrative content is spoken rather than written. Taken together, Mayer presents a strong, evidence-based rationale for narration paired with strong complementary visual support. In fact, it is exactly this format that one can see on the news each evening.

What Can Stephen Colbert Teach Us About PowerPoint?

Perhaps we can learn something from the evolution of another information-delivery device: real and fake television newscasts. If CNN could make as much money just running the printed banner that currently runs at the bottom of the screen (aka the "crawl") without the major expense of a newscaster, they would. If pictures and text, or pictures and a voice-over, would be sufficient, networks would welcome the savings in anchorperson salaries. But there seems to be something important about a live person, or at least a visible talking head, that connects the viewer to the information.

The narration works better than a printed banner for a number of reasons, many of which have been mentioned in this chapter. While newscasters have access to their notes via a teleprompter or written on paper, the viewer is never shown these notes. Rather, the use of text is minimal, and text is typically used to emphasize or complement the narration. In many stories where it makes sense, multimedia content in the form of video and simulations is used to add depth or support to a story. Lastly, complementary graphics are usually displayed over the shoulder of the anchor to reinforce the narrative content, co-occupying the attentional space—as I recommend you do with your slides. The graphics are typically used to facilitate, rather than deliver, the story's core content: they are not in direct competition with the anchor. This is an area where the free-market forces of network television and the literature on multimedia information delivery converge.

With Great Power Comes Great Responsibility

After the first few dates, PowerPoint becomes both comforting and seductive. It gives you a safe, structured, and predictable interaction. It playfully tempts you to add sounds, transitions, and pictures. The relationship can be creative and exciting. You can dress it up, take it out, and people's heads will turn. It is easy to lose yourself in this new relationship and, for once, hand control over to this wonderful new partner. In the end, though, you have to live with what you have created and what you have let yourself become. Have you lost your identity and effectiveness as a formidable teacher, becoming a passive enabler to a young program with no experience or mind of its own?

It is important always to be diligent when using technology. Although I have suggested that teaching style interacts with the use of technology, I have not discussed how teaching style may be affected by the presence of new pedagogical tools. PowerPoint can take a class to a new level if it is used strategically and complements the teacher's style. However, this is a double-edged sword. If teachers are not cognizant of the reciprocal effects of this technology, it is easy to adapt to the technology rather than to adapt the technology to fit their own style and purposes. Teachers who once were spontaneous and narrative have become scripted and stiff using PowerPoint. New technologies can change style so much for some, in fact, that the change in teaching style may be responsible for many effects often attributed to the technology (e.g., Anthis, 2009). It is very important to plan your course with a strong vision, pulling in technology strategically and only as it facilitates your learning goals.

After the initial courtship, each of us forges a relationship with the technology that is ideally based upon its effects, functions, and success (Barbour, 1992). Whole-hearted adoption or rejection of technology based on assumptions that it is either globally beneficial or globally detrimental is not a realistic appraisal of this relationship. Technology is what we make it, plain and simple: the difference is with the user and the context. As in any good relationship, living with PowerPoint entails a bit of work.

PowerPoint, then, may be more like a toddler than a partner. It can be mischievous, and sometimes you have to wonder who really is in charge. It has strong default tendencies that offer some structural advantages for teachers paired with potential hurdles for learners. With vision, knowledge of the medium, and a little discipline, we can help shape this program into a responsible classroom asset.

References

Anthis, K. (2009). *Is it the clicker, or is it the question? Untangling the effects of student response system use.* Poster Presented at 31st Annual National Institute on the Teaching of Psychology, St. Petersburg, FL.

Bagui, S. (1998). Reasons for increased learning using multimedia. *Journal of Educational Multimedia and Hypermedia, 7,* 3–18.

Barbour, I. (1992). *Ethics in an age of technology: The Gifford Lectures, Volume Two.* San Francisco: Harper Collins.

Bartsch, R. A., & Cobern, K. M. (2003). Effectiveness of PowerPoint presentations in lectures. *Computers & Education, 41*(1), 77–86.

Chandler, P., & Sweller, J. (1991). Cognitive load theory and the format of instruction. *Cognition and Instruction, 8,* 293–332.

Clark, J. M., & Paivio, A. (1991). Dual coding theory and education. *Educational Psychology Review, 3,* 149–170.

Craig, R. & Amernic, J. (2006). PowerPoint presentation technology and the dynamics of teaching. *Innovations in High Education, 31,* 147–160.

Craik, F. I. M., & Lockhart, R. S. (1972). Levels of processing: A framework for memory research. *Journal of Verbal Learning and Verbal Behavior, 11,* 671–684.

Daniel, D. B. (2005a). Using technology to ruin a perfectly good lecture. In: B. Perlman, L. McCann, & B. Buskist (eds.), *Voices of NITOP: Favorite talks from the National Institute on the Teaching of Psychology* (pp. 119–130). Washington, DC: American

Daniel, D. B. (2005b). Evil Technology: Nature or Nurture? In: T. Zinn, B. K. Saville, & J. E. Williams (eds.), *Essays from Excellence in Teaching,* 5. Retrieved May 15, 2009, from http://teachpsych.org/resources/e-books/eit2005/eit05-10.html

Daniel, D. B., & Poole, D. A. (2009). The ecology of pedagogy: How collaborative research can prevent us from harming students. *Perspectives on Psychological Science, 4*(1), 91–96.

Fletcher, J. D. (2003). Evidence for learning from technology-assisted instruction. In: H. F. O'Neil, Jr., & R. S. Perez (eds.), *Technology applications in education: A learning view* (pp. 79–99). Mahwah, NJ: Lawrence Erlbaum Associates.

Hackforth, R. (tr. and ed.). (1972). *Plato's Phaedrus.* Cambridge: Cambridge University Press.

Hardin, E. (2007). Presentation software in the college classroom: Don't forget the instructor. *Teaching of Psychology, 34*(1), 53–57.

Harp, S. F., & Maslich, A. A. (2005). Methods and techniques: The consequences of including seductive details during lecture. *Teaching of Psychology, 32*(2), 100–103.

Kavale, K. A., & Forness, S. R. (1987). Substance over style: Assessing the efficacy of modality testing and teaching. *Exceptional Children, 54*(3), 228–239.

Kozma, R. (1991). Learning with media. *Review of Educational Research, 61,* 179–211.

Ludwig, T. E., Daniel, D. B., Froman, R., & Mathie, V. A. (2004). *Using multimedia in classroom presentations: Best principles.* Retrieved May 19, 2009, Society for the Teaching of Psychology Web site: http://teachpsych.org/resources/pedagogy/ classroommultimedia.pdf

Mayer, R. E. (2001). *Multimedia learning.* New York: Cambridge University Press.

Mayer, R. E., Griffith, E., Jurkowitz, I. T. N., & Rothman, D. (2008). Increased Interestingness of extraneous details in a multimedia science presentation leads to decreased learning. *Journal of Experimental Psychology: Applied, 14*(4), 329–339.

Mayer, R. E., Heiser, J., & Lonn, S. (2001). Cognitive constraints on multimedia learning: When presenting more material results in less understanding. *Journal of Educational Psychology, 93,* 187–198.

Mayer, R. E., & Moreno, R. (1998). A split-attention effect in multimedia learning: Evidence for dual processing systems in working memory. *Journal of Educational Psychology, 90,* 312–320.

Mayer, R. E., Moreno, R., Boire, M., & Vagge, S. (1999). Maximizing constructivist learning from multimedia communications by minimizing cognitive load. *Journal of Educational Psychology, 91,* 638–643.

Najjar, L. J. (1996). Multimedia information and learning. *Journal of Multimedia and Hypermedia, 5,* 129–150.

Paivio, A. (1986). *Mental representations: A dual coding approach.* Oxford, England: Oxford University Press.

Savoy, A., Proctor, R. W., & Salvendy, G. (2009). Information retention from PowerPoint™ and traditional lectures. *Computers & Education, 52*(4), 858–867.

Shwom, B. L., & Keller, K. P. (2003). The great man has spoken. Now what do I do? A response to Edward R. Tufte's "The cognitive style of PowerPoint." *Communication Insight, 1,* 1–15. Retrieved on May 24, 2009, from: http://www.communi-partners.com/documents/ComInsV1._000.pdf

Stahl, S. A. (1999, Fall). Different Strokes for Different Folks? American Educator, retrieved May 20, 2009, from: http://www.aft.org/pubs-reports/american_educator/ fall99/DiffStrokes.pdf

Szabo, A., & Hastings, N. (2000). Using IT in the undergraduate classroom: should we replace the blackboard with PowerPoint? *Computers in Education, 35*(3), 175–187.

Tufte, E. (2003, Nov. 9). PowerPoint is evil. *Wired.* Retrieved July 2, 2004, from http:// www.wired.com/wired/archive/11.09/ppt2.html

Wolf, M., & Ashby, A. (2006). A brief history of time, phonology, and other explanations of developmental dyslexia. In: K. W. Fischer, J. H. Bernstein & M. H. Immordino (eEds.), *Mind, brain, and education in reading disorders.* Cambridge, UK: Cambridge University Press.

Worrell, F. C., Casad, B. J., Daniel, D. B., McDaniel, M., Messer, W. S., Miller, H. L., Prohaska, V., & Zlokovich, M. S. (2009). Promising principles for translating psychological science into teaching and learning. In: D.F. Halpern (ed.), *Undergraduate education in psychology: a blueprint for the future of the discipline.* Washington, DC: American Psychological Association.

Technology: Applications In and Outside the Classroom

7 Comprehensive Hybrid Course Development

Charles M. Harris and Ulas Kaplan

Hybrid courses combine out-of-class computer-based teaching and learning with traditional face-to-face classroom experiences. Comprehensive hybrid courses incorporate an extensive range of methods and practices utilized in both face-to-face and online teaching and learning. They offer students the familiar experience of direct interaction with instructors and peers and the significant flexibility of online learning. Hybrid courses offer instructors opportunities to incorporate a variety of instructional technologies to accommodate students with diverse abilities for learning. Because comprehensive hybrid courses require less physical classroom space, institutions can offer additional courses without the cost of expanding their physical facilities.

Developing comprehensive hybrid courses is consistent with the many initiatives calling for education to more fully implement information literacy by increasing the emphasis on fluency with information technologies (Association of College and Research Libraries, 2000; Johnson, Levine, & Smith, 2009; National Research Council, 1999; Southern Association of Colleges and Schools, 2006; Southern Regional Education Board, 2007; Western Cooperative for Educational Telecommunications, n.d.). A programmatic emphasis on fluency with information technologies facilitates a lifelong learning process for instructors to continually build on their knowledge of current and emerging information technologies and apply that knowledge to the design and delivery of their courses.

In *Being Fluent With Information Technology* (1999), the National Research Council's Committee on Information Technology Literacy articulated priorities for each of three essential and interrelated types of knowledge: (a) contemporary skills, (b) foundational concepts, and (c) intellectual capabilities. Contemporary skills are required to use particular hardware and software. Foundational concepts include ideas and processes for designing and operating information technologies. Intellectual capabilities enable efficient, effective problem solving based on a synthesis and interpretation of contemporary skills and foundational concepts. Whereas contemporary skills will change with new generations of hardware and software, foundational concepts and intellectual capabilities are timeless and allow fluent use of information technologies.

Comprehensive hybrid courses that integrate face-to-face and online components are ideally structured for implementing fluency-oriented instruction. McKeachie (1999) discusses five conditions that should be met to increase successful experiences for students and instructors: (a) all students must have access to the technology at appropriate places and times, (b) students must have access to the specified software applications and resources, (c) technical support must be available for students at study times, (d) institutions must assign staff time appropriately, and (e) time and resources must be available for faculty development of necessary skills. The conditions specified by McKeachie illustrate the complexity of developing and delivering hybrid courses. Success will be, in large part, contingent on easy access to technical resources and the availability of institutional support for instructors and students.

Thankfully, the Pew Internet & American Life Project describes students of the "Net Generation" as accustomed to accessing information by means of the Internet and embracing technology as a viable means of achieving their goals of experiential learning and social interaction through person-to-person communication and dialogue with instructors (Jones, 2002). Dunn, McCarthy, Baker, Halonen, and Hill (2007) constructed quality benchmarks for undergraduate psychology programs with a continuum of performance ranging from underdeveloped to distinguished. For technology-related student-learning outcomes, distinguished psychology programs provide opportunities for students to develop technological expertise as part of their professional development.

Conceptualizing a Hybrid Course

Theoretical Framework

Holmberg (1989) postulates that understanding theoretical formulations of the nature of teaching and learning is central to the instructional process. We see in Vygotsky's (1962) *social constructivism* the complementary roles of instructors and students in the interactive processes of teaching and learning. The major theme of Vygotsky's sociocultural theory is that social interaction plays a fundamental role in the development of cognition. Vygotsky believed everything is learned on two levels: learning occurs initially through interaction with others and is subsequently integrated into an individual's mental structure. The educational implications of Vygotsky's theory are that learners should be provided socially rich environments in which to explore knowledge domains with their peers and instructors. Access the URL (http://webpages.charter.net/schmolze1/vygotsky/vygotsky.html) for an elaborate exploration of Vygotsky and his theory.

Modeling, social interaction, and experiential learning are key concepts in Vygotsky's theory that are also valued by college students of the Net Generation, as documented by the Pew Internet & American Life Project (Jones, 2002). By integrating traditional face-to-face and online components, the structure of hybrid courses is well suited for applying the theoretical concepts within Vygotsky's social constructivism. We understand that the selection of Vygotsky's guiding theoretical principles reflects our assumptions about teaching and learning and that others might find conceptual support in other theoretical formulations. For example, information-processing theory and Piaget's theory of cognitive constructivism independently include relevant concepts for developing hybrid courses. However, we do not believe that instructors and students are well served by the external–internal dichotomy of information-processing theory versus Piagetian mentalistic constructivism.

Selection of a theoretical frame of reference establishes a context for the construction of process goals that facilitate student thinking and learning (McKeachie, 1999). Process goals transcend specific course content by providing a base of concepts and skills for transforming information into personal knowledge about self and others in relation to the social and physical worlds. For guidance in constructing process goals, we recommend Chickering and Gamson's (1999) seven principles of good practice in undergraduate education: (a) encourages faculty–student interaction, (b) encourages cooperation among students, (c) encourages active learning, (d) gives prompt feedback, (e) emphasizes time on task, (f) communicates high expectations, and (g) respects diverse talents and ways of learning. Access the URL (http://www.winona.edu/president/seven.htm) for elaborations of each of the seven principles. The overarching goal when developing hybrid courses is for principles of sound pedagogy to drive both course design and the incorporation of instructional technology.

Course Design

This chapter is based on our experience with a hybrid course. Students attend class once each week and access all other course components online. The online components are accessed through Blackboard, our campus-wide course-management system, and include narrated PowerPoint-based lectures, podcasts, a blog, and links to course-related information, course documents, external resources, and inventories accessed through the instructor's course Web site. Successful hybrid course design begins with a comprehensive re-examination of the goals, objectives, content, textbook, assignments, and schedule of a traditional face-to-face course. The decision to assign a portion of face-to-face class time to online experiences should include consideration of course goals and the instructor's philosophy of teaching. Along with McKeachie (1999), we recommend Zimbardo and Newton's (1975) protracted schedule for course design in order to allow adequate time for conceptualizing and integrating online and face-to-face components of a hybrid course. Our proposed timeline and activities for hybrid course design are approximations and should be adjusted when necessary to accommodate different levels of teaching experience and technological expertise. We recommend constructing a checklist or spreadsheet to systematically monitor the timely accomplishment of the many tasks involved in the development of a comprehensive hybrid course.

Approximately 3 months before the hybrid course begins, implement the following:

- Publicize the course as a hybrid to establish commitment to the project.

- Re-examine course goals and objectives to ensure continuity and consistency between the face-to-face and online components of the hybrid course.
- Select a textbook that relates to course goals and objectives and that includes supplementary resources for instructors and students in a hybrid course.
- Identify the personnel who provide technical support for online courses.
- Schedule training to become proficient with the instructional technologies selected for the hybrid course.
- Convey to students the minimum computer equipment and skills required for successful performance in a hybrid course.

Approximately 2 months before the hybrid course begins, implement the following:

- Determine the schedules for content, assignments, and performance assessment for each week of the course.
- Specify the content and begin developing the face-to-face lectures.
- Begin development of the online lectures.
- Construct a syllabus that specifies the purpose, goals, objectives, methods, and performance assessment as well as requirements and due dates for all assignments.
- Consult an instructional technologist to discuss options for facilitating online interactions and ensuring accessibility for students with visual, auditory, motor, and cognitive impairments.
- Inform students that successful completion of a hybrid course will require effective and disciplined study and time-management skills.

Approximately 1 month before the hybrid course begins, implement the following:

- Verify access to technical support personnel for the duration of the hybrid course.
- Review the syllabus for completeness and accuracy.
- Continue developing the face-to-face and online lectures.

- Begin constructing quizzes, tests, and examinations.
- Inform students that, one week prior to the beginning of the hybrid course, they will have access to the syllabus and detailed instructions for navigating among the online components of the course.

Approximately 1 week before the hybrid course begins, implement the following:

- Use the course-management system to make the syllabus and detailed instructions for locating and navigating among the online components of the course available to students.
- Schedule technical support personnel to be present during the first class.
- In preparation for the first face-to-face class, construct a detailed, sequential list of activities that includes presenting concise instructions for accessing and navigating among the online components of the hybrid course.

Instructional Technologies

Course-management software is designed with many features so that it can be marketed to as many users as possible. Therefore, choosing an appropriate course-management system is the seminal task when selecting instructional technologies for accomplishing the goals of a hybrid course (Elbaum, McIntyre, & Smith, 2002). One may select from a variety of course-management systems, such as Angel, Blackboard Academic Suite, Moodle, TopClass, WebCT, or another system adopted by an institution. We recommend that readers view the respective Web sites for detailed descriptions of distinctive features of these portal systems. To complement the course-management system, the teacher should identify ancillary technologies for (a) information dissemination with links to any Web-based source, (b) asynchronous and/or synchronous communication, (c) narrated online lectures that are comparable to face-to-face lectures, (d) small-group experiential learning, (f) electronically processed writing assignments, and (g) performance assessment (Shank & Sitze, 2004). We selected the following up-to-date technologies as of this writing: Blackboard Academic Suite 8.0, PowerPoint 2007, Adobe Presenter 7, Respondus 4.0, Google Blogger, GarageBand 3.0, and Adobe Acrobat 9. Readers should always check on availability of the latest versions of such technologies.

Blackboard Academic Suite 8.0 is a course-management system with tools that facilitate student engagement, collaboration, and critical thinking, along with smart grading capabilities. Functions include (a) information dissemination, (b) scalable e-mail, (c) discussion boards, (d) small-group activities, (e) file sharing and transmission of written reports, and (f) performance assessment with instant feedback for students and summary statistics for instructors. See the URL (http://www.blackboard.com/sites/release8) for additional information.

PowerPoint 2007, part of Microsoft Office, is a presentation program developed for the Microsoft Windows and Mac computer operating systems. PowerPoint presentations consist of a number of individual slides that contain text, graphics, movies, or other objects that can be arranged freely on the slides. A PowerPoint presentation can be printed, displayed live on a computer, or published online as a Webcast. See the URL (http://office. microsoft.com/en-us/powerpoint/default.aspx) for additional information.

Adobe Presenter 7 converts PowerPoint presentations into Web-based multimedia lectures. PowerPoint presentations incorporate narration, interactivity, and distribution of content for a uniform viewing experience. After installation, Adobe Presenter appears as an option on the PowerPoint toolbar. See the URL (http://www.adobe.com) for additional information.

Respondus 4.0 is a Windows-only application for offline creation and management of exams. Similar to a word processor, the Respondus Editor includes a spell checker, table editor, equation editor, and full media support. Respondus can import content from a word processor and seamlessly publish directly to Blackboard, eCollege, WebCT, and other e-learning systems. Unfortunately for Mac users, as of this writing Apple does not offer assessment creation software. See the URL (http://www.respondus.com) for additional information.

Google Blogger is a free Google service for creating blogs and Web sites. Blogger features Web-standards–compliant templates, individual archive pages for posts, comments, posting by e-mail, a drag-and-drop template editing interface, reading permissions for creating private blogs, and new Web feed options using RSS (Really Simple Syndication) linkage to automatically receive information from selected blogs and other Web sources. See the URL (https://www.blogger.com/start) for additional information.

GarageBand 3.0 is a robust Apple recording utility ideal for recording audio podcasts that can be linked through course-management systems, such as Blackboard, and published on blogging services such as Blogger. Podcasts can be shared by creating an RSS file from your blog. See the URL (http://www.apple.com/support/garageband/podcasts/recording) for additional information. Windows users can create a podcast with Mac-based GarageBand, save the podcast on a USB or flash drive, and upload the podcast to a Windows application. A second option is to use Windows-based Mixcraft by Acoustica. See the URL (http://www.acoustica.com/mixcraft/features.htm) for additional information.

Adobe Acrobat 9 creates portable document files (PDFs) that preserve the look and integrity of your original documents. Unlike Word documents, the content of PDF files cannot be modified or deleted. PDF files can be accessed and read regardless of hardware and software platforms. Course documents, spreadsheets, presentations, brochures, photographs, rich graphics, and more can be electronically converted into PDFs. See the URL (http://www.adobe.com) for additional information.

Constructing a Hybrid Course

Throughout the construction of hybrid courses the focus should be, at least, on equivalency and, optimally, on improving the processes and outcomes typical of traditional face-to-face courses. Optimal outcomes can be obtained by ensuring that principles of sound pedagogy direct the selection and use of technologies that support the online components of a hybrid course. To that end, Chickering and Gamson's (1999) seven principles of good practice in undergraduate education are applicable to discipline-based, multidisciplinary, and interdisciplinary hybrid courses. The following strategies and techniques, presented for each of the seven principles, are ways to achieve the dynamic interaction that is valued by college students of the Net Generation (Jones, 2002) and that is central to Vygotsky's (1962) social constructivism.

Principle 1: Encouraging Student–Faculty Interaction

Interaction between instructors and students is an essential element of the processes we label *teaching and learning* (Holmberg, 1989). Because the distance-learning component of a hybrid course significantly reduces the amount of face-to-face interaction, alternatives for access to instructors are necessary. Our model for a hybrid course includes several technologies that support asynchronous online interaction. Blackboard, the campus-wide course-management system at James Madison University, features multiple functions supporting asynchronous interaction. Several Blackboard functions support instructor-to-student and student-to-student text-based communication. Using Adobe Acrobat, instructors convert and publish text-based information, in secure PDF format, through a variety of Blackboard functions such as Announcements, Faculty Information, Course Information, and Course Documents. A prime feature of Blackboard's Communication function is the option to simultaneously e-mail all students or a select subset of students. Student-to-student communication is supported by the main menu Discussion Board and by the Group Pages small-group Discussion Board. By publishing PowerPoint-based lectures online, Adobe Presenter supports asynchronous interaction among students and instructors. Instructors produce Web-based lectures in which narration is synchronized with the corresponding PowerPoint-based text and ancillary linkages. Using the control panel and slide bar, students have the following options: (a) pausing the lecture to take notes, (b) reversing the lecture to replay a specific section, and (c) fast-forwarding the lecture. Inclusion of the instructor's voice and a photograph, for an otherwise text-based experience, are distinctive features of Presenter-supported PowerPoint-based lectures. Hearing the instructor's voice and seeing the instructor's face enhances rapport and establishes a personal connection among students and instructors.

Principle 2: Encouraging Cooperation Among Students

Cooperative learning experiences are consistent with learning in Vygotsky's social constructivism (Tudge & Scrimsher, 2003; Bodrova & Leong, 2003). Cooperative learning activities that incorporate group rewards and require individual accountability are effective techniques for increasing student participation and for improving motivation to learn (Bearison & Dorval, 2002; Slavin, 1995). Strategies for implementing online, asynchronous cooperative learning include STAD (Student-Team Achievement Divisions), the jigsaw classroom (Aronson & Patnoe, 1997), learning together, group investigation, and cooperative scripting (Santrock, 2001). Student-to-student interaction through the online learning component within a hybrid course compensates for the reduction of face-to-face interaction typical of conventional classroom settings.

The Group Pages option on the Communication page of Blackboard supports asynchronous, small-group cooperative learning experiences. Organizing students into small collaborative groups increases dialogue among students about complex concepts and issues within a hybrid course. Within each small group, members communicate by e-mail, a discussion board, and file exchange functions that are unique to their group. For example, in a hybrid lifespan development course, small-group assignments that offer a variety of learning outcomes include dialogue and group reports on issues such as (a) the compatibility or incompatibility of beliefs and practices supporting the concepts of women's rights and fetal rights, (b) the advantages and disadvantages for college students of the practices when dating vs. hooking up, and (c) arguments for and against the right to die as a universal, human right. A general outcome of cooperative learning assignments is improved communication skills as students develop increased clarity in expressing their questions and comments about complex issues.

Principle 3: Encouraging Active Learning

Blackboard functions support a variety of active learning experiences through self-paced assignments and practice exercises constructed by the instructor or selected from a standard textbook. For example, active learning is facilitated by posting practice exercises under the Assignments function. Also, practice quizzes with answer keys can be posted under Course Documents. We recommend using Respondus for offline construction of tests and quizzes. Blackboard allows a variety of options when constructing a test—for example, setting a 70-minute time limit for a 50-item test. Another option is making all items visible for the duration of the test or restricting viewing to individual items with no opportunity to return to an item after a response has been entered. Posting explanations for correct and incorrect responses to test items encourages students to practice self-monitoring and further review of the concepts being assessed. Active learning is facilitated within a hybrid course by efforts to minimize the perception that distance learning experiences tend to be impersonal and individually isolating (Shank & Sitze, 2004). Such misperceptions can be minimized when a high level of interaction among instructors and students is complemented with clearly stated learning objectives, well-designed assignments, and frequent opportunities for students to select self-paced practice exercises.

Principle 4: Giving Prompt Feedback

Experiential learning that features a rapid pace and immediate responses is valued by contemporary college students. With texting, tweeting (which uses Twitter microblogging software for brief messages of 140 characters or less), blogging, instant messaging, chat rooms, e-mail, and streaming video through iPods and cell phones, instant feedback is a common life experience for contemporary students (Jones, 2002; Pew Internet & American Life Project, 2009). Blackboard provides timely feedback to students, collectively and individually, through a variety of functions: e-mail, discussion boards, the Assignments function, and test scoring and reporting. The Communication function supports e-mailing all or any subset of students. Discussion boards allow instructors and peers to respond immediately to comments or queries by individuals or groups of students. When a student submits a report through the Assignments function, the instructor evaluates the report, the grade is immediately posted in the instructor's Gradebook, and the student immediately receives the grade and the instructor's critique that is comparable to comments on hard-copy papers submitted in a conventional course. For tests with only selected-response items, Blackboard's test scoring function immediately posts grades in the instructor's Gradebook and for students under My Grades. For tests with short-answer items and essays, the process is the same as when reports are submitted through the Assignments function. Also, Blackboard's test scoring function allows student to view feedback on both correct and incorrect responses for each test item. Blackboard's multiple functions for prompt feedback make it possible for students to regularly monitor their learning and performance. Just-in-Time Teaching (JiTT) is a Web-based teaching and learning strategy in which instructors provide prompt feedback to students (Benedict & Anderton, 2004). When the JiTT feedback model is used within our hybrid course, questions or problems can be posted under Assignments in Blackboard. Students enter their responses by a predetermined time prior to the beginning of the next class session. Instructors identify areas of understanding and misunderstanding in student responses and adapt their lectures accordingly.

Principle 5: Emphasizing Time on Task

Traditionally, the concept of *time on task* is narrowly defined to mean the amount of time elapsed between the initial task involvement and the termination of involvement (Santrock, 2001). By expanding the concept of *time on task* to include the *timeliness* of student activity (Harris, Mazoue, Hamdan, & Casiple, 2007), instructors can implement the full range of online resources within a hybrid course. Whereas *time* addresses the amount of time directed toward a task, *timeliness* addresses the relation of the task to cognate concepts within the unit or course. From the perspective of Vygotsky's (1962) social constructivism, individual factors to be considered for promoting task-related time and timeliness include a student's prior knowledge, problem-solving skills, and motivation for a specified task. A variety of strategies and techniques are available for facilitating task-related *time* and *timeliness* in hybrid courses. Blackboard offers several asynchronous functions for promoting both duration and quality of time on task. Prior to the first class, instructors can convey to students the basic skills and type of technology necessary for successful performance in hybrid courses. During the course, the Announcements function is appropriate for posting timely, but not time-sensitive, information such as recommendations for time management of a specific assignment. For time-sensitive information such as impending deadlines, the e-mail option under the Communication function is effective for informing all students, a subset of students, or individuals. To improve quality of time on task, the Assignments function requires students to enter a response to a specific task, problem, or issue in order to be able to exit the activity. Requiring students to enter an analysis and critique tends to promote a thoughtful reading and comprehension of the assigned task, problem, or issue.

Principle 6: Communicating High Expectations

The cumulative effect of implementing the five principles of good practice in undergraduate education conveys high expectations for student performance in hybrid courses. Instructors can also convey explicit expectations about individual responsibility and performance. Before the first class, instructors can post a syllabus that clearly depicts equivalency between the hybrid course and the same course offered in a traditional setting. Also prior to the beginning of the course, instructors can refute common misperceptions about hybrid courses (Harris et al., 2007): (a) hybrid courses are not easier than traditional courses, (b) hybrid courses are not student-paced, lacking scheduled submissions and specified deadlines, (c) hybrid learning is not lacking feedback and mentoring by instructors, and (d) hybrid courses are not correspondence courses, lacking interaction with instructors and other students. A recurring theme throughout these recommendations is a consistently high level of instructor involvement in the online component of hybrid courses. Also, frequent instructor involvement meets the expectations of the socially oriented college students of the Net Generation.

Principle 7: Respecting Diverse Talents and Ways of Learning

Web-based tools such as Google Blogger, for constructing course-related blogs, and GarageBand, for constructing audio podcasts, are viable technologies for engaging students in diverse ways of learning. Blogs are ideal for engaging students on complex and controversial topics. By requiring participation on a blog to be anonymous, comments are issue-oriented and not merely expressions of agreement or disagreement with other members of the class. Linking to brief surveys from a blog facilitates an expanded discussion of complex and controversial issues. Such open, issue-oriented dialogue is a formative educational experience for student development of substantive, task-related critical thinking. Podcasts present narrated instructions and comments by the instructor and ideally complement text-based information in order to accommodate students with differing learning styles.

Designers of online learning experiences within hybrid courses are responsible for providing equal access for students of all abilities. Updates about applications of the Americans with Disabilities Act (http://www.usdoj. gov/crt/ada) and its oversight by the federal Office of Civil Rights (http:// www.ed.gov/about/offices/list/ocr/index.html) are accessible through their respective Web sites. Comprehensive guidelines for accessing the content of online applications are under development by the Web Accessibility Initiative (http://www.w3.org/WAI, of the World Wide Web Consortium). We recommend that designers of hybrid courses consult these resources in the early stages of course design and throughout the process of course development. The challenge of integrating principles of sound pedagogy and multiple technologies within hybrid learning experiences is made more complex by diversity in students' abilities to learn. Designers of hybrid learning experiences must give deliberate attention to ensuring that their courses support optimal achievement for all students by accommodating students with visual, auditory, motor, and cognitive impairments.

Summary

There are philosophical and practical reasons why comprehensive hybrid courses are becoming common offerings by institutions of higher education. Several regional accrediting boards are calling for education to extend information literacy programs by emphasizing fluency with information technologies. The Horizon Report (Johnson, Levine, & Smith, 2009) describes contemporary college students as wanting to be active participants in the learning process, with a need for control in their learning environments comparable to the control they have in accessing the expanding universe of information available through the Internet. Students in the Net Generation readily accept information technologies as viable resources for managing their personal, educational, social, and career-related experiences.

In contrast, the inconsistent level of technological proficiency among college and university instructors is a critical issue for institutions of higher education (Johnson, Levine, & Smith, 2009). Institutions must identify and implement new instructional models that will engage their students. To remedy the disparity between student and faculty readiness for fluency with information technologies, institutions must commit to the concept, allocate faculty assignments appropriately, and provide adequate financial support (McKeachie, 1999). Institutions have multiple options for demonstrating commitment to offering fluency-oriented courses and curricula. Incorporating specific, fluency-oriented language into institutional mission and vision statements would be a first step. Concurrently, fluency-supportive budgets must be established within all administrative units of the institution. Operationally, the allocation of faculty assignments for developing and conducting hybrid courses must be accompanied by employment of competent, accessible technical support personnel such as instructional technologists, hardware technicians, and software systems analysts. In conclusion, developing and implementing comprehensive hybrid courses is one of many strategies available to institutions of higher education committed to preparing students for full participation in this Information Age.

Recommended Readings

Dziuban, C., Hartman, J., & Moskal, P. (2004). Blended learning. *EDUCAUSE Center for Applied Research*, 2004(7).

Garrison, D. R., & Vaughan, N. D. (2008). *Blended learning in higher education: Framework, principles, and guidelines*. San Francisco: Jossey-Bass.

References

Aronson, E., & Patnoe, S. (1997). *The jigsaw classroom: Building cooperation in the classroom*. New York: Addison Wesley Longman, Inc.

Association of College and Research Libraries. (2000). *Information literacy competency standards for higher education*. Chicago: American Library Association.

Bearison, D. J., & Dorval, B. (2002). *Collaborative cognitition*. Westport, CT: Ablex.

Benedict, J. O., & Anderton, J. B. (2004). Applying the just-in-time teaching approach to teaching statistics. *Teaching of Psychology, 31*, 197–199.

Bodrova, E., & Leong, D. J. (2003). Learning and development of preschool children from the Vygotskian perspective. In A. Kozulin, B. Gindus, F. S. Ageyev, & S. M. Miller (eds.), *Vygotsky's educational theory in cultural context*. New York: Cambridge University Press.

Chickering, A. W., & Gamson, Z. F. (1999). Development and adaptation of the seven principles of good practice in undergraduate education. *New Directions for Teaching and Learning*, No. 80. San Francisco: Jossey-Bass.

Dunn, D. S., McCarthy, M. A., Baker, S., Halonen, J. S., & Hill IV, G. W. (2007). Quality benchmarks in undergraduate psychology programs. *American Psychologist, 62*, 650–670.

Elbaum, B., McIntyre, C., & Smith, A. (2002). *Essential elements: Prepare, design, and teach your online course*. Madison, WI: Atwood.

Harris, C. M., Mazoue, J. G., Hamdan, H., & Casiple, A. R. (2007). Designing an online introductory statistics course. In: D. S. Dunn, R. A. Smith, & B. C. Beins (Eds.), *Best practices for teaching statistics and research methods in the behavioral sciences*. Mahwah, NJ: Lawrence Erlbaum Associates, Publishers.

Holmberg, B. (1989). *Theory and practice in distance education*. London: Croom Helm.

Johnson, L., Levine, A., & Smith, R. (2009). *The 2009 Horizon Report*. Austin, TX: The New Media Consortium.

Jones, S. (2002). *The Internet goes to college: How students are living in the future with today's technology*. Washington, DC: Pew Internet & American Life Project.

McKeachie, W. J. (1999). *Teaching tips strategies, research, and theory for college and university teachers*. Boston: Houghton Mifflin Company.

National Research Council. (1999). *Being fluent with information technology*. Washington, DC: National Academy Press.

Pew Internet & American Life Project. (2009). *Twitterpated: Mobile Americans increasingly take to tweeting.* Retrieved July 31, 2009, from, http://pewresearch.org/pubs/1117/twitter-tweet-users-demographics

Santrock, J. W. (2001). *Educational psychology.* Boston: McGraw-Hill.

Shank, P., & Sitze, A. (2004). *Making sense of online learning: A guide for beginners and the truly skeptical.* San Francisco: Pfeiffer.

Slavin, R. E. (1995). *Cooperative learning: Theory, research, and practice* (2nd ed.). Boston: Allyn & Bacon.

Southern Association of Colleges and Schools, Commission on Colleges. (2006). *Distance education policy statement.* Southern Association of Colleges and Schools Commission on Colleges. Retrieved April 20, 2009, from http://www.sacscoc.org/pdf/081705/distance%20education.pdf

Southern Regional Education Board. (2007). Principles of good practice. *SREB Electronic Campus Initiatives.* Retrieved April 20, 2009, from http://www.ecinitiatives.org/publications/principles.asp

Tudge, J., & Scrimsher, S. (2003). Lev S. Vygosky on education: A cultural-historical, interpersonal, and individual approach to development. In: B. J. Zimmerman & D. H. Schunk (eds.), *Educational psychology: A century of contributions.* Mahwah, NJ: Erlbaum.

Western Cooperative for Educational Telecommunications. (n.d.). Best practices for electronically offered degree and certificate programs. *Western Cooperative for Educational Telecommunications.* Retrieved April 20, 2009, from http://www.wcet.info/resources/accreditation/Accrediting%20-%20Best%20Practices.pdf

Zimbardo, P. G., & Newton, J. W. (1975). *Instructors's resource book to accompany psychology and life.* Glenview, IL: Scott, Foresman.

8 Academic Advising with a Developmentally Organized Web Site

Drew C. Appleby

A wide variety of individuals can deliver academic advising in a broad assortment of settings and with the assistance of a diverse array of technologies. Advisees can receive information, insight, or direction about personal, academic, or career matters during one-on-one meetings with faculty (Hemwall, 2008), professional academic advisors, professional counselors, graduate students, undergraduate peer advisors, and advising support staff (Self, 2008); in groups (King, 2008); and in the classroom (Appleby, 2010). Advising can also take place within a technological context and, according to Leonard (2008, p. 292), "Technology has had and will continue to have a profound effect on academic advising. In fact, there is probably nothing else that has had as significant an impact on advising in the past ten years as the introduction of new technologies."

Twenty-two years ago, I described an advising strategy that involved a simple microcomputer application designed to aid the academic advising process, make students more responsible for their educational choices, increase computer literacy, promote career- and graduate-school planning, provide mentoring, increase the quality of letters of recommendations and résumés, and facilitate student recruitment (Appleby, 1989). During the ensuing two decades, academic advisors have begun to utilize an extraordinary range of technologies, including degree audit programs, student information systems, career guidance programs, transfer articulation systems, Webinars, instant messaging, social networking sites, e-mail, listservs, course-management systems, podcasts, online orientation programs, blogs, RSS news feeds, and advising Web sites (Leonard, 2008). The purpose of this chapter is to describe the developmentally organized advising Web site (http://www.psych.iupui.edu/undergraduate) I created to provide online advising to students during the full course of their undergraduate experience. The remaining sections of this chapter represent the portions of my Web site in the order they appear in a graphic (Figure 8.1) that students use to navigate the site. The Introduction section appears on the same page as the graphic. I wrote all of the sections in the second person to personalize their messages to students.

Many of the documents in my site are general enough to be used by any undergraduate psychology department and can be copied and used in their original form (e.g., *Areas of Specialization in Psychology That Require Graduate School* and *Occupations of Interest for Psychology Majors from the Dictionary of Occupational Titles*). Other documents contain information specific to the IUPUI Psychology Department (e.g., *The IUPUI Psychology Department's Undergraduate Curriculum* and *The Distinctive Features of*

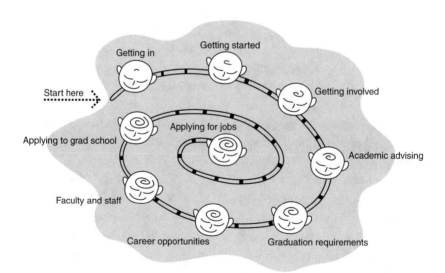

Figure 8.1 The graphic (created by Malene Abell) that appears on the first page of the advising Web site.

IUPUI's Undergraduate Psychology Program) and can serve as organizational templates for the creation of similar documents by other psychology or non-psychology departments. There are also documents that can serve as provocative stimuli for faculty discussions in any academic department about issues that are crucial to the unique missions of academic programs (e.g., *The Mission Statement of the IUPUI Psychology Program* and *The Student Learning Outcomes of the IUPUI Undergraduate Psychology Program*). Finally, the organizational structure of the site can be used by any academic department that wishes to inform its students about the developmental nature of their undergraduate education.

Introduction to the Web Site

Earning a bachelor's degree from the Indiana University-Purdue University Indianapolis (IUPUI) Department of Psychology is an academic journey composed of a series of stages that require thoughtful planning, careful preparation, and dedicated action. This Web site will help you understand the step-by-step nature of this process and introduce you to the resources that can make your journey to a degree in psychology a successful and self-actualizing experience. You can learn about these stages and resources by clicking on the spiraling heads in the graphic below that are labeled Getting In, Getting Started, Getting Involved, Academic Advising, Graduation Requirements, Career Opportunities, Faculty and Staff, Applying to Grad School, and Applying for Jobs.

Getting In

There are thousands of undergraduate psychology departments in the United States, and they are all different. To find out if our department would be a good fit for you, please read *Are You Considering Psychology as Your Major at IUPUI?* If you and our program are a good fit, read the *Mission Statement of the IUPUI Psychology Program* and the *Distinctive Features of IUPUI's Undergraduate Psychology Program* to discover the guiding principles of our program and the ways in which it sets itself apart from other psychology programs. You should also read *The Student Learning Outcomes of the IUPUI Undergraduate Psychology Program* so you are fully aware of the types of knowledge and skills you can develop as you progress through our curriculum. If you like what you read about our program, please go to *IUPUI's Enrollment Services Office* to learn how to apply for admission to the university, and then read the *Criteria for Acceptance into the Purdue School of Science as a Psychology Major* to see if you qualify to be admitted to IUPUI as a psychology major.

Getting Started

Your first year in college is crucially important, and it is absolutely essential to understand that this year will not simply be an extension of high school. Please read about *How Do First Year College Students Perceive the Differences Between High School and College* and view the PowerPoint presentation titled *Advice for First Year College Students From an Academic Travel Agent* to discover the very real academic differences you will experience when you become a college freshman and the strategies that can enable you to adapt successfully to these differences. Once you have adjusted to the culture of higher education, it will be time for you to identify the types of careers you can enter; become aware of the knowledge, skills, and characteristics (KSCs) necessary to enter these careers; and develop plans of action to acquire these KSCs. Please read *The Savvy Psychology Major* to understand how you can accomplish these essential tasks.

Getting Involved

Becoming actively involved in your undergraduate education will help you develop a greater sense of belongingness in the Psychology Department, provide you with opportunities to develop the KSCs you will need to attain your educational and career goals, and make you aware of the people who can help you accomplish your goals. One of the advantages of IUPUI is its large size, which means there are many more academic, research, social, and professional opportunities for involvement available to psychology majors at IUPUI than at smaller colleges and universities. A three-part strategy to take advantage of these opportunities is to (1) **become aware** of them, (2) **decide** which of them will be most valuable for you, and (3) **become actively involved** in those opportunities that will help you develop the KSCs you will need to enter the graduate program or career of your choice. This section of the Web site will help you accomplish the first stage of this strategy (i.e., becoming aware of these opportunities), your academic advisor can guide you during the second stage, and it will then be your responsibility to accomplish the third stage. One very important way to increase your awareness of what is going on in the department is to become a member of the department's listserv, which is an electronic e-mailing system that allows the department to send messages to all psychology majors who have become members. These messages are about important topics such as department events, internships, jobs, scholarships, new courses, or academic policy changes. To learn about the listserv, read *FAQs About the Psychology Department Listserv.*

Psychology is the scientific study of behavior and mental processes. This means that scientific research is at the core of our discipline. The IUPUI Psychology Department is one of only 5% of all the psychology departments in the United States that exist within schools of science with other empirical sciences such as biology, chemistry, and physics. This emphasis on science means our faculty are actively involved in research and there are many opportunities for psychology majors to learn how to perform research and to collaborate with faculty on cutting-edge research projects. To learn about how IUPUI psychology majors can take advantage of these opportunities, read *Undergraduate Research Opportunities.* To learn how to obtain funding to perform an undergraduate research project, read *Funding Opportunities for Undergraduate Research.* If graduate school is part of your plans, it will be imperative for you to develop research skills and to have your letter of recommendation writers provide evidence that you possess these skills. Neither of these will be possible unless you engage in research during your undergraduate career. You will also want to present the results of your research to your peers when you have completed it. Read *Undergraduate Research Conferences* to discover three opportunities to do so.

Another way to get involved is by becoming a teaching assistant (TA). Like performing research, becoming a TA provides you with the opportunity to work closely with a faculty member, develop valuable career- and gradu-ate-school-related skills, help your fellow students, and strengthen your knowledge in a particular area of psychology. The document titled *FAQs About the Role of a Teaching Assistant* will answer the three following ques-tions: How can I become a TA? What does a TA do? What are the benefits of being a TA?

Our department has an Advising Office staffed with undergraduate peer advisors (PAs). Read the Description of *IUPUI's Peer Advisor Training Program* to learn why the National Academic Advising Association recognized our training program for these PAs as a "Best Practice."

You can also increase your involvement in the Psychology Department by becoming an active member of Psychology Club or Psi Chi, the international honor society in psychology. Read *FAQs About Psi Chi and Psychology Club* to become familiar with these organizations. Also read *Career-Related Skills That Can Be Developed by Psi Chi Officers* to learn how the skills that club officers develop while they are performing their duties are the same skills they will need to enter and thrive in today's competitive job market.

Academic Advising

Academic advising is a crucial part of your undergraduate education because it enables you to understand (1) what classes you will need to graduate, (2) in what order you should take these classes, and (3) how these classes can help you develop the KSCs you will need to gain entrance to and succeed in the graduate program or career to which you aspire. Please read the IUPUI Psychology Department Advising Office's *Academic Advising Syllabus* to gain an understanding of the purpose of our advising program and the ways it can help you become a successful psychology major. This syllabus is composed of the following sections:

1. Mission, Student Learning Outcomes, and Assumptions of the IUPUI Psychology Advising Office
2. What Is a Savvy Psychology Major?
3. The Dangers of Self-Advising
4. Ten Reasons Why Psychology Majors Graduate Later Than They Plan
5. Academic Advising Resources
6. Faculty, Staff, and Peer Advisors
7. IUPUI's School of Science Academic Advising Network
8. Expectations and Responsibilities of Advisors and Advisees
9. How to Prepare for a Meeting With Your Advisor
10. Academic Advising Events and Calendar
11. Three-Year Schedule of Psychology Classes

Graduation Requirements

Successful psychology majors know **what** courses they must take to graduate, **when** to take these courses, **why** they must take these courses, and **how** the successful completion of these courses will prepare them for their educational and occupational futures. Please read *The IUPUI Psychology Department's Undergraduate Curriculum* to discover the answers to these crucial what, when, why, and how questions.

Our department offers both a Bachelor of Arts (BA) and a Bachelor of Science (BS) in Psychology. Although the differences between these two degrees are small, it is important to be aware of them so you can choose the degree whose requirements will better prepare you for your future. Read *Should I Pursue a BS or a BA Degree in Psychology at IUPUI?* to discover these differences.

Once you have chosen your degree (BA or BS) and determined what courses you must take to complete it, the next step is to create a semester-by-semester plan to finish your degree. Please read *Four-Year Graduation Plans from Past and Present University Bulletins* to view samples of these plans you can use as models to create your own unique plan to graduate. Many IUPUI psychology majors have job and/or family obligations that prevent them from taking the 15 or 16 hours per semester required to graduate in eight consecutive semesters. The Psychology Department has created a *Four-Year Fast Track Plan for a BA in Psychology* that enables its busy students to graduate in four years by taking a reduced class load during their fall and spring semesters and enrolling in summer school classes.

The final document that will enable you to graduate on schedule is the *School of Science Requirements for a BA or BS Degree in Psychology*. This document discusses important issues such as number of credit hours and grade point average required to graduate, residency requirements, pass/fail options, and courses for which no credit is granted.

Several other documents answer questions about graduation require-ments. The first answers the question, can psychology majors graduate with Honors? The answer to that question is a definite YES, and the information you will need to understand our program is included in the *IUPUI Psychology Department's Honors Program*. Not all psychology departments require a capstone class and not all that do provide their students with a choice of three capstone experiences like our department does. To discover what a capstone class is, understand which capstone to take, and know when to take it, read *Your Capstone Class*. If you are interested in earning a minor in psychology, please read *How to Earn a Minor in Psychology* and *How to Request a Final Psychology Minor Audit*. One of the unique features of our department is that its majors can earn a concentration in one of four areas of specialization in psychology that correspond to our graduate programs. Please read *Psychology Major Concentrations* and the *Application for a Concentration* for a descrip-tion of these concentrations and the document to apply for one.

A final document you should read is the *Graduation Checklist*. This list contains the procedures you must follow during the semester before you graduate to make sure your graduation actually takes place.

Career Opportunities

According to the most recent edition of the National Center for Education Statistics Web site, more than 92,500 students graduate every year in the United States with a BA or BS in Psychology (Snyder & Dillow, 2010) and then either enter the work force or continue their education in graduate or professional school. To view a list of areas of psychology that require gradu-ate school, read *Areas of Specialization in Psychology That Require Graduate School*. If you would like to discover where IUPUI psychology alumni have gone to graduate school and into what graduate/professional programs they have been accepted, read *Graduate Programs of IUPUI Psychology Majors*.

Areas of employment for those with a Bachelor's Degree in Psychology are almost limitless, but a good way to investigate specific occupations that psychology majors can enter is to read *Occupations of Interest for Psychology Majors from the Dictionary of Occupational Titles*. This list contains concise descriptions of 130 occupations that psychology majors can and have entered. These descriptions are composed of the skills that people employed in these occupations must be capable of demonstrating on the job. The advantage of this type of skill-centered description is that it enables job-seeking psychology majors to (1) choose the classes and extracurricular activities that can help them to develop these skills during their undergraduate careers and then (2) be able to prove their possession of these skills by providing appropriate evidence on résumés and during interviews. The bottom line of any job interview is, "Do you possess the skills that are required to perform competently in this job?" The information in this document will provide you with a list of these skills so you can be ready, willing, and able to answer this crucial question in a confident and competent manner. A specific list of careers held by IUPUI psychology majors can be viewed at *Jobs Held by IUPUI Psychology Alumni With a Bachelor's Degree*. One excellent source of information for students who are interested in a career that requires graduate school, but who find they must end their education with a bachelor's degree, can be found at Occupational Outlook Handbook *Links to Specialized Career Paths in Psychology*.

A valuable source of information for students who are trying to decide about going to graduate school or applying for a job immediately after graduation is *Do You Prepare for Graduate School and a Job in the Same Way?* Another source of information for career-exploring psychology majors is a PowerPoint presentation titled *JagJobs*, which describes the online career exploration site provided by the IUPUI Career Center. A final resource for career-exploring psychology majors is the *IUPUI Office of Career and Employment Services*, which contains a wealth of human, printed, and electronic resources.

Faculty and Staff

The most valuable resources of any psychology department are its faculty and staff. These are the people who will share their **knowledge** of psychology with you, provide you with opportunities to develop crucial psychological **skills**, model the **characteristics** you will need to succeed in your future profession, and provide you with the **support and mentoring** you will need to succeed as a psychology major. Please read the *Faculty* and the *Staff* sections of our department's Web site to discover who these people are, what they do, and the services they can provide. Once you have familiarized yourself with our faculty and staff, the next step is to begin to use this knowledge to make wise choices about the classes you will take, the activities in which you will participate, and the advising and mentoring support you will need as you progress through your undergraduate journey.

Applying to Graduate School

If your career goal requires a graduate degree, it will be extremely important to become familiar with the graduate school application process because it is very complex and quite different from applying to undergraduate school. Familiarity with the application process will enable you to know not only **what to do—but also what not to do**—as you apply to graduate school so your chances of gaining admittance to the program of your choice are maximized. Two must-view PowerPoint presentations are *The Graduate School Application Process* and *The Graduate Record Exam*. These two presentations will systematically introduce you to the A-to-Z steps you should follow as you apply to graduate school and prepare for the Graduate Record Exam (GRE), which is the entrance exam required by the vast majority of psychology graduate programs. Knowing what to do during the application process is extremely important, but knowing what not to do is equally important. To find out what not to do when you apply to graduate school, please view the PowerPoint presentation titled *The Kisses of Death in the Graduate School Application Process.*

Another valuable resource for preparing for the GRE is a PowerPoint titled *How to Do Your Best on the GRE* produced by the Educational Testing Service (ETS), the company that publishes the GRE. Sarah Reed from the IUPUI Career Center narrates the PowerPoint slides. ETS trained Sarah to help students develop the test-taking skills that should enable them to score up to their potential on the GRE.

A bachelor's degree in psychology can provide a strong foundation for entrance into professional graduate programs such as dentistry, law, medicine, occupational therapy, optometry, pharmacy, physical therapy, and veterinary medicine. *Information for Psychology Majors Who Plan to Enter Professional Graduate Programs* provides Web addresses that will lead you to information sheets for these programs offered by Indiana University, Purdue University, and Butler University. These sheets contain the following types of information about each of these programs:

1. The nature of the profession
2. Career opportunities for those with a degree in this profession

3. The skills and characteristics of successful program applicants
4. Courses needed in addition to those required for a BA or BS in psychology
5. Suggested electives and extracurricular activities
6. Number of required undergraduate hours
7. Admissions tests
8. Letters of recommendation
9. Admissions criteria (e.g., minimum GPA and test scores)
10. Application deadlines
11. Contacts for further information

The final link on this page will take you to an extensive table of *Topics About Graduate School and Their Hot Links* created to help you gather information from the Internet that will enable you to accomplish the following:

1. Understand what graduate programs are looking for in applicants
2. Obtain strong letters of recommendation
3. Learn what undergraduate courses are expected by graduate programs
4. Write an effective personal statement
5. Decide between a PhD and a PsyD
6. Create an effective curriculum vitae (the academic equivalent of a résumé)
7. Choose the right graduate program for you
8. Make a successful transition to graduate school once you have been accepted

Applying for Jobs

Although a Bachelor's Degree in Psychology does not prepare its owner to be a psychologist, there are an almost limitless number of psychology-related jobs that psychology majors can enter. Psychology-related jobs are those that require the skills that psychology majors can acquire if they take full advantage of the opportunities provided by their undergraduate educations.

Job Skills Valued by Employers Who Interview Psychology Majors is an article that describes the types of skills that employers look for during the hiring process, such as the ability to speak articulately, write clearly, think critically, solve problems creatively, and demonstrate strong interpersonal skills. The Internet has become an amazing source of information for job seekers, and you will find a long list of Web sites that can help you to identify, understand, choose, and apply for jobs in *Internet Sources of Information for Job-Seeking Psychology Majors*. These sites will help you accomplish the following job-related activities:

1. Discover the types of jobs available to psychology majors
2. Decide what career is right for you
3. Write an effective résumé and cover letter
4. Learn how to dress for your interviews
5. Anticipate the questions interviewers are likely to ask
6. Prepare for and participate successfully in job fairs
7. Be aware of career-related workshops on campus
8. Find what jobs are available
9. Develop a network

A Collegial Offer

Academic advising is a teaching and learning process (Appleby, 2008). My Web site is a teaching tool I created to provide potential and current IUPUI psychology majors with a comprehensive opportunity to learn about our academic program; the stages of their undergraduate education; the ways in which they must change as they progress toward graduation; the resources that can help them make these changes; the personal, educational, and occupational goals they can attain as a result of these changes; and the strategies they can use to successfully attain these goals. In keeping with the applied focus of this book, I would like to offer you any of the information contained in my site that could benefit your students, your colleagues, your program, and your institution. All I ask in return is appropriate credit for the materials you use and any constructive feedback you receive about my materials so I can continue to improve and refine the design and contents of my Web site. If I can be of any assistance to you regarding the contents of this chapter or my site, please do not hesitate to contact me at dappleby@ iupui.edu.

References

Appleby, D. C. (1989). The microcomputer as an academic advising tool. *Teaching of Psychology, 16*(3), 156–159.

Appleby, D. C. (2008). Advising as teaching and learning. In: V. N. Gordon, W. R. Habley, T. J. Grites, & Associates (eds.), *Academic advising: A comprehensive handbook* (2nd ed.). San Francisco: Jossey-Bass.

Appleby, D. C. (2010). Advising in the classroom: A career exploration class for psychology majors. In D. S. Dunn, B. C. Beins, M. A. McCarthy, & G. W. Hill (eds.), *Best practices for teaching beginnings and endings in the psychology major: Research, cases, and recommendations.* New York: Oxford University Press.

Hemwall, M. K. (2008). Advising delivery: Faculty advising. In: V. N. Gordon, W. R. Habley, T. J. Grites, & Associates (eds.), *Academic advising: A comprehensive handbook* (2nd ed.). San Francisco: Jossey-Bass.

King, N. S. (2008). Advising delivery: Group strategies. In: V. N. Gordon, W. R. Habley, T. J. Grites, & Associates (eds.), *Academic advising: A comprehensive handbook* (2nd ed.). San Francisco: Jossey-Bass.

Leonard, M. J. (2008). Advising delivery: Using technology. In: V. N. Gordon, W. R. Habley, T. J. Grites, & Associates (eds.), *Academic advising: A comprehensive handbook* (2nd ed.). San Francisco: Jossey-Bass.

Self, C. (2008). Advising delivery: Professional advisors, counselors, and other staff. In: V. N. Gordon, W. R. Habley, T. J. Grites, & Associates (Eds.), *Academic advising: A comprehensive handbook* (2nd ed.). San Francisco: Jossey-Bass.

Snyder, T. D., & Dillow, S. A. (2010). *Digest of educational statistics: 2009* (Table 286: Bachelor's degrees conferred by degree-granting institutions by sex, race/ethnicity, and field of study: 2007-08). Retrieved June 16, 2010, from http://nces.ed.gov/programs/digest/d09/tables/dt09_286.asp?referrer=list

9 Enhancing Student Engagement and Learning Using "Clicker"-Based Interactive Classroom Demonstrations

Gary M. Muir and Anne M. Cleary

An instructor presents a question on the screen during class: "Are there more words that start with the letter L, or are there more words that have L as the third letter?" Students begin using clickers to indicate their responses, pressing "A" for "More words start with L" and "B" for "More words have L as the third letter." After everyone has responded, the instructor presents a bar graph on the screen depicting the percentage of students who pressed "A" or "B." The graph shows that more students pressed "A" than "B," demonstrating the students' use of the *availability heuristic* (Tversky & Kahneman, 1974), the tendency to base decisions on the ease with which one can think of examples. People tend to answer that there are more words that start with "L" because it is easier for people to think of examples of words that start with the letter L than examples of words that have L as the third letter. In fact, there are more words that have L as the third letter. This scenario is only one example of the many ways that clickers—or "classroom response systems"—can enhance student engagement and learning through the use of interactive classroom demonstrations.

Classroom Response Systems

Classroom response systems (CRSs), also known as wireless response systems, personal response systems, or just "clickers," are becoming increasingly popular on college campuses (e.g., Beatty, 2004; Caldwell, 2007; Furlong, 2007). Students use handheld devices or clickers to respond to questions, the instructor's computer records each clicker response via a receiver unit, and software quickly aggregates a summary of the responses for presentation on a projector screen.

The Most Common Uses of CRSs

A review of the literature suggests that clickers are commonly used for polling student attitudes and testing their knowledge of course content (see Bruff, 2009, for an excellent recent guide to teaching with clickers). For example, Zhu (2007) asserted that common uses of clickers include assessing student misconceptions at the start of class, assessing students' understanding of material, initiating class discussion, administering tests and quizzes, collecting feedback on teaching, taking attendance, and recording participation. The present chapter focuses on a use for clickers that receives considerably less attention in the literature: actively engaging students in the processes of research data collection and interpretation. Although articles have mentioned the potential use of CRSs in conducting classroom experiments (e.g., Draper et al., 2002), most research on CRSs in college classrooms focuses on the aforementioned uses listed by Zhu (e.g., Caldwell, 2007; MacArthur & Jones, 2008).

Novel Uses of CRSs

A vast body of research involves the collection and aggregation of responses from large groups of people at once. Because clicker systems are designed for this purpose, they are well suited for research data collection in the classroom. Clickers can be used to actively illustrate research methods, replicate findings, or even test novel hypotheses in the classroom setting. In these ways, data collected from student clicker responses can be used to actively engage students in the processes by which behavioral scientists collect and analyze their data and arrive at their conclusions. In addition to the behavioral sciences, teachers from other disciplines can use CRSs to learn about their students and inform teaching. Importantly, using student-generated data promotes active learning. Instead of merely reviewing data from previous research, students are actively engaged in the process by which the data were derived. Actively engaging students during class time is thought to facilitate learning (McKeachie, 1999); therefore, active involvement in the research process via clickers should be beneficial to student learning. This chapter focuses on three general domains of CRSs: (1) using student-generated data to illustrate various statistics, (2) using student-generated data to engage students in replications of known findings, and (3) using student-generated data to engage students in the testing of novel hypotheses.

Using CRSs to Illustrate Statistics

Basic statistics are essential to understanding behavioral science. Knowledge of basic methods used to describe numerical data and the implications of these different methods enable students to critically evaluate data presented in journals and the popular media. Unfortunately, not all students are motivated to learn statistics. To overcome these barriers, we can teach descriptive statistics in an engaging and interactive way. The statistics instructor could also choose to conduct inferential statistics (for example, t-tests) using data collected with clickers. Clickers provide an opportunity to teach descriptive statistics by allowing students to participate in both the collection and analysis of data in the classroom.

When the first author teaches descriptive statistics in "Principles of Psychology" (an introductory psychology course), he first presents a brief lecture defining key terms for measures of central tendency (mean, median, and mode), variability (range, standard deviation), and association (correlation coefficient), followed by graphical examples of data distributions that are normal, positively or negatively skewed, and bimodal. This lecture component emphasizes the appropriateness of specific measures of central tendency and variability when describing different distributions. Students then generate their own data distributions using the clickers.

For example, the first author asks female students to use clickers to submit their height using a rating scale of one to nine (e.g., 1 = <5'0", 2 = 5'0"–<5'2", and so on). Responses will typically generate data that approximate a normal distribution (Fig. 9.1a) and the clicker software displays the data to the class as a frequency histogram. The same exercise is then conducted with males, who are typically the minority in the class, and the male distribution (Fig. 9.1b) is compared against the female height distribution. The class uses the data to discuss issues regarding sampling. (e.g., "How confident would we be in describing the height of males in our class if only three males had clicked in?," "What if every male in the world had provided data?," "What would the distribution look like if males and females responded together?"). In addition, the first author asks a number of opinion-based questions using a nine-point Likert scale (i.e., 1 = *Strongly Disagree*; 5 = *Neither Agree nor Disagree*; 9 = *Strongly Agree*) in an attempt to generate distributions of differing shapes. For example, the question, "The invasion of Iraq was a mistake," has reliably generated a negatively skewed distribution (Fig. 9.1c). Students describe the shape of the distribution and which measures of central tendency and variability would best represent the data.

Also, answers to some questions are specifically paired to illustrate positive or negative correlations. It is important to note that the type of questions asked is critical in determining the resulting distribution's shape. Our experience has been that questions based on more controversial issues (e.g., "The country made the right choice by returning George W. Bush to the presidency") will generate more polarized (and animated) responses from students than less controversial questions (e.g., "Winter is my favorite season in Minnesota"). If controversial issues are used, however, it is essential that the instructor not indicate approval or disapproval for any answer while discussing results with the class.

The instructor calculates scatter plots of the students' responses (Fig. 9.2) and correlation coefficients between pairs of questions using Excel or another statistical package following class. These data are then shared and discussed with students during lecture on scatter plots and correlation coefficients in the subsequent class period. Although we have not yet tried this, a relatively simple Excel macro could allow these analyses to occur within the same class period as the data collection.

CRS Use in Replicating Known Behavioral Research Findings

In addition to illustrating statistics, clickers can be used to replicate well-known findings (e.g., the levels-of-processing effect), and data collection via clickers leads to effect sizes comparable to those reported in the literature

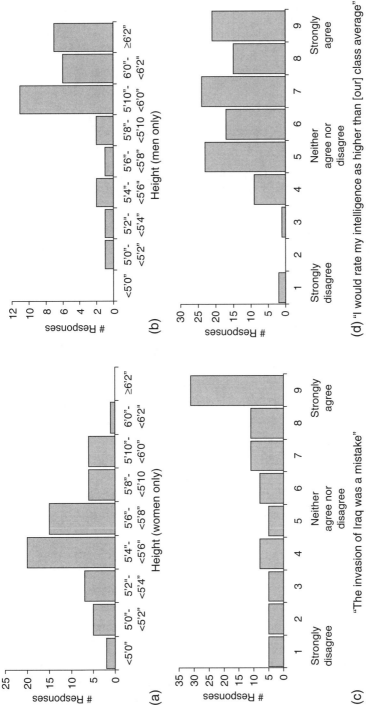

Figure 9.1. Examples of frequency histograms generated by student responses using clickers. A. Height of only females in the class (n = 62). B. Height of only males in the class (n = 31). C. All students' responses to the statement "The invasion of Iraq was a mistake" (n = 89). These data can be used to prompt discussions about types of distributions, measures of central tendency and variability, and sampling issues. D. All students' responses to the statement "I would rate my intelligence as higher than [our] class average" (n = 112), reflecting the "better than average" phenomenon.

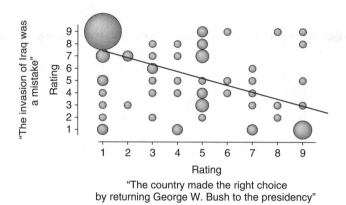

Figure 9.2. Scatter plot and regression line for student ratings (1 = *Strongly Disagree*; 5 = *Neither Agree nor Disagree*; 9 = *Strongly Agree*) of the two statements "The country made the right choice by returning George W. Bush to the presidency" and "The invasion of Iraq was a mistake" shows a strong negative correlation (*r* = –.54). The size of each sphere reflects the number of respondents selecting the pair of ratings at its center point.

(Langley, Cleary, & Kostic, 2007). Thus, instructors can replicate previous research findings using student-generated data. Replication of research findings is a key component of many science classes, particularly classes with laboratory components. Clicker systems' potential for replications should be especially useful for large-enrollment classes where most laboratory activities are not feasible. This section describes eight examples of behavioral research findings that could be replicated in classroom settings: the false-memory phenomenon, the levels-of-processing phenomenon, the fundamental attribution error, the "better than average" phenomenon, the Stroop effect, and the serial position effect, as well as two replications of effects frequently discussed in economics: the prisoner's dilemma and the ultimatum game.

The False Memory Phenomenon

Cleary (2008) reported an in-class replication of the false-memory phenomenon, which is the finding that participants claim to remember a word that was not studied when the word is strongly associated with the list of studied words (Roediger & McDermott, 1995). Cleary (2008) presented her class with a study list of words followed by a recognition memory test. The study words were five of the original word lists used by Roediger and McDermott (the "anger" list, the "fruit" list, the "spider" list, the "king" list, and the "high" list);

these lists were read aloud to the class. Each word on the recognition test appeared singly on the screen in front of the class, and the presentation order of the words was random. Of the test words presented on the recognition test, five came from the study lists that the instructor previously read to the class (e.g., "mad"), five did not come from the study lists but were related to studied lists (e.g., "anger"), and five were new words not related to studied words (e.g., "rough"). For each test word, students used their clickers to respond "A" when they believed the item was studied and "B" when they believed the item was not studied.

Immediately following the recognition test, the instructor imported data from students' responses into an Excel spreadsheet that had been previously set up with the formulas needed to compute the mean proportion of items judged to be studied in each of the three conditions (studied items, critical non-studied items, and unrelated non-studied items). The instructor then used the overall means to create a graph in Excel to display to the class. Finally, the instructor analyzed the data in front of the class using statistical software. Results showed that students were indeed significantly more likely to judge critical lures (i.e., non-studied words that were closely related to all of the studied words) as having been studied than unrelated lures. Cleary demonstrated that a commonly reported effect in the literature (the false-memory effect) can be replicated using clickers in a group setting.

The Levels-of-Processing Effect

The levels-of-processing (LOP) effect (e.g., Craik & Tulving, 1975) indicates that deeply processing list items in terms of their meaning generally leads to better memory than shallow processing of the items in terms of their physical features (e.g., letters). Cleary (2008) replicated this effect in the classroom. Students read a single word and judged whether or not it fit into a sentence (e.g., "He put the dishes in the _____") using "A" for yes and "B" for no. As a second condition, students read a single word and clicked to report whether the word was in capital letters ("A" for yes and "B" for no). Several randomly ordered examples of these two conditions prompted choices from students. The instructor then used Excel to compute the mean proportion of items judged to have been studied in each condition. Students were significantly more likely to judge words as having been studied when they had previously made a sentence judgment for the word than when they had previously judged whether the word was in capital letters, illustrating the LOP effect.

The "Fundamental Attribution Error"

Humans appear to be motivated to make attributions about the causes of others' behavior (Heider, 1958). Previous studies have shown, however, that these attributions are not always accurate and are prone to systematic biases that are dependent upon the circumstances. For example, the fundamental attribution error (FAE) explains a tendency for people to attribute strangers' behavior to stable, internal sources (i.e., personality) rather than to situational, external factors (i.e., the conditions under which they are meeting; Ross, 1977). To demonstrate the FAE using clickers, students divide into pairs where one is the "Quizmaster" and the other a "Contestant" (in an adaptation of Ross et al., 1977). The Quizmasters ask Contestants five challenging (but not impossible) general-knowledge questions generated by the Quizmasters. Quizmasters then score the Contestants' responses after all five questions have been asked. Next, the instructor asks all students to "privately write down a rating of your own general knowledge ability compared to that of your partner." (1 = *much worse than partner*; 5 = *same as partner*; 9 = *much better than partner*). Writing a rating forces students to commit to a value they cannot later change. Next, Quizmasters and Contestants anonymously click in with their ratings. The results consistently show that Quizmasters, on average, rate their general knowledge as much *higher* than their partners. In contrast, Contestants consistently rate their general knowledge as *lower* than their partners when using the clickers to anonymously provide ratings.

This result occurs because students fail to adequately take into account the situational variable of role when assessing the general knowledge of their partners relative to their own. Instead of acknowledging that the randomly selected Quizmasters knew all the answers *because they generated the questions*, both groups consistently made internal attributions, either attributing the Quizmasters' ability to answer all the questions to their higher general-knowledge ability, or attributing the Contestants' typically poor performance to their lower general-knowledge ability.

The "Better Than Average" Phenomenon

Studies have shown that students from Western cultures tend to rate themselves as better than the average college student (Cross, 1977). This "better than average" phenomenon is not confined to student's perceptions of their academic ability but also extends to ratings of other attributes of value to the rater (Mezulis et al., 2004). This statistical impossibility must therefore be an overestimation of ability on the part of a large number of individuals.

It is useful to replicate the "better than average" phenomenon in class as a means to illustrate how our self-perceptions may be unrealistically biased. To replicate the finding, students anonymously respond using the clickers to the statement "I would rate my intelligence as higher than [our] class average" (1 = *Strongly Disagree*; 5 = *Neither Agree nor Disagree*; 9 = *Strongly Agree*). The results are extremely robust, with successful replication of the phenomenon every time (e.g., a typical class response is shown in Fig. 9.1d). Another example would be to have students rate their sense of humor compared to the class average.

The Stroop Effect

The Stroop effect (Stroop, 1935) is one of the most popular and robust demonstrations in psychology. In this task, participants try to name the ink color of a word as quickly as possible. Results show that if the ink color matches the word (e.g., "green" written in green ink) then response times are facilitated relative to the time required to name the ink color of a color block. In addition, if the ink color does not match the word (e.g., "green" written in red ink), response times are significantly longer because automatic reading of the word interferes with naming the ink color. Clickers that can quickly record response times (i.e., some radiofrequency [RF] clickers) would be needed to replicate this phenomenon, or any other experiment based on reaction-time data. One option is to initially present a column of color blocks and ask students to click "1" when they have finished quietly naming aloud the color ink for each block in the entire column. The average time to complete the task for that column could then be compared to the average time taken to name the ink color of subsequent columns of "color" words that matched the word's ink color and "color" words that *did not* match the ink's color. Once again, a spreadsheet program could then be used to analyze differences in response times as a function of the different stimulus types.

The Serial Position Effect

Bill Hill of Kennesaw State University has effectively used clickers to replicate the serial position effect (G. W. Hill, personal communication, July 22, 2009). Briefly, the serial position effect is where items at the end and beginning of a long list presented serially are better remembered than those items in the middle (e.g., Murdock, 1962). Hill presented students with a long list of words serially and then asked students to write down as many words as possible from the list. Using clickers, students then identified which words from the list they had correctly recalled (e.g., "Did you recall THREAD?" with students clicking "yes" or "no"). Results show that students typically remember more words accurately from the beginning (i.e., the primacy effect) and the end (i.e., the recency effect) of the original word list than words in the middle.

Examples of Replications Used in Economics: The Prisoner's Dilemma and the Ultimatum Game

Although the majority of replications using clickers presented in this section have been used to demonstrate psychological phenomena, similar uses for clickers have been reported from other disciplines. Hinde and Hunt (2006) described a replication of the prisoner's dilemma in which students make the choice to play cooperatively or competitively against the instructor using clickers. Students see the "payoff" schedule for their responses as a 2 × 2 table with columns and rows labeled C(ooperation) and D(efection). Students are the "column" player and the instructor is the "row" player. Students try to get the most number of points for themselves as possible. The instructor constructs the payoff matrix similarly to other examples of the prisoner's dilemma: If both players cooperate, they gain three points each; if only one defects, the defecting player receives five points while his or her partner receives none; if both players defect, they both receive only one point. Students then make a choice each round using the clickers to play cooperatively (by clicking *C*) or competitively (by clicking *D*). The overall responses of students in the class are then displayed, and students record their payoff for each round. After several rounds, the overall results demonstrated that students who chose to play cooperatively had a better outcome (i.e., higher number of points) both for themselves and their partner (the instructor) than those students who more often choose to play competitively.

A final example from economics involves text messaging on a mobile phone to enable pairs of students to communicate while playing the ultimatum game (Cheung, 2008). The game requires students to make decisions about allocating resources. Pairs of students divide up a known sum of hypothetical money between them by having one student offer some amount to his or her partner, who can accept or refuse the amount offered. If the offer is accepted each student gets the amounts proposed in the division, and if the offer is refused then both get nothing. An alternative method to text messages would be to have half the students (player 1s) make offers of between $1 and $9 (out of a total pool of $10) to their partners (player 2s) using the clickers, where the clicker responses are visible on the screen and are identifiable by players 1's clicker number. Player 2s would then find their partner's clicker number on the screen to see the amount they had been offered. Player 2s could then indicate acceptance of the offer by choosing the same number as the offer or reject the offer by selecting 0 (or an invalid option) on his or her clicker. An Excel macro could be used to determine whether the two responses in the round matched (i.e., were accepted) or not (i.e., were rejected) and whether the difference was a function of the amount offered. Results show that although the purely rational choice would be to accept any non-zero amount offered, participants will typically refuse low offers (thereby ensuring that both parties receive nothing), perhaps on the basis of perceived unfairness (Cheung, 2008).

CRS Use for Conducting Student-Devised Studies

Another potential use of CRSs is to conduct studies or experiments devised by students and using members of the class as the research participants. This section describes several potential in-class activities. The second author has used CRSs to engage students in novel hypothesis testing in two classes: a Cognitive Psychology class and a Research Methods in Psychology class.

Example 1: Do Pictures Benefit Memory for Words?

In cognitive psychology, students generate a novel hypothesis that can be tested using the CRS as a methodological tool. The students submit suggestions that are reviewed by the instructor and a graduate teaching assistant (TA), who work together to choose the study to be conducted in class. The winning idea from one particular semester was the hypothesis that presenting pictures along with study words would lead to better memory for the words than presenting the words alone. Thirty words appeared individually on a projector screen. Fifteen of these words were accompanied by color drawings of words; for example, the word rose was accompanied by a colored drawing of a red rose above the word. Fifteen of the words were unaccompanied by pictures. Following the study list, the instructor presented the class with a randomly ordered recognition test containing the 30 studied words along with 15 non-studied words. For each test word presented on the screen, the class used their clickers to respond "A" for "studied" and "B" for "non-studied."

Following the test but prior to displaying the results, the instructor encouraged a discussion about what students thought the hypothesis for the study was and whether they thought it would be supported. Next, the instructor analyzed the data in class using pre-created spreadsheets in Excel that contained the formulas necessary for computing the mean proportions of items labeled as "studied" in each of the three test conditions (studied with a picture, studied without a picture, and non-studied). Although the results did not support the hypothesis in this instance (the means were roughly equal in the picture/word and the word-only conditions), students discussed ideas about why the hypothesis was not supported.

Example 2: Do Judgments About Oneself Lead to Better Memory than Judgments About Others?

The self-reference effect is the finding that relating items to oneself leads to better memory for the items than other encoding methods (for an exception related to evolutionary theory, see Nairne, Thompson, & Pandeirada, 2007). One semester, the student-generated idea in the cognitive psychology class was the following hypothesis: Self-reference should be better than an "other" reference when the "other" is a loved one, and as an extension of the theory, an "other" reference should lead to better memory when the "other" is a loved one than when the "other" is someone less well known.

Students read 18 individually presented words on the projector screen. Six of the words were accompanied by the question, "How relevant is this word to you?" Six were accompanied by the question, "How relevant is the word to your loved one?" Six were accompanied by the question, "How relevant is this word to the CSU track coach?" The order of the words in the list was random. For each word presented, students used their clickers to respond to the question in the following way: A = *not at all,* B = *not very,* C = *somewhat,* and D = *extremely.* Following the study list, the class viewed a recognition test list containing 24 randomly ordered words. For each word presented on the screen, students pressed "A" to indicate "studied" and

"B" to indicate "non-studied." The instructor then asked the students what they thought the hypothesis for the study was and whether they thought it was supported by the results. The instructor performed the data analysis after class and discussed it with the class during the next class period. The overall data pattern supported the hypothesis: Memory was best for items previously judged in terms of their relevance to the self, followed by items judged in terms of their relevance to a loved one, followed by items judged in terms of their relevance to the CSU track coach. Thus, the pattern of the means was in the predicted direction. However, the effects did not reach significance: the comparison between self-reference and loved-one decisions was marginally significant ($p = .07$) but would likely have become significant with an increase in power (i.e., a larger number of student participants). It is unclear whether the other pairwise comparisons would have reached significance with greater power. While the comparison between coach and self-reference decisions may have ($p = .09$), the comparison between coach and loved-one may not have ($p = .63$), although a linear contrast analysis suggested that a linear trend (from coach to loved-one to self-reference decisions) may have emerged with more participants ($p = .09$). Though power may have been an issue in this particular example (where only 24 students participated), power would be less of an issue in large lecture-style classes, where 100 or more students may be present for any given clicker activity.

Novel Hypothesis Testing in a Laboratory-Style Class

In the second author's Research Methods in Psychology class, students worked in groups throughout the semester to complete a novel study. Many students relied on the CRS as a tool for carrying out their own experiments using the other class members as their research participants. Examples of activities carried out by students for their group projects are described below.

In one group project, students used the CRS to examine the hypothesis that color would help memory for location information. Participants viewed a 4×5 grid on the projector screen. A different picture appeared in each cell of the grid, and the pictures were revealed one column at a time for several seconds each. In one condition, each column in the grid appeared in a different color. Each black-and-white line drawing appeared in the center of a colored cell within the grid. In the other conditions, the students presented the columns in white. Students read a passage as a distractor task following the encoding phase. Then, students received a test of memory for picture location. To test memory for picture location, on each test trial, students saw a picture and indicated by using their clickers which column the picture had appeared in (a = 1, b = 2, c = 3, d = 4). After everyone had responded to this question, a second question appeared asking students to indicate in which row the picture had appeared (a = 1, b = 2, c = 3, d = 4, e = 5). In support of the group's hypothesis, student participants performed significantly better at the location memory task when different colors were used for each column.

Other examples of ways in which the students used the CRS to carry out their group projects include the following. A couple of student groups studied eyewitness memory. Students in the class first viewed a video, then received either misinformation or an accurate control set of information. Finally, using clickers, they completed a test on memory for the actual event. Another group conducted a study of the effects of attractiveness on recognition memory for faces. Participants used clickers to rate the attractiveness of the faces during the study phase and then received a clicker-administered recognition memory test. Yet another group examined whether the perceived disability of a perpetrator of a crime would affect the harshness of the punishment recommended for that crime. The students indicated their recommended punishment for a crime through survey questions answered using the clickers.

Student Assessment of Clicker Efficacy

Results from a survey conducted in the first author's Principles of Psychology course in spring 2008 following the descriptive statistics and fundamental attribution error clicker demonstrations (above) showed that 100% of 80 student respondents (23 males and 57 females from a class of 100) agreed with the statement "When we used clickers to demonstrate a topic, they increased my interest in the topic." Further, 97.5% of students agreed that "When we used clickers to demonstrate a concept, I found them beneficial to my learning." As one student commented with respect to the descriptive statistics demonstration, "It reinforces the connection between people and numbers. I can understand the concepts better when I can see where they come from." Finally, 100% of students agreed with the statement "I liked using clickers in this class." Similar survey reports on clicker use in replications of experiments are described by Cleary (2008). Furthermore, a survey conducted in the second author's Cognitive Psychology class indicated that 20 of 21 respondents found clicker use in novel hypothesis testing to be a worthwhile activity. Student comments included, "I think it was a good activity because it gave us a chance to participate in a memory experiment like the ones we talk about in class," "It's interesting to see the results of the experiment and it's also interesting to see what kind of experiment a peer came up with," "I liked the way the experiment was done with the clickers. It shows immediate results. Also, I like doing experiments thought up by students that are new," and, "I think this was a worthwhile activity. It allowed us to see how a true experiment is carried out. It was also interesting because the results came back the opposite of what I had predicted." Although these data are subject to the limitations associated with self-report, they indicate that students see positive value in using clickers in the classroom.

Our assessment of the effects of clickers in our classes has been limited to student self-report data. Although these results show strongly and consistently positive responses from students, the challenge ahead (and our future goal) is to obtain performance measures on the impact of clickers on learning. In their review, Fies and Marshall (2006) identified as missing from the clicker literature "tightly controlled comparisons in which the only difference is the use, or lack of use, of [clickers]" (p. 106). Although such studies are now beginning to be conducted (e.g., Crossgrove & Curran, 2008; Freeman et al., 2007; Morling et al., 2008; Stowell & Nelson, 2007), major methodological challenges remain, such as the use of appropriate control groups to attribute any differences observed to the use of clickers. It is also important to note, however, that the most important benefits associated with the use of clickers may not be using the clickers themselves, but rather with changes in the instructor's classroom pedagogy that accompany their use (Burke da Silva, Wood, & Menz, 2007).

Conclusions

Clicker technology provides an opportunity for students in the classroom to be active participants in demonstrations, replications of previous findings, and novel hypothesis testing in ways that increase engagement and provide the potential to enhance learning. In addition, clickers can be employed creatively across a wide range of subjects and disciplines. As one student surveyed about the effectiveness of the interactive clicker-based demonstrations said, "It is much easier to recall a concept or theory if there is an activity or demonstration linked to it." Clickers offer an excellent opportunity to connect students to content and increase their engagement in learning.

References

Beatty, I. (2004). Transforming student learning with classroom communication systems. *Educause Research Research Bulletin,* 2004, 1–13. http://www.educause.edu/ir/library/pdf/ERB0403.pdf

Bruff, D. (2009). *Teaching with classroom response systems: Creating active learning environments.* San Francisco: Jossey Bass.

Burke da Silva, K., Wood, D., & Menz, R. I. (2007). Are the benefits of clickers due to the enforcement of good pedagogy? In: *Enhancing Higher Education, Theory and Scholarship, Proceedings of the 30th HERDSA Annual Conference [CD-ROM],* Adelaide, 8–11 July.

Caldwell, J. E. (2007). Clickers in the large classroom: Current research and best-practice tips. *Life Sciences Education, 6,* 9–20.

Cheung, S. L. (2008). Using mobile phone messaging as a response medium in classroom experiments. *Journal of Economic Education, 39*(1), 51–67.

Cleary, A. M. (2008). Using wireless response systems to replicate behavioral research findings in the classroom. *Teaching of Psychology, 35,* 42–44.

Craik, F. I. M., & Tulving, E. (1975). Depth of processing and the retention of words in episodic memory. *Journal of Experimental Psychology: General, 104,* 268–294.

Cross, P. (1977). Not can but will college teachers be improved? *New Directions for Higher Education, 17,* 1–15.

Crossgrove, K., & Curran, K. L. (2008). Using clickers in nonmajors- and majors-level biology bourses: Student opinion, learning, and long-term retention of course material. *CBE—Life Sciences Education, 7,* 146–154.

Draper, S. W., Cargill, J., & Cutts, Q. (2002). Electronically enhanced classroom interaction. *Australasian Journal of Educational Technology,* 18(1), 13–23.

Fies, C., & Marshall, J. (2006). Classroom response systems: A review of the literature. *Journal of Science Education and Technology, 15,* 101–109.

Freeman, S., O'Connor, E., Parks, J. W., Cunningham, M., Hurley, D., Haak, D., Dirks, C., & Wenderoth, M. P. (2007). *Prescribed active learning increases performance in introductory biology. CBE-Life Sciences Education, 6,* 132–139. http://www.lifescied.org/cgi/reprint/6/2/132

Furlong, K. (2007, April 30). With classroom response systems, new wave of learning is only a "click" away. *Vanderbilt Register.*

Heider, F. (1958). *The psychology of interpersonal relations.* New York: Wiley.

Hinde, K., & Hunt, A. (2006). Using the personal response system to enhance student learning: Some evidence from teaching economics. In: Banks, D. A. (ed.), *Audience response systems in higher education: applications and cases*. Hershey, PA: Information Science Publishing.

Langley, M. M., Cleary, A.M., & Kostic, B. (2007). On the use of wireless response systems in experimental psychology: Implications for the behavioral researcher. *Behavior Research Methods, 39*, 816–823.

MacArthur, J. R., & Jones, L. L. (2008). A review of literature reports of clickers applicable to college chemistry classrooms. *Chemistry Education Research and Practice, 9*, 187–195.

McKeachie, W. J. (1999). *Teaching tips*. Boston: Houghton Mifflin.

Mezulis, A., Abramson, L., Hyde, J. S., & Hankin, B. L. (2004). Is there a universal positivity bias in attributions? A meta-analytic review of individual, developmental, and cultural differences in the self-serving attributional bias. *Psychological Bulletin, 130*, 711–746.

Morling, B., McAuliffe, M., Cohen, L., & DiLorenzo, T. M. (2008). Efficacy of personal response systems ("clickers") in large, introductory psychology classes. *Teaching of Psychology, 35*(1), 45–50.

Murdock, B. B., Jr. (1962). The serial position effect of free recall. *Journal of Experimental Psychology, 64*, 482–488.

Nairne, J. S., Thompson, S. R., & Pandeirada, J. N. S. (2007). Adaptive memory: Survival processing enhances retention. *Journal of Experimental Psychology: Learning, Memory, and Cognition, 33*, 263–273.

Roediger, H. L. III., & McDermott, K. B. (1995). Creating false memories: Remembering words not presented in lists. *Journal of Experimental Psychology: Learning, Memory, and Cognition, 21*, 803–814.

Ross, L. (1977). The intuitive psychologist and his shortcomings: Distortions in the attribution process. In: L. Berkowitz (ed.), *Advances in experimental social psychology* (vol. 10, pp. 173–220). New York: Academic Press.

Ross, L. D., Amabile, T. M., & Steinmetz, J. L. (1977). Social roles, social control, and biases in social-perception processes. *Journal of Personality and Social Psychology, 35*, 485–494.

Stowell, J. R., & Nelson, J. M. (2007). Benefits of electronic audience response systems on student participation, learning and emotion. *Teaching of Psychology, 34*(4), 253–258.

Stroop, J. R. (1935). Studies of interference in serial verbal reactions. *Journal of Experimental Psychology, 18*, 643–662.

Tversky, A., & Kahneman, D. (1974). Judgments under uncertainty: Heuristics and biases. *Science, 185*, 1124–1131.

Zhu, E. (2007). Teaching with clickers. *University of Michigan Center for Research on Learning and Teaching Occasional Papers*, 22.

10 The *What? How?* and *Which?* of Course-Management Systems

Michelle A. Drouin

"I was absent last week, did I miss anything?" asks Jason, a student in my face-to-face class.

"Hmm..." I say and then pause. I understand that Jason really wants to know what he missed and how he can gain access to what he missed, but the question always vexes me. Does Jason think I canceled class because of his absence? Of course he missed something!

"Well Jason, you missed three lectures," I say. "The lecture outlines are in Blackboard, but you should try to get the lecture notes from another student."

"Alrighty," Jason mutters and goes back to his seat.

Neither of us is happy with this exchange. Jason probably wants me to recount the three lectures for him (preferably in written, outline form), and I want to be able to give Jason a better alternative than "make a friend and ask for notes," especially if he has a legitimate reason for his absence.

Unfortunately, the frustrating "Did I miss anything?" question and interchanges that follow are common in my face-to-face classes, occur sometimes in my hybrid classes, but never surface in my classes that are delivered online through a course-management system (CMS). This is just one of the many reasons I cherish my CMS and why you should learn more about yours.

What is a CMS?

Course-management systems (CMSs) are packaged software systems (e.g., Blackboard) that allow the creation of online learning environments. Many instructors, especially new technologically savvy instructors, use one or more CMSs with relative ease (e.g., Beatty & Ulasewicz, 2006; Papastergiou, 2007), but some instructors hesitate to use CMS for a number of reasons, including discomfort with technology and desire to protect intellectual property (Chisholm, 2006). With online course offerings becoming more prevalent in academic institutions (Allen & Seaman, 2007), even instructors hesitant to use CMS are sometimes forced to reevaluate their attitudes and beliefs toward instruction to accommodate today's learners. Moreover, once involved in creating courses delivered through CMS, instructors must learn new pedagogical approaches, as creating an engaging learning experience poses different types of challenges when students are not physically present (Angeli, Valanides, & Bonk, 2003). In this chapter, I will provide an overview of CMS, discuss some of the instructional approaches relevant to CMS, and introduce the tools that I consider indispensable in supporting instruction in face-to-face (FTF) and online courses.

Which CMS?

There are many CMSs available. Some, such as Angel, Blackboard, and Desire2Learn, require commercial licenses and are typically purchased by institutions; others, such as CourseWorks, Moodle, and Sakai, are open-source (i.e., systems that have no license fees) and can be used by individuals or institutions (EduTools, 2009). Two of the more popular CMSs in North America and Europe are Blackboard, the leading commercial CMS, and Moodle, the leading open-source software package (The Campus Computing Project, 2008; Trotter, 2008). Blackboard dominates the higher education market in the United States: more than 50% of the institutions surveyed in 2008 indicated that it was the sole CMS used on their campus (The Campus Computing Project, 2008). However, the survey also showed that many institutions have shifted from commercial CMS to open-source CMS, and about a fourth of those surveyed intend to do so within the next 5 years. This shift is likely due to cost, quality, and ease of use issues. Although there are no site-license fees, open-source CMSs are not free because information technology

(IT) service teams are still needed to administer, maintain, and troubleshoot the systems. However, as more universities adopt open-source CMS, operating issues can be communicated across campuses, which may cut down on costs, and the programs can be refined for ease of use. Thus, in the next 5 years, there might be a change in the landscape of higher education away from commercial CMS toward open-source CMS.

All CMSs provide course developers with a variety of tools, such as e-mail, grade books, chat rooms, content areas, and assessment functions (EduTools, 2009; Hayes, 2000), that require no programming skill on the part of the developer. However, not all CMSs offer the same tools, and some have better features than others. For example, not all CMSs have a whiteboard application (i.e., an online chalkboard that has both typing and drawing features) and although most CMSs have an e-mail tool, not all have a searchable address book within that tool. For a side-by-side comparison of the tools and features of the popular CMSs, visit the EduTools Web site at: http://www.edutools.info/item_list.jsp?pj=4. I could use pages of text to describe the pros and cons of the various CMSs, but most instructors use the CMS that is either purchased for or managed by their campus. Thus, I will shift my discussion to the aspects of CMS that instructors are able to control: CMS tools and instructional strategies.

How Do Teachers Choose the "Right" CMS Tools and Instructional Strategies?

Choosing the "right" tools to use in a CMS environment depends largely on one's instructional strategies. So before we discuss tools, let's first turn our attention to instructional strategies.

Choice of CMS Instructional Strategies

When building their online courses, many instructors use the same instructional strategies as they use in their FTF courses. For example, instructors building a CMS-delivered course might use their existing FTF course materials (e.g., PowerPoint slides, exams, and assignments) and might try to implement the same types of activities (e.g., lectures and within-class discussions). When instructors take this approach to building their CMS-delivered course, there is likely to be continuity between online and FTF sections in terms of course content, which seems like a desirable outcome for those wishing to provide an equivalent experience to their online and FTF learners. However, this begs the question: Are the online and FTF environments equivalent? And, for that matter, should similar instructional strategies be employed in both settings?

The question of whether the FTF environments are "equivalent" is one that is debated and will not be resolved here. However, there are many similarities between the two environments. For example, there are learning objectives, learning activities, and means of assessing student performance in both FTF and CMS-delivered courses. That said, there are also some notable differences. The most obvious difference is that the instructors and students are physically present in the FTF classroom, but they are not physically present in the online classroom. Not surprisingly, these "classroom" differences create different challenges for instructors (Angeli et al., 2003). For example, as illustrated in the vignette at the beginning of this chapter, instructors may not have as many online resources for their FTF students as they do for their online students when students have "missed class," which challenges instructors to find alternate ways to help FTF students access the material they have missed. On the other hand, some activities might be more challenging for instructors to implement in their online classrooms than in their FTF classrooms. For example, it may be difficult for instructors to organize interactive learning activities for students in the online classroom, whereas this type of group work is relatively easy to organize in a FTF classroom. Therefore, before applying a FTF instructional strategy to the online classroom, one must consider how differences in an online classroom might affect the implementation of a FTF instructional strategy.

Let's consider this question in terms of a specific instructional strategy. One frequently cited instructional model is based on *social constructivism*, or the idea that students learn best through active participation and the exchange of information with others (Vygotsky, 1978). According to Vygotsky, knowledge is constructed within social contexts; learning cannot be separated from the environment within which it occurs; and collaboration within social environments is essential to learning. Social learning instruction methods are considered part of "good practice" in undergraduate education (e.g., Chickering & Gamson, 1987), but will these same social learning methods work in a CMS-delivered course?

Many researchers say "yes," and there is empirical research that emphasizes the importance of social interaction in online learning environments to promote learning (e.g., Garrison, Anderson, & Archer, 2001; Hull &

Saxon, 2009). In fact, there are even social interaction models that have been applied specifically to computer-mediated communication (CMC) environments. For example, Moore (1989) subdivided the interactions that take place in an active learning environment into *learner–content*, *learner–instructor*, and *learner–learner* interactions. Within this model, effective interactions between these three entities are essential to the construction of knowledge. Presumably, these effective interactions could take place in any learning environment (FTF or online) and would promote student learning. However, as some studies have shown (e.g., Papastergiou, 2007), social learning strategies are not always easy to implement in online environments.

Papastergiou (2007), an instructor teaching computer science education, was accustomed to using social constructivist learning strategies in her FTF classroom and tried to implement these same strategies in a hybrid class on the same topic. However, she found that the CMS lacked features that she needed to support her instructional goals (e.g., notification system that would alert her of students' latest updates to the assignments, discussion, and workgroup sections). She also noted that attempting to implement a social constructivist approach online required significantly more of her time and effort than when she used the approach in her FTF courses. Consequently, Papastergiou asserted that the social learning method was difficult to employ via CMS.

Considered together, these studies (e.g., Garrison, Anderson, & Archer, 2001; Hull & Saxon, 2009; Papastergiou, 2007) give a mixed review of the social learning strategy for online learners, suggesting that it is effective, but it may be more difficult to implement online than FTF. More generally, these studies emphasize how important it is for online instructors to be thoughtful about their choice of instructional strategies and to assess the effectiveness of those strategies. Also, the studies highlight an important point: the FTF and online classrooms are different venues, specifically with regard to social interaction.

Although many online learners believe that social interaction is important (e.g., Drouin, 2008; Ouzts, 2006), they usually do not engage in the same types of social learning activities as FTF learners (Kearnsley, 2000; Reeves, Herrington, & Oliver, 2004), and they may not need or want the same types of interactions that are present in the FTF classroom (Drouin, 2008). Instructors who try to engage online students in social learning activities may become disheartened when they find that their online students prefer to work independently, log on asynchronously, and communicate with fellow classmates via threaded discussions rather than synchronous chats (Butler & Pinto-Zipp, 2006). However, rather than becoming disheartened, instructors must recognize that the main reasons students enroll in online courses are because they have time restrictions and online courses are "convenient" (Butler & Pinto-Zipp, 2006). Thus, instructors may have to adjust their instructional methods accordingly.

Unfortunately, there is no one-size-fits-all instructional strategy for CMS environments. My recommendation to novice online instructors is to try out the instructional strategy that you currently use in your FTF classroom. If you find that strategy ineffective or too labor-intensive, make adjustments. My only cautionary advice concerns social interaction: be mindful of the types of social learning activities you employ in the CMS classroom, as it seems especially important to create an online learning environment where there is enough interaction for some and not too much for others.

Choice of CMS Tools

Just as choosing the appropriate instructional strategy is important to the delivery of a course, so too is selecting the appropriate tools for that course. This is true in both FTF and CMS settings. However, some first-time CMS users are overwhelmed by the sheer number of tools available in their CMS courses, and others are unsure of how to align the tools to their instructional goals. If we return to Moore's subdivision of the types of interactions that occur in active learning environments and map specific tools to those interactions (see Table 10.1 for interactions, tools, and my frequency of use of these tools in FTF and online courses), we can see that this could be quite confusing.

First, it's evident that more than one CMS tool can be used to support each mode of interaction (e.g., e-mail and discussion boards both facilitate *student–student* interaction), and many tools serve multiple functions (e.g., discussion boards facilitate *student–student, student–instructor*, and *student–content* interactions). Second, researchers have suggested that instructors align the tools they use with their instructional goals (Dick & Carey, 1996) but that they should avoid using too many CMS tools, because too many tools might interfere with, rather than promote, learning (Koszalka & Ganesan, 2004). Thus, it's no surprise that novice CMS instructors may feel anxious when setting up their courses for the first time.

Unfortunately, this anxiety may actually paralyze some instructors into stagnation—maintaining instructional methods or tools that are outdated or

Table 10.1

MS Tools and Frequency of My (or My Students') Tool Usage Categorized by Interaction Types

		Frequency of Tool Usage	
Type of Interaction	Compatible Tools	FTF	Online
Student–Student			
Bidirectional interaction	E-mail	Rarely	Rarely
between students	Discussion board	Rarely	Always
	Chat	Rarely	Sometimes
	Assignments	Never	Never
Student–Instructor			
Interaction between	E-mail[a]	Sometimes	Sometimes
student and instructor;	Syllabus[b]	Always	Always
may go between student	Chat[a]	Rarely	Rarely
and instructor inter-	Announcements[b]	Always	Always
changeably[a] or from	Assessments[b]	Never	Never
instructor only[b]	Discussion board[a]	Rarely	Always
	Assignments[a]	Never	Rarely
	Calendar[b]	Never	Never
Student–Content			
Interaction between	Content pages	Sometimes	Always
student and course	Assessments	Always	Always
content; student must	Media library	Never	Always
initiate interaction	URL links	Sometimes	Always
	Discussion board	Rarely	Always
	Assignments	Never	Rarely

[a]Interactions may originate from student or instructor.
[b]Interactions may originate from instructor only.

ineffective while avoiding new technologies that may improve their teaching effectiveness. Instructors hoping to move beyond this stagnation often turn to instructional designers, seasoned online instructors, and the online pedagogical literature to take the tentative first steps in course building. By using these resources, instructors can be strategic in selecting their CMS tools so that their instructional goals are supported and the environment facilitates learning for the population of learners engaged in the course.

So, *Which* CMS Tools Are Best?

Let me give a disclaimer: There is no exact recipe for creating the perfect CMS-delivered course! Instructors need to use the tools that they feel are most appropriate for their content, teaching style, and students. That said, as a seasoned online instructor, I have a lot of experience using CMS (WebCT initially and now Blackboard Vista) to manage and deliver course content to my FTF and online learners. Through trial and error, I've found some tools are more important and helpful to my teaching than others, and I will detail those here. However, keep in mind that my instructional approach is based on a social learning model (which works for me, but I'm not suggesting you adopt it), and I've needed to revise this approach slightly for my classes delivered entirely through CMS.

In the next few sections, I will give some specific CMS tool recommendations (see also Table 10.1). First, I will present my bare-bones approach (i.e., the skeletal CMS features that can be employed in almost any course), and then I will present a more detailed approach, targeted specifically to instructors delivering classes wholly within the CMS.

The Bare-bones Approach

Instructors wishing to familiarize themselves with a CMS may choose to implement just some "bare-bones" tools to supplement their FTF courses as a precursor to developing a wholly online course. I believe a core group of features would likely be useful for all courses, whether they are wholly online or FTF with a supplemental CMS component.

Nearly every course would be complemented by the use of a CMS *grade book*. Within CMS systems, instructors can post grades for exams and assignments and students can log in with their usernames and passwords to access these grades (listed in the order they appear in the grade book). This instructional feature is incredibly easy to implement when the university system uploads the class roster automatically, and although slightly less convenient when instructors must upload the rosters manually, it is still a relatively straightforward, password-protected way to administer grades.

Another useful CMS tool is the *announcements* feature. Instructors can post announcements for the whole class and can even elect that these announcements "pop up" when students log in to the CMS. This feature helps instructors keep in touch with students and maintain a social presence in the course. It can also be useful for the organized or forgetful instructor, as within Blackboard (and many other CMSs) instructors can choose to release an announcement at a specific time and date, and announcements can be created and timed for release even before the semester begins.

Similar to e-mail outside of CMS, *e-mail within CMS* provides a medium for student–student and student–instructor exchanges. The attractive feature of e-mail within the CMS (over e-mail outside of the CMS) is that it provides a simple course-specific communication medium. Also, with a searchable address book, which is a feature of some CMSs, students can easily find the e-mail address of other students in the course, the TA, or the instructor.

The *syllabus* tool is often little more than a content page with the title "syllabus." But as it has its own designated icon within CMS, the syllabus tool is one that is easy to implement and useful for students. Also, posting the syllabus within the CMS makes it possible for students to access it at any time, but the information is restricted to course members, thereby protecting intellectual property.

The More Detailed Approach

In addition to the "bare-bones" tools I employ to support FTF courses, I consider a number of CMS tools integral to my delivery of online courses. These tools are all Blackboard tools, as this is the CMS that my university uses; however, similar tools exist in other CMSs. Please refer back to Table 10.1 to see a list of the tools that I use often in my online courses. As shown, there are many tools that I use either "very often" or "always" in my online courses, and these tools are not always the same tools that I use in my FTF courses.

Although I rarely use the *discussion board* in my FTF classes, I always use it in my online courses as a way for students to interact with each other and the course content. I post questions for every chapter, and these questions are designed to elicit both task-oriented and social-emotion-oriented replies (as per Gorsky & Capsi, 2005 and Liu & Ginther, 1999). Also, the questions are designed to be thought-provoking and sometimes controversial (Blignaut & Trollip, 2003). I assign students course credit (totaling 5% of the students' grades) for participating in these discussions, and I require them to post a "meaningful and relevant" response to six topics throughout the semester. I give only these general guidelines and no specific grading rubric.

Generally, this approach works quite well with most of my psychology students. Although they are required to post only 6 responses per semester, about one third of the students in my online courses post more than 12 responses (as shown by Blackboard logs), which is substantially greater than the minimum requirements. These results are especially encouraging when one considers that previous researchers (e.g., Bullen, 1998; Hara, Bonk, & Angeli, 2000) have found that students tend to contribute only until they have satisfied minimum requirements. Nevertheless, other online instructors have employed different discussion board techniques (e.g., using more concrete rubrics to "grade" discussion posts, or requiring participation as a greater percentage of course grades) with success as well. So, there are many approaches to discussion boards that may work well in a given CMS course.

Content pages can hold many different types of information (e.g., text, audio, or video files); *media libraries* hold only media (e.g., audio and video files); and *URL links* lead students to external Web pages (e.g., a publisher's Web site, which may contain interactive activities, such as quizzes and flash-cards, designed to support learning). I have grouped several course tools together because these tools are all used to deliver course content, and also because these features could, in some cases, be used interchangeably to deliver the same content. For example, in my online courses, I use a variety of media (e.g., audio files, video files, screen captures) to deliver my course content. These media files can be embedded in a content page, downloaded from a media library folder, or accessed through a URL link. In each case, my students are able to access the same material, but they are just accessing the material from different locations. My choice of where to upload my file is based on two criteria: how easy it will be to find and how easy it will be to access. In most cases, I embed files within Blackboard (rather than on an external Web link) so that students do not have to click back and forth. I also make herculean efforts to be sure that the files can be opened by all students (e.g., those with different computer operating systems and software packages, pop-up blockers, slow Internet connections) by including alternate file types (e.g., both Microsoft Word and Adobe documents) and trying the links on several different computers while I am building my course.

With regard to specific media, I advise instructors to deliver their course content in any way they think is appropriate. Content delivery methods range from the basic (e.g., static content pages containing reading material) to the embellished (e.g., streaming video lectures and interactive online activities).

There is some evidence that suggests that media-rich content (including animations, simulations, and audio files) is well received by students and helps to promote learning (Lam & McNaught, 2006). However, the quality of the media appears to be an important factor in influencing student learning outcomes (Lam & McNaught, 2006). In my media-rich online courses, students have expressed satisfaction with particular media features, such as:

- *Video lectures.* I use streaming videos (videos that do not download, but rather stream continuously and play as they arrive at the student's computer) to deliver my online course lectures. By using a program called Mediasite, students are not only able to see my PowerPoint slides (as they could with Adobe Presenter or Impatica), but they are also able to see video of me delivering the lectures. Adobe Presenter and Impatica are also great tools for content delivery, but with these programs, students are able to see only the PowerPoint slides with accompanying audio. Mediasite also has a synchronous feature (that I don't use) so that students could log in and view the lecture when the instructor is delivering it live. These lectures are stored on a university server and cannot be downloaded or saved by the individual students, which protects intellectual property. Moreover, even students with very slow Internet connections can access the streaming videos without encountering complications related to bandwidth (i.e., the rate at which data is transferred).
- *Supplementary videos.* To elaborate on course concepts, I often post supplementary video clips. These clips can be from external URL links, such as YouTube, Discovering Psychology online series, or Nova, or can be from digital files uploaded into the CMS. *Note*: Before uploading video files into the CMS, see an instructional designer about copyright laws and the "fair use" act.
- *Interactive exercises.* Interactive exercises (such as quizzes, crossword puzzles, and flashcards) can be great interactive tools for students. As most publishers offer interactive exercises on their Web sites as complements to their textbooks, instructors can easily embed the URL links into their content pages.

There are some instructor-only tools that are not included in Table 10.1 that I consider integral to my online course delivery. The first is *student tracking*. In the FTF environment, an instructor might notice when a student has been absent for a few weeks, but a CMS environment provides no automatic cues to the instructor that a student has been missing. However, within the CMS, instructors can get valuable information about their students' attendance and participation. For example, an instructor can see when the student logged in for the first time and logged in for the last time, and how much time he or she has spent in that course during a particular window of time. The tracking feature can also provide individual tool usage information, such as how many URL links and content pages the student accessed, how many discussion board posts the student submitted and accessed, and how many e-mails the student read and sent. Thus, by using this tracking tool, instructors can see whether students are participating "actively" in the course or not.

Some instructors choose to access the tracking data only at the end of the course to see, for example, how many discussion board posts the students submitted throughout the semester. However, other instructors monitor student participation regularly and send e-mails to students who are not participating at an appropriate level. Whether this prompting leads to greater retention in these courses is an empirical question that needs exploration.

The other instructor-only tool that I find indispensable in my online CMS courses is *selective release*. The selective release tool is used primarily by instructors who are running an instructor-paced course (i.e., the instructor releases the course information, assignments, and exams at a particular time) rather than a self-paced course (i.e., the student accesses the course materials at any time). Some instructors use the self-paced format and believe that it's in the best interest of the students if they can set their own pace for learning, based on their own time commitments and personal obligations. However, others believe that allowing students to self-pace increases the opportunity for procrastination (Glick & Semb, 1978), and if the instructor does not help pace the students, fewer will succeed in the course. I subscribe to the latter belief and therefore find selective release to be an invaluable tool. Through selective release, I am able to coordinate the release of my materials so that they emerge in a systematic, precise, and organized manner. Moreover, I can plan this release of materials before the class has even started; as such, it is a tool that is appreciated by both the extremely well organized and the extremely forgetful.

Let me give an example of a situation for which I find selective release useful: online assessments. When I am preparing the course in the CMS prior to the start of the semester, I coordinate the assessments so that they are released (i.e., they "pop up" on the home page) according to the dates signified on the syllabus. Then, I coordinate the learning content modules so that Unit 1 is displayed on the home page, but subsequent units are released at the same time as the assessment for the preceding unit. Finally, I write two announcements, one sent the week before the exam stating that the exam is the next week, and one sent after the exam is released to remind students of the exam deadline. By coordinating the release of material in this manner, students are able to view only the information that I think is relevant, and changes to the home page are obvious cues to new content, activities, or assessments. Moreover, the course is dynamic, and I impress upon the students that I am present and available. Also, by organizing these release dates before the semester has begun, I never forget to release an exam!

Ok, So What Next?

As I've shown, there are some CMS tools that both FTF and online instructors could use with relative ease to enhance their teaching and course administration, such as e-mail, announcements, and the grade book. Others, like content delivery tools, selective release, and student tracking, are much more likely to be used in online courses than in FTF courses. Meanwhile others, like the discussion board, can serve to enhance instruction in both FTF and online courses. The most appropriate tools to use in any given course depend upon the course content and the instructor's pedagogical approach.

Once instructors have decided which tools seem to be most appropriate for their CMS courses, their next step should be to implement those tools and measure their effectiveness. Some of the recent online pedagogical literature examines the effectiveness of CMS instructional methods and tools. There are also online resources, such as Quality Matters (www.qmprogram.org), that offer information (in the form of training and a rubric) to instructors hoping to design quality online courses. These literature and Web resources can be helpful in a general sense, but specific information about the effectiveness of any CMS tool or pedagogy can be obtained only when instructors evaluate their own courses in a systematic manner.

Instructors must assess their courses and instructional strategies for several reasons. First, just as PowerPoint might be an extremely effective method of FTF content delivery for one instructor and an extremely poor method of delivery for another, individual instructor variability may increase or decrease a tool's effectiveness in any CMS-delivered course. Second, course content is likely to vary at least minimally, and often significantly, from course to course. Even two instructors teaching the same course—child development, for example—might employ two completely different instructional methods. Whereas one instructor might have students rear a virtual child and complete various assignments related to this experience, another might have students debate theoretical perspectives on development through a series of discussion board posts. These activities are likely to correspond to the instructional approaches of the different instructors, and particular CMS tools might support one approach better than the other (see Hardin, 2007).

Moreover, in light of the emphasis on formative feedback to increase instructor effectiveness (see, for example, Wininger & Norman, 2005), every instructor should be engaging in systematic assessment of his or her class-room practices, whether that classroom exists in the FTF or CMS environment. For example, instructors could measure achievement outcomes in different versions of the same course that utilize different CMS tools. They could also administer surveys to gauge students' satisfaction, sense of community, and perceptions of learning. Or, they could have their course reviewed by a peer as part of a formative assessment process. Regardless of the method of assessment, instructors should be mindful that are many ways to gain feedback on the quality of a course and that measures of student learning and achievement are integral to formative assessment.

In sum, when one considers the differences between FTF and online classes, and the different ways in which CMS can be used to support FTF and online instruction methods, it is likely that there is no single approach that will work best in all environments. However, by starting with my "bare-bones" approach, progressing to include more tools and strategies, and continually assessing the effectiveness of those tools and strategies, instructors can learn *what* CMS tools are available and useful to them, *how* to best address the learning needs of their students, and *which* tools and approaches work best in their own CMS-delivered courses.

References

Allen, I. E., & Seaman, J. (2007, October). Online nation: Five years of growth in online learning. Needham, MA: Sloan-C. Retrieved June 10, 2009, from http://www.sloanconsortium.org/publications/survey/pdf/online_nation.pdf

Angeli, C., Valanides, N., & Bonk, C. (2003). Communication in a web-based conferencing system: The quality of computer-mediated interactions. *British Journal of Educational Technology, 34*, 31–43.

Beatty, B., & Ulasewicz, C. (2006). Online teaching and learning in transition: Faculty perspectives on moving from Blackboard to the Moodle learning management system. *TechTrends, 50*, 36–45.

Blignaut, S., & Trollip, S. R. (2003). Developing a taxonomy of faculty participation in asynchronous learning environments—an exploratory investigation. *Computers and Education, 41*, 149–171.

Bullen, M. (1998). Participation and critical thinking in online university distance education. *Journal of Distance Education, 13*, 1–32.

Butler, T. J., & Pinto-Zipp, G. (2006). Students' learning styles and their preferences for online instructional methods. *Journal of Educational Technology Systems, 34*, 199–221.

Chickering, A. W., & Gamson, Z. F. (1987). Seven principles for good practice in undergraduate education. *American Association of Higher Education Bulletin, 39*, 3–7.

Chisholm, J. K. (2006). Pleasure and danger in online teaching and learning. *Academe, 92*, 6. Retrieved March 19, 2009, from http://www.aaup.org/AAUP/pubsres/academe/2006/ND/Feat/chis.htm

Dick, W., & Carey, L. (1996). *The systematic design of instruction* (4th ed.). New York: Addison Wesley Longman.

Drouin, M. A. (2008). Do students need sense of community in online learning environments? Sense of community and student satisfaction, achievement, and retention in an online course. *Quarterly Review of Distance Education, 9*, 267–284.

EduTools. (2009). *CMS: Product List*. Retrieved April 24, 2009, from http://www.edutools.info/item_list.jsp?pj=4

Garrison, D. R., Anderson, T., & Archer, W. (2001). Critical thinking, cognitive presence, and computer conferencing in distance education. *American Journal of Distance Education, 15*, 7–23.

Glick, M., & Semb, G. (1978). Effects of pacing contingencies in personalized instruction: A review of the evidence. *Journal of Personalized Instruction, 3*, 36–42.

Gorsky, P., & Caspi, A. (2005). Dialogue: A theoretical framework for distance education instructional systems. *British Journal of Educational Technology, 36*, 137–144.

Hara, N., Bonk, C. J., & Angeli, C. (2000). Content analysis of online discussion in an applied educational psychology course. *Instructional Science, 28*, 115–152.

Hardin, E. E. (2007). Presentation software in the college classroom—don't forget the instructor. *Teaching of Psychology, 34*, 53–57.

Hayes, R. (2000). Exploring discount usability methods to assess the suitability of online course delivery products. *The Internet and Higher Education, 2*, 119–134.

Hull, D. M., & Saxon, T. F. (2009). Negotiation of meaning and co-construction of knowledge: An experimental analysis of asynchronous online instruction. *Computers and Education, 52,* 624–639.

Kearnsley, G. (2000). *Online education: Learning and teaching in cyberspace.* Belmont, CA: Wadsworth.

Koszalka, T. A., & Ganesan, R. (2004). Designing online courses: A taxonomy to guide strategic use of features available in course management systems (CMS) in distance education. *Distance Education, 25*, 243–256.

Lam, P., & McNaught, C. (2006). Design and evaluation of online courses containing media-enhanced learning materials. *Educational Media International, 43,* 199–218.

Liu, T., & Ginther, D. (1999). *A comparison of the task-oriented model and the social-emotion-oriented model in computer-mediated communication.* Paper presented at the Southwestern Psychological Association Conference, Albuquerque, NM.

Moore, M. G. (1989). Three types of interaction. *The American Journal of Distance Education, 3*, 1–6.

Ouzts, K. (2006). Sense of community in online courses. *The Quarterly Review of Distance Education, 7*, 285–296.

Papastergiou, M. (2007). Use of a course management system based on Claroline to support a social constructivist inspired course: A Greek case study. *Educational Media International, 44,* 43–59.

Reeves, T., Herrington, J., & Oliver, R. (2004). A development research agenda for online collaborative learning. *Educational Technology Research and Development, 52,* 53–65.

The Campus Computing Project. (2008, October). *The 2008 national survey of information technology in U.S. higher education.* Retrieved June 10, 2009, from http://www.campuscomputing.net/sites/www.campuscomputing.net/files/2007-CCP_0.pdf

Trotter, A. (2008). Blackboard vs. Moodle: Competition in course-management market grows. *Education Week, 2,* 21. Retrieved March 19, 2009, from http://www.edweek.org/dd/articles/2008/06/09/01moodle.h02.html

Vygotsky, L. S. (1978). *Mind in society.* Cambridge, MA: MIT Press.

Wininger, S. R., & Norman, A. D. (2005). Teacher-candidates' exposure to formative assessment in educational psychology textbooks: A content analysis. *Educational Assessment, 10*, 19–37.

11 Interact! Teaching Using an Interactive Whiteboard

Matthew B. Sacks and Benjamin A. Jones

Instructors in all disciplines are charged with creating a classroom environment conducive to learning and open to discussion. They must disseminate course-related information, review important findings from the field, and convince their students that the theories and research from generations past still hold meaning in contemporary society. How, then, do teachers engage their students in meaningful educational interactions that can stir the passions of young minds? This book offers instructors several different tools and methods of engagement that serve to create a passionate and inquisitive classroom milieu. The current chapter offers yet another tool for the instructor's toolbox: an innovative classroom presentation device that is interactive and versatile and encourages active student involvement in the learning process. In this chapter we will introduce readers to the Wiimote Interactive Whiteboard (WIWB). The WIWB is a novel technological tool designed for use across disciplines within higher education. We will review the history of interactive whiteboards (IWBs) and their use in college classrooms and will describe the innovative functions of the WIWB, followed by several suggestions for the successful implementation of WIWBs in college courses.

History of IWBs

The term "interactive whiteboard" is used to describe electronic presentation equipment that allows users to directly manipulate and interact with images displayed on the surface of an IWB. IWBs can be freestanding or mounted onto a wall, with the most common installation being at the front of a classroom, replacing the traditional whiteboard or blackboard. Using an IWB, an image can be directly manipulated in the same fashion that images are manipulated on a computer screen. IWBs have been used in higher education settings dating back to the late 1990s (for a review, see Higgins, Beauchamp, & Miller, 2007). Previous literature suggests that IWBs are an effective educational tool leading to student benefits in motivation, attention, and enjoyment (Beeland, 2002; Hall & Higgins, 2005; Weimer, 2001). Using IWBs makes it possible to perform actions such as annotating and altering lecture materials, saving these materials, and re-using them for future classes (Glover & Miller, 2002).

Despite reports on the benefits of IWBs, several factors limit their use in today's college classroom. The current cost of commercial IWBs ranges from $1500 to $7500 ("What Does it Cost to Purchase Whiteboards," 2008), financially restricting their availability to collegiate instructors. The successful implementation of IWBs often requires training and support for instructors (Armstrong et al., 2005) because of the new and unfamiliar software. These factors have thus limited the dissemination of IWBs into college classrooms and have stunted the growth of the medium's pedagogical utility.

Creation of the WIWB

In November 2006, the Nintendo Corporation released the Wii videogame console, eventually selling over 34 million units in less than 2 years (Nintendo Co. Ltd., 2008). The Wii system comes with a remote controller (a Wiimote) that combines a traditional game control keypad with a digital camera sensitive to light with an infrared (IR) filter. In addition, accelerometers digitally transmit the three-dimensional positioning and motion of the unit via Bluetooth wireless connectivity. Soon after the release of the Wii, computer programmers began to experiment with the Wiimote and its interface with computers. In December 2007, Johnny Chung Lee created a computer program that calibrated the IR camera data to a flat surface and registered a mouse click command at the relative location where IR light is detected (Lee, 2007). An IR light source is then used as a virtual pen to draw on and interact directly with images projected onto a wall. Lee demonstrated the program on YouTube, explaining the production and use of the WIWB. The video, "Low-Cost Multi-touch Whiteboard using the Wiimote," has since been viewed over 3.3 million times (Lee, 2007).

Lee introduced the world to the possibilities of the WIWB, which can now be created for less than $100 (Table 11.1). Using Lee's original work, other programmers have created new programs that have made it more user-friendly and functional (Boon Jin, 2010; Schmidt, 2008). Today, the WIWB is not only considerably less expensive than professional IWBs, but it has also successfully mimicked the functions of a commercial IWB while offering unique functionality above that of commercial IWBs. Boon Jin (2010) recently developed the "Smoothboard" program with the needs of teachers and pre-senters in mind. For example, the program allows for customizable settings for separate programs (e.g., PowerPoint, Google Earth).

The WIWB's low cost and ease of use make it an ideal classroom tool for collegiate instructors. Instructors with basic familiarity and expertise in working with computers will find the production of the WIWB to be moder-ately difficult. Detailed instructions exist online (see Jones, 2008 http://www. boonjin.com/smoothboard/index.php?title=Main_Page) that describe how to install the adapter and connect the Wiimote to a computer and set up for use with a Whiteboard program. An online message board (http://www. wiimoteproject.com/wiimote-whiteboard/) allows teachers to post questions and receive answers from a thriving international community of software programmers and developers as well as other instructors and users.

Table 11.1
Wiimote Interactive Whiteboard Components

Component	Cost
Nintendo Wiimote	~$40 (available for purchase separate from the full Wii system)*
Bluetooth adapter	~$25 (internal in most modern laptops)*
Infrared LED pen	~$20 (can be built for ~$5)*
Whiteboard software program	Free, or donations can be made to the software authors (Boon Jin, 2010; Lee, 2007; Schmidt, 2008)

* These items may be purchased on eBay for less money.

The use of a WIWB in a classroom setting is both intuitive and dynamic, mostly because it is based on users' existing operating environment (e.g., Linux, Windows, Mac OS), requiring little acquisition of new software operation skills. The Wiimote is placed with the IR-sensitive camera directed toward a wall or whiteboard and is connected to a computer via Bluetooth. The instructor may then use an IR-Pen to manipulate images projected onto the wall or whiteboard. The IR-Pen interaction provides the same interaction that occurs between a mouse pointer and images on a computer screen. The difference with the WIWB is that the instructor's actions and movements are in full view of the students in the classroom. Instructors can use most of the same gestures and functions that they know from years of working with a computer mouse (including "right-click" functions when using the Smoothboard program). This intuitive functioning contrasts favorably with many professional IWBs, which require the instructor to learn program-specific gestures and operations (Armstrong et al., 2005).

When introduced into the classroom setting, the WIWB is typically viewed as something of an oddity, as students are accustomed to seeing a Wiimote used only for playing video games. After a full disclosure of the purpose and function of the WIWB, students typically sit quietly whispering to their neighbors as the instructor uses the IR-Pen to move images around the screen, add written comments to slides, and interact with other presentation materials. It is important that instructors set aside time to briefly describe to students how the WIWB will be used to enhance classroom presentations, and assist them in the learning process. The following section of this chapter presents several examples of classroom activities that can be implemented using the WIWB. For the purposes of this chapter, we will focus upon examples from psychology lectures, but these activities are easily transferred to other disciplines. These illustrations are by no means comprehensive: this section is meant to serve as a point of departure from which instructors can create novel interactive teaching experiences in their own classrooms.

Classroom Examples

Many instructors provide their students with handouts based upon the slides or other materials presented in class, to assist students in taking notes on the topic of the day. With the WIWB, instructors have the added ability to give students immediate access to notes and annotations that are created during the course of a given classroom session. Such a function allows students to focus more upon their own learning process rather than frantically trying to scribble down every word that the instructor writes on the board.

Freud's Topographical Model of the Mind

For example, imagine a psychology instructor is discussing Sigmund Freud's topographical model of the mind. One option is to present the students with a detailed diagram using the "iceberg" metaphor to designate the different elements of the model: "Conscious" is the small bit of the iceberg above the water line, "Preconscious" is just below, and "Unconscious" is the largest portion of the iceberg, existing entirely underwater. This presentation can be enhanced and moved into a more interactive modality by using a WIWB. Using a program such as Microsoft PowerPoint, the instructor could draw an iceberg (using the Insert Freeform Line function), or show a plain image of an iceberg in the water. As the concepts involved in Freud's topographical model are introduced, the teacher could use the IR-Pen to write in the model's terms, or ask different students to come to the front of the class and write in their guesses of where the terms should be placed. As the discussion progresses, notes on additional ideas and examples can be written in and/or images can be dragged across the model using the IR-Pen.

Classical Conditioning

The classical conditioning process of learning (Pavlov, 1927) can also be explained using the WIWB. An instructor could begin such a presentation by showing images of a dog, food, and a bell, along with the basic classical conditioning terms (unconditioned stimulus, conditioned response, etc.). By moving the images and words around the screen with the IR-Pen, the instructor could create the context and recipe for Pavlov's classical conditioning study in an interactive and fluid manner. This presentation and the Freud example both succeed in creating a dynamically interesting classroom experience that allows for more interaction between the teacher, the learner, and the material. Instructors from other disciplines can use this same method for presenting an endless variety of topics.

Animated Neurotransmitters

The WIWB can also be used to enhance a lecture on the neurotransmitter reuptake process. Using PowerPoint, an instructor can prepare a slide before class that depicts a presynaptic neuron releasing neurotransmitters from its synaptic vesicles across the synapse and locking onto the postsynaptic neuron. Simple PowerPoint animation movements can move small circles, representing neurotransmitters, down from the presynaptic neuron to the postsynaptic neuron, and then back up again during the reuptake process. All of the shapes for the vesicles and neurotransmitters serve as a palette that can be moved from one side of the slide to the other. During class, the instructor presents this slide (in the "Normal" view; this view allows for better movement of objects) and explains the various pieces of the puzzle: the neural impulse moving along the presynaptic neuron's axon, the synaptic vesicles releasing the neurotransmitters into the synapse, and the "lock and key" fitting of neurotransmitters into postsynaptic receptor sites. During the lecture, the instructor or students can use the IR-Pen to drag and drop the shapes representing the impulse, vesicles, and neurotransmitters into their proper (predesignated) locations. By switching to the "Slide Show" view, the teacher then uses the IR-Pen to click through the prepared animation sequence, which will animate these shapes, displaying a visually stimulating representation of the reuptake process. Instructors from a variety of disciplines could use this type of presentation method to create lively and active classroom experiences (e.g., mapping the movement of Allied forces during D-Day; displaying the movement of Saturn's moons).

Spatial Movements

The Wiimote also has the ability to transmit information regarding its three-dimensional location and movement. De Steur's "Wiimote Commander" program (2008) offers instructors the ability to track the position and speed of up to seven separate Wiimotes as well as controlling their lights and sounds. Dynamic interactive learning environments can be created using such programs. For example, in a classroom discussion of the functions of the brain, psychology professors may highlight the tasks of the hippocampus, including its role in processing spatial information. An instructor can enhance this discussion by comparing the functioning of the hippocampus to the intricate circuitry of the Wiimote accelerometers. One possible demonstration is to have a good-natured student (or instructor) hold a Wiimote on top of his or her head as he or she walks about the classroom, turning and moving his or her head in different directions. As this happens, the Wiimote Commander program can simultaneously project an image of the positioning of the Wiimote. The instructor can use the immediate visual display to discuss the nature of the brain's own sensory processing system and how the hippocampus relays information about the body's position in three-dimensional space to the rest of the brain and to the motor system. The Commander program can also compile all of the motion and position data, which can then be graphed visually with a spreadsheet program (e.g., Microsoft Excel). Such a method again incorporates a visually dynamic presentation with increased student involvement. Physics and geometry lessons could also make use of this program to present information.

Displaying Disorders

WIWB-based presentations can help enhance the presentation of disorders such as schizophrenia, a mental illness characterized by bizarre symptoms such as hallucinations and delusions. The WIWB can be used in a number of classroom activities to expose students to an experience approximating that of someone with schizophrenia. One such activity involves the use of the three-dimensional online virtual world "Second Life" (Linden Lab, San Francisco, CA; see also Chapter 19 in this volume). In this virtual world, researchers have created a virtual hospital ward environment designed to simulate the auditory and visual hallucinations experienced by individuals with schizophrenia (Yellowlees & Cook, 2006). Using the WIWB, the instructor invites students to the front of the classroom, where they maneuver through this virtual hospital ward, interacting with objects in the environment that simulate experiences such as intrusive voices and visual hallucinations (e.g., an image in a mirror slowly begins to decay and bleed). (*Editor's note: This Second Life schizophrenia environment does contain some elements that play upon common misconceptions regarding the disorder, such as violent imagery.*) To make the experience more immersive, students can also wear headphones to make the simulation sounds louder than ambient classroom noises.

A slightly more elaborate exercise involves the presentation of a video created by Janssen Pharmaceuticals, the producers of the antipsychotic medication Risperdal. The video is a first-person "3D theater experience" also designed to simulate the visual and auditory hallucinations experienced by individuals with schizophrenia (Janssen, 2009). Instructors can extract audio files from the video to be used in concert with the Wiimote Commander program. By strategically placing several Wiimotes around the classroom (perhaps under cover of darkness, with lights turned down for the showing of the video), and using the Wiimote Commander program, instructors can have several Wiimotes play these audio files while the Janssen video is shown. Thus, the intrusive voices portrayed in the video are heard coming from several locations throughout the classroom, creating a rather immersive environment for the students and allowing them to gain a better understanding of the experience of hallucinations and their possible negative impact. For either of these classroom activities, it is recommended that instructors warn their students about the nature of these activities prior to starting.

Brain Structures Revealed

One of the more unusual features of the WIWB is the ability to manipulate three-dimensional objects and images in an interactive, intuitive fashion. In the field of psychology, one topic that lends itself to three-dimensional explorations in the classroom is biopsychology. Lessons on the complex structure and anatomy of the human brain may be enhanced via interactive presentations with the WIWB. A number of Web sites and software programs offer users the ability to interact with two- and three-dimensional brains (Table 11.2).

Table 11.2
WIWB Applications

Coronal Atlas Human Head and Brain
http://www.thehumanbrain.info/head_brain/hn_coronal_atlas/coronal.html
Harvard Whole Brain Atlas
http://www.med.harvard.edu/AANLIB/home.html
National Geographic "Mapping Memory in 3D"
http://ngm.nationalgeographic.com/2007/11/memory/brain-interactive
PBS 3-D Brain
http://www.pbs.org/wnet/brain/3d/

The "Brain Voyager Brain Tutor" (Brain Innovation B.V., Maastricht, Netherlands, 2003) is a software program that can be used with the WIWB to interactively view and manipulate a three-dimensional human brain. Instructors may use this program to discuss the location and major functions of the different lobes of the brain. Instructors or students can use the IR-Pen to rotate the brain, zoom in, and select different locations to display information about the specific brain structures. Once again, this type of presentation affords students a more hands-on, interactive learning experience that will assist them in understanding the intricate biology of the brain. The WIWB's ability to wirelessly track the IR-Pen's movements and commands makes it extremely useful in the interaction with many types of three-dimensional images and programs. Enterprising instructors can take this WIWB-brain example one step further to create an even greater level of student involvement. Using a ceiling-mounted projector, an instructor may display images horizontally onto the floor or vertically onto the wall. Mounting an IR-Pen onto an extension (e.g., securely attaching it to a yardstick) will allow for direct interaction with this floor-projected brain image while standing upon it. Students may get up from their seats and quite literally walk from one section of the projected brain to another, pointing at neurological structures, asking questions, and discussing concepts, all while standing on the brain image.

Demonstrating Research Methods or Collecting Data

Many basic science experiments make use of complicated programs and procedures to test research participants. Discussing such research in the classroom can be greatly enhanced through interactive teaching methods such as those available through the WIWB. For example, a Continuous Performance Task (CPT) is a test in which a continuous stream of information (typically letters or numbers) is presented to an individual, who is asked to respond to a given target (an "X" or other item) embedded within the information stream. Response times are collected and used to assess the individual's information processing abilities. Psychology instructors can use the WIWB along with a research program such as E-Prime (2004) to create a CPT for use in a classroom presentation. The instructor can run a preprogrammed visual CPT that displays a series of letters one at a time, with the letter "X" appearing every few letters. A student is to press a button on the Wiimote every time he or she sees an "X." After the CPT demonstration, the instructor immediately transfers the E-Prime data to a graphical program to display the student's reactions times to the entire class. This procedure should allow the class to gain a better understanding of the research paradigm and of the processing speed concept. Other research protocols can be similarly demonstrated in this interactive fashion.

A final recommendation for using the WIWB in the college classroom involves the recording of class activities. Many instructors already use "webcams" to record classes for use in later semesters or to make available to students who missed a particular class. However, a standard complaint about these recordings is that they are frequently captured too far away from the activity at hand, or the video resolution makes it difficult to understand what the instructor wrote or projected on the board. With the WIWB, all activities occur within a digital environment. A desktop recording program, such as Hyper Cam (2007), can be used to record onscreen movements along with recording the audio of the lecture and discussion in the classroom. This procedure gives instructors the ability to create high-quality digital copies of specific lectures, or portions of lectures ("micro-lectures"), for immediate posting on course Web sites, or for use in future classes.

Assessment

To continue to gain information on the usefulness of WIWBs in the classroom, we recommend that instructors solicit WIWB-specific feedback from their students. Both authors have used WIWBs in classroom settings (collegiate, high school, and middle school), with students verbally reporting high levels of interest and attention. Sacks (2008) reported on the use of the WIWB in several sections of introduction to psychology and abnormal psychology courses. Students (n = 24) filled out anonymous questionnaires at the end of each semester, responding to specific questions about the utility of the WIWB in class. Results showed that 70.8% of the sample rated the WIWB as an effective teaching tool, 95.8% reported high levels of interest, 70.8% reported high levels of attention, and 75% reported high levels of enjoyment. Although the self-report data are encouraging, future studies are necessary to determine whether WIWB use actually enhances student learning outcomes. As more instructors come to adopt WIWBs in their own classrooms, it is possible that more thorough assessments will offer additional data on how WIWBs can best be used to enhance the learning environment.

Conclusion

As the nature of learners has evolved, there has been a dynamic shift in the role of educators from disseminators of information to engagers and facilitators of the learning process. Most collegiate lecture content is typically displayed on blackboards, with students acting as passive consumers of the distributed information. Traditionally, the role of the college instructor has been to teach while speaking from behind a lectern that separates the learners from the content. The WIWB appears to successfully engage today's college students, who have now become accustomed to interacting with everything from computers to cell phones. The WIWB allows students to actively engage with content in a dynamic fashion, intuitively moving objects, drawing, taking notes, and discussing material in a lively and substantive way. The future of the WIWB in higher education will depend upon the creativity, ingenuity, and initiative of college instructors, their students, and a thriving community of software programmers and educators focused on creating interactive technology for all learners.

References

Armstrong, V., Barnes, S., Sutherland, R., Curran, S., Mills, S., & Thompson, I. (2005). Collaborative research methodology for investigating teaching and learning: the use of interactive whiteboard technology. *Educational Review, 57*(4), 457–469.

Beeland, W. D. (2002). *Student engagement, visual learning and technology: can interactive whiteboards help? Action Research Exchange,* 1(1). Retrieved from http://chiron.valdosta.edu/are/Artmanscrpt/vol1no1/beeland_am.pdf

Boon Jin, G. (2010). Smoothboard (Version 2.0) [Computer software]. Singapore: Author. Available online at: www.smoothboard.net

Brain Voyager Brain Tutor. [Computer software]. Maastricht, Netherlands: Brain Innovation B.V. Available online at: http://www.brainvoyager.com/

E-Prime (Version 1.1) (2004). [Computer program]. Pittsburgh, PA: Psychology Software Tools.

De Steur, F. (2008) Wiimote Commander [Computer software]. France: Author. Available online at: http://wiimotecommande.sourceforge.net/

Glover, D., & Miller, D. (2002) The interactive whiteboard as a force for pedagogic change: the experience of five elementary schools in an English education authority. *Information Technology in Childhood Education, 1*, 5–19.

Hall, I., & Higgins, S. (2005). Primary school students' perceptions of interactive whiteboards. *Journal of Computer Assisted Learning, 21,* 102–117.

Higgins, S., Beauchamp, G., & Miller, D. (2007). Reviewing the literature on interactive whiteboards. *Learning, Media and Technology, 32*(3), 213–225.

Hyper Cam (Version 2.14.02) (2007). [Computer program]. Murrysville, PA: Hyperionics Technology. Available online at: http://www.hyperionics.com

Janssen Pharmaceuticals. (2009, January 11). *A Virtual Hallucination: Mindstorm.* Retrieved from http://www.janssen.com/janssen/mindstorm_video.

Jones, B. *Smoothboard Wiki.* Retrieved February 8, 2009, from http://www.boonjin.com/smoothboard/index.php?title=Main_Page

Lee, J. C. (2007). Wiimote Whiteboard [Computer software]. Pittsburgh, PA: Author. Available on-line at: http://johnnylee.net/projects/wii/

Lee, J. C. (Director). (2007). *Low-Cost Multi-touch Whiteboard using the Wiimote.* Retrieved January 11, 2009, from http://www.youtube.com/watch?v=5s5EvhHy7eQ

Nintendo Co. Ltd. (2008, October). Consolidated financial highlights. Minami-ku, Kyoto, Japan.

Pavlov, I. P. (1927). *Conditioned reflexes.* London: Oxford University Press.

Sacks, M. B. (2008, October). *Interact! Teaching psychology using a low-cost interactive whiteboard.* Paper presented at Getting Connected: Best Practices in Technology-Enhanced Teaching & Learning in Psychology, Society for the Teaching of Psychology, Atlanta, GA.

Schmidt, U. (2008). Wiimote Whiteboard [Computer software]. Germany: Author. Available online at: http://www.uweschmidt.org/wiimote-whiteboard

Second Life (2003). [Computer software]. San Francisco: Linden Lab. Available online at: http://www.secondlife.com

Weimer, M.J. (2001). The influence of technology such as a SMART board interactive whiteboard on student motivation in the classroom. Retrieved on September 10th, 2009, from http://downloads01.smarttech.com/media/sitecore/en/pdf/research_library/k-12/the_influence_of_technology_such_as_a_smart_board_interactive_whiteboard_on_student_motivation_in_the_classroom.pdf

What Does it Cost to Purchase WHITEBOARDS? (2008, February). *Training and Development, 62*(2), 96.

Yellowlees, P. M., & Cook, J. N. (2006). Education about hallucinations using an Internet virtual reality system: a qualitative survey. *Academic Psychiatry, 30,* 534–539.

12 Motivating Student Engagement with MySpace and Web-Enhanced Research Labs

Kim A. Case and Beth Hentges

Students today live in an environment in which reading and writing,

through digital media as well as traditional texts, are pervasive.

The challenge for teachers is to connect literacy skills that students

develop in their social environment with the literacy environment

of the school

(CONSIDINE, HORTON, & MOORMAN, 2009, P. 471).

As our society becomes increasingly dependent on technology, many students are becoming extremely comfortable in online environments. Unfortunately, technology sometimes pulls student engagement away from the college course. Although the struggle to maintain student interest is far from a novel problem, students' passion for technology adds a new wrinkle. The old adage, "if you can't beat them, join them" seems particularly apt here.

College instructors can use technology with which students are comfortable to motivate engagement in the learning process. This chapter focuses on two distinct ways of using technology to enhance student engagement: social networking sites (e.g., MySpace, Facebook, Friendster) and course-management systems (e.g., Blackboard, WebCT). These are useful tools for motivating deeper engagement with course materials, increasing student interest in learning in online and face-to-face courses, and mentoring student researchers. In this chapter, we describe a MySpace media assignment designed to engage students in learning as they present their work on Web pages. We also explore the use of course-management systems for expanding student engagement in research experiences. Implications for teaching and learning in relation to each instructional approach are discussed.

Student Engagement: A Brief Overview

Student engagement has received increased attention in institutions of higher learning in terms of individual class instruction, institutional assessment, and accountability (Kuh, 2009). Although there is disagreement over the precise definition of engagement (Salinero & Beardsley, 2009), researchers use the term to reflect the level of students' involvement in their own learning (Kuh, 2009). Students, particularly younger students who grew up familiar with the Internet, already engage with technology as one of their primary sources of information. However, schools and instructors frequently block the use of the Internet as a source of information. This practice may be for a number of reasons, including the perception that the Internet contributes to increases in academic dishonesty (Selwyn, 2008), inaccurate information, and instructors' personal discomfort with technology. Thus, education suffers from a divide between student approaches to knowledge acquisition and educational-system expectations. It is important for instructors to create a bridge between the technology students regularly access and the more traditional classroom experience (Considine, Horton, & Moorman, 2009). Given that Internet-based activities permeate many aspects of daily life, weaving technology into education is no longer a luxury, but a necessity (Considine, Horton & Moorman, 2009; Salinero & Beardsley, 2009).

Students and Social Networking Sites

Social networking sites such as Facebook, MySpace, and Friendster allow people to establish and maintain social connections over vast distances via the Internet. These sites typically allow individuals to post personal information, text, photos, and videos to participate in multimedia communication with one another. Approximately 75% of online adults 18 to 24 years old and 57% of online adults 25 to 34 have a social networking site profile (Lenhart, 2009). Among college-age adults, 68% of full-time students and 71% of part-time students utilize social networking sites. In contrast, only 28% of non-students maintain a profile (Lenhart, 2009). Because a large percentage of students use social networking sites, these sites provide an opportunity for expanding the classroom community and enhancing student engagement beyond the face-to-face mode.

Most of the research on the link between social networking sites and academics emphasizes involvement of students in the sites and potential problems such as privacy issues (Cain, 2008). In addition, there is some concern about students sharing overly personal or damaging information through social networking sites (Cain, 2008). Although all the major social networking sites offer privacy settings that allow the user to control profile access, many users fail to restrict public access (Lenhart, 2009). Thus, information shared by students becomes public to virtually anyone, even though they may perceive it as private (Cain, 2008). Some academic institutions have disciplined students for certain information (e.g., revealing or embarrassing pictures, threats of crime, bigoted comments, or admission of violations of university policies) placed on social networking sites (Cain, 2008), although most students believe that faculty and university administrators should not search student profiles.

As one solution to too much self-disclosure, it is possible to create multiple online profiles for different purposes. Over half of social network users have more than one profile, using each one for different purposes, such as keeping in touch with different networks or separating personal and professional profiles (Lenhart, 2009). Regardless of judicious use of profiles, time spent networking may detract from activities more conducive to academic success. Concerns with problematic Internet use, particularly "Internet addiction," is an extreme example of the potential problem (Kim & Davis, 2009). Some students may be unable to regulate their use of social networking sites and spend more time than they can afford on the sites.

A MySpace Assignment: Enhancing Student Engagement and Interaction

As students spend more time communicating through social networking forums such as Facebook and MySpace, instructors are beginning to consider the pedagogical possibilities (Aragon, 2007; Gainer, 2008). Social networking sites are potential teaching tools for increasing student interest and involvement with course materials. Given that such sites are structured for social connection, they offer students opportunities to expand the classroom and share their learning experiences.

Over several years of teaching in psychology and women's studies, I (first author) became increasingly disappointed with the structure of course papers. The more papers I graded and returned, the more I doubted the pedagogical rewards of providing detailed feedback that many students never read. Furthermore, traditional course papers failed to support my goals of encouraging student engagement and creating learning communities. Although I read every paper, students never received peer feedback or benefited from the work of their classmates. In addition, 20% to 25% of students per semester requested my advice on how to share what they learned in the course with family, friends, or the wider community. Some students urged family members to read essays from the course. One ambitious student even coordinated bringing a national speaker to her internship site (a counseling center) after reading an essay on domestic violence as part of her coursework. However, most students seemed unsure of how they might create meaningful ways to educate others using the knowledge they gained in the course. The structure of the MySpace assignment (below) addresses all three problems with embedded student feedback loops, shared learning, and opportunities for raising awareness beyond the classroom walls.

Rather than restricting students to presenting their findings in a final paper to the instructor, online MySpace presentations allow students to educate each other and encourage knowledge sharing with those outside the literal or virtual classroom. In contrast to student presentations (face-to-face or online) that rarely involve sustained discussion, social networking forums automatically provide outlets for student interaction for an extended period, perhaps even after the course ends. Students benefit from receiving immediate and direct peer feedback as well as instructor feedback in a form that students read (if the instructor chooses to participate). Through the use of social networking sites, students may also choose to share their coursework or research outcomes with the public. All of these benefits support a learning community model that encourages higher rates of student interaction by emphasizing student-centered learning. In addition, this approach provides students with the opportunity to create educational materials for public consumption and commentary.

My first use of the MySpace project occurred in a fully online diversity course that required students to observe a form of media (e.g., magazines, music videos, commercials) and present a critique of media images of race and gender. Previously, this media critique took the form of a course paper submitted to the instructor at the end of the term. Project components included the following: (a) each student observed and analyzed media images of race and gender, (b) students created individual MySpace sites presenting their research findings, (c) each student viewed and added at least 10 class-mates' projects as "friends" so that projects become linked in MySpace, (d) students used the comment function to provide feedback to at least 4 other students, and (e) each student produced a reflective essay explaining his or her MySpace project design and submitted this to the instructor.

Students received media-project instructions with deadlines for each portion of the assignment to keep them moving toward successful comple-tion of the project. A MySpace project prototype, developed by a teaching assistant, provided students with ideas for using the social networking site to present their work. The prototype included not only critical analysis com-mentary but also images and videos to illustrate creative ways of displaying media observation findings. For example, the prototype included images of magazine advertisements as well as video clips of television commercials, music videos, and scenes from television sitcoms to provide ideas to students conducting observations across a variety of media. Along with the prototype, students made use of online discussion boards in WebCT designed to guide them through the MySpace project. As students posted questions about con-tent or more technical questions, the instructor and teaching assistant responded within 24 hours. Classmates also commonly answered questions in support of each other on this discussion forum.

MySpace Project Outcomes

The students' MySpace projects varied in terms of the placement of content and the use of examples to support their findings. Although some students used the main MySpace profile page to present media observation findings, most of them used the blog function to house the majority of the written content. The blog area in MySpace enabled students to present longer sum-maries with deeper analyses of themes identified during their media observa-tions. For example, one student created separate blogs of approximately four paragraphs each addressing racial images, gender images, a summary of underlying media messages, and her analysis of the impact of magazine images on the psychology of race and gender. Projects also commonly included embedded videos (usually from http://www.youtube.com) as examples of children's cartoons, music videos, commercials, and television sitcoms perpetuating or challenging racial and gender stereotypes. To illustrate the prevalence of gender roles in television commercials, another student provided a video sampling of dishwashing liquid, laundry detergent, and vacuum advertisements that indicated these are solely the tasks of women. Finally, some students provided links from the MySpace project to other relevant educational Web sites.

Student interaction increased dramatically as a result of the MySpace assignment. Students far exceeded the requirement of adding a minimum of 10 classmate Web sites to their own projects by adding between 12 and 25 classmate projects. They created a web of projects connecting students as they viewed findings from the spectrum of media sources covered by other students in the course. Further, project instructions required students to provide commentary on at least four classmate Web sites. However, the overwhelming majority commented more often, with some leaving comments on over 20 MySpace pages. In terms of peer feedback, students received an average of nine comments on their own individual project Web sites. These comments led to further discussion of media images and how they affect our thoughts and behaviors. For example, after reading one student's blog post in MySpace about portrayals of women of color in magazines, another student posted a comment asking the class a thought-provoking question about possible solutions. This sparked a lengthy discussion among five more students that lasted for 2 weeks after the official semester ended. Almost 40% of the students chose to link their project page with friends and family external to the course.

Student MySpace Project Feedback

Responses to a brief survey during the last week of the term (N = 21) demonstrated that students enjoyed the overall assignment, offering comments to others, and receiving comments from peers. One student exclaimed she "enjoyed this project more than [any project she] ever had before!" Students indicated that creating the MySpace project, viewing classmates' pages, and receiving comments from others helped them learn and apply course concepts. For example, a student wrote, "the media project promoted utilization of what we were learning and [she] enjoyed viewing other student work." Another reported that "once [she] was able to view other students' pages, [she] began to see the big picture." Students also reported that the project helped them get to know others in the online course, potentially serving as a buffer to the isolation students often experience in online learning environments.

After experiencing the MySpace assignment, students expressed a desire to share future course work online in order to raise awareness of social issues and educate others. Some students also shared that they "plan to keep the page once the class is over," indicating that commitment to the project extended beyond the limited life of the course itself. Overall, students recommended using this project in future sections of the same course and endorsed converting the assignment for use in other courses.

When asked how they might alter the MySpace assignment, a few students suggested using a group project model to alleviate anxiety among students unfamiliar with the social network. Several students also requested a battery of MySpace tutorials for those with less Web site experience. These ideas contributed to the summary of pedagogical implications included in the section below.

MySpace Assignment Pedagogical Implications

Although the first iteration of this project assignment appeared successful based on student outcomes and feedback, some alterations may benefit the instructor and enhance student learning. To assist with the implementation of this project, faculty members may consider (a) using a teaching assistant to help answer practical and technical questions about creating the page; (b) providing students with video tutorials (perhaps created using Adobe Captivate [http://tryit.adobe.com/us/captivate] or Camtasia Studio [http://www.techsmith.com/camtasia]) addressing how to get started, embed videos, and add images to the page; (c) formatting this assignment as a group project to reduce student anxiety; or (d) providing students with access to several prototype MySpace project pages that include ideas about how to present their findings.

This project in its current form includes an individual student media analysis paper followed by a group MySpace project incorporating findings from four or five students. As they navigate the two-step process, students gain valuable writing experience individually but also benefit from using technology to create a presentation of their findings. For students unfamiliar with MySpace or those generally afraid of technology, group support during the site-creation phase appears to reduce anxiety and promote effective peer modeling and student-to-student technological support.

Given that many faculty members teach face-to-face, Web-enhanced, blended (hybrid), and fully online courses, this technological transformation of course papers provides the flexibility of use in a variety of course formats. Face-to-face students may use the MySpace assignment as a tool for in-class presentations followed by online peer feedback and discussion. Of course, fully online courses can make use of the project because it does not require a face-to-face presentation. In fact, instructors might consider connecting with teachers in similar courses at other educational institutions to enable MySpace (or another social network) project commentary among students from multiple universities. For those instructors encouraging student exposure to cross-cultural perspectives, this assignment model could facilitate valuable global learning communities as well.

Mentoring Student Researchers in a Web-Enhanced Learning Environment

As seen with the MySpace assignment, technology can increase student engagement in classroom material and with fellow students outside the classroom. While there are many obvious applications of technology for classroom assignments, teachers can also use the Web to engage students in learning outside of formal course instruction. Research labs are one area where maintaining social communications between students and teachers is particularly important (Ryser, Halseth & Thien, 2009). Although research labs certainly provide students with experiential learning, it can sometimes be a struggle to develop student "interaction mechanisms" (Ryser, Halseth & Thien, 2009, p. 261) where students engage in collaborative learning. Course-management software can be used to enhance communication and collaborative learning within a research laboratory.

Most universities provide course-management systems (e.g., Blackboard, WebCT, or Sakai) to instructors for face-to-face, Web-enhanced, and online courses. A recent study by Elicker, O'Malley, and Williams (2008) suggests these interactive online sites aid student learning in terms of increased grades and course satisfaction. However, faculty can also imagine and design new spaces within these online systems for teaching and learning that occurs outside their courses. For example, to enhance student engagement in research, I (first author) developed a WebCT space for my research assistants to facilitate ongoing communication about our various studies. The students participate in continuous online discussions about journal articles, the internal-review process, study design and methodology, data-collection problems and solutions, and more. This online laboratory provides a central location for not only the calendar for data collection, but also editing of surveys and conference posters, for example. Four major goals drove the original design of this online space for research assistants. I wanted to (1) save the students and the instructor time, (2) provide students with a library of information and resources, (3) create a space for continuous open communication, and (4) establish a community of learners that engage with one another at each stage of the research process.

Structure of the Web-Enhanced Research Lab

By moving the majority of resources and communication online, we reduced weekly face-to-face meetings to every 2 weeks. During the weeks we do not physically meet, each student posts an online summary of the research he or she has completed and asks questions for group feedback. One student noted that this format "allows us to be in contact so much faster" than when the lab met only face-to-face. Because many students work full time, devote time to family responsibilities, and commute to campus for classes, time-saving solutions provide a broader range of students with the valuable opportunity of conducting research with faculty. For example, one research assistant is a full-time graduate student raising two children who lives 40 miles away from the university. Using the learning-management system as a major portion of the research lab learning environment allows participation in the research for a diverse group of students.

Due to the hybrid research lab, student researchers gain immediate and unlimited access to rich resources they need throughout a particular study. For example, students may find journal article references along with article summaries written by previous research assistants as well as guides and external links about APA style. Of course, this WebCT site also houses practical resources, such as the data-collection schedule, a calendar of meetings and conference deadlines, and a hyperlink to the online participant pool Web site. In addition, documents relevant to the internal review board (IRB) process, including previous IRB applications and consent forms, aid student learning about participant protections and ethical guidelines for research practices. When students reach the stage of statistical data analysis using SPSS, they access a folder of video tutorials walking them through each step for creating new variables or conducting t-tests, for example. The site also offers professional development via links to associations and tips for applying to graduate school. Students appreciated having "outside links, documents, and our calendar all available 24-7." Although each student may not directly engage in each step of the research project during a given semester, the students may freely access previous conference presentations, publications, and grants produced by our lab. One student who advanced to co-authoring journal articles found it helpful to "access useful documents while creating posters and writing manuscripts." The quiz and assignment functions within the course shell also provide news ways to teach about research. New research assistants are required to master a quiz regarding confidentiality, debriefing procedures, and data-collection procedures. When student researchers complete reflection essays on a conference experience as part of the lab, they easily submit those into the assignment page in WebCT. All of these course-management tools enhance student engagement with hands-on research and introduce new avenues for deeper learning.

Student engagement is extended with enhanced communication. As one of the student researchers noted, "Communication is the key to success in these complex research studies and WebCT allows for complete communication between all of us." Based on personal observations, communication among student researchers increased dramatically due to our WebCT research site. As the principal investigator, I regularly post announcements regarding procedural changes, reminders, and notices such as potential conferences for presenting findings from the lab. The discussion board provides an organized central location for student collaborations on creating posters, study design decision making, coordinating conference travel, and even grant writing. Another student appreciated that "rather than waiting until lab meetings to communicate news, updates, urgent messages ... we are able to post messages on WebCT for instant access." The online lab meetings that occur every 2 weeks keep all researchers in touch with current trends in data collection and analysis. As an added bonus, the course-management system restricts all research communication such as posts and e-mails to the lab Web site rather than using private e-mail accounts or other dispersed methods of communication. This practice ensures that discussions and research-related e-mails are housed in one accessible location. In addition, instructors can archive discussion boards that are outdated or that may be useful for pedagogical research purposes.

As a result of incorporating the course-management system into the research lab, the students successfully built a strong community of support and collaborative learning. The site regularly serves as a space for students to brainstorm together, "share ideas, ask questions, and … resolve problems faster" (research assistant) if an obstacle arises. For example, when a participant failed to follow the instructions provided, the student researcher posted the problem on WebCT as a discussion thread. Within 24 hours, several students responded with ideas about how to handle the situation if it occurs in the future. One student reported that "when one asks a question, it usually enlightens all of us, especially new people to the lab." Discussion board forums about student hypotheses for an upcoming experiment led to an online debate about expected outcomes. This online environment supported the development of a community of researchers by enhancing learning through discussions, encouraging group problem solving, and creating a space for veteran student researchers to train new researchers. As students graduate and leave the lab group, many also leave behind long-term contributions that benefit new students for several years. For example, the first student lab supervisor created detailed step-by-step tutorials explaining best practices for conducting a literature review using the library databases. In addition, she created a tutorial on entering information into the software program *Endnote*, which allows indexing and organization of research references. Incoming student researchers regularly access tools created by former lab members.

Pedagogical Implications of the Hybrid Research Lab

Student engagement in the research lab increased after implementing the online lab space. Research assistant attendance rates at physical meetings and online (asynchronous) meetings improved tremendously. Students' increased participation and communication includes daily discussion board contributions, questions, and feedback to each other. In addition, the students completed more tasks on time. Increased task completion may be due to the public online announcement of each individual's duties, creating an increased sense of responsibility to peers. Thus, instructors may enhance student engagement using the tools available through course-management systems.

Instructors interested in utilizing course-management systems such as Blackboard and WebCT for teaching student researchers may consider additional options for enhancing learning. Although my research lab never used the instant messaging chat rooms in WebCT, students could potentially use this function for synchronous teamwork such as planning the results section of a conference poster or debating possible study outcomes. Another potential assignment could be a scavenger hunt for resources found in the system. For example, the instructor may send student researchers on a scavenger hunt throughout the lab's course-management system shell requiring them to find specific information within the latest IRB application, locate a regional conference for presenting the lab's next study, or find the section of the consent form that explains the right to withdraw. Such an assignment lends itself to customization to fit the needs of any research lab. Finally, the quiz function in most course-management systems provides easy and accessible ways to get students more involved in learning about the research process. A quiz might describe previous studies conducted in the lab and ask students to label dependent and independent variables, submit their own hypotheses, and write a short essay outlining the possible confounds of a study.

Overall, the flexibility that learning-management systems afford instructors in their courses can also be harnessed for teaching students as they earn hands-on research experience. With the support of an online research-lab environment, instructors may enhance student communication, engagement, and performance.

Conclusions

In this chapter, we examined a MySpace project as part of a course and Web involvement outside of a traditional course. Assessment of student learning as a result of the MySpace project may be evaluated through student feedback and instructor rubrics. Pre-test and post-test surveys would allow comparison of student knowledge of course concepts before and after the project. Although not a direct measure of learning, open-ended questions requesting student feedback about how the assignment contributed to their learning may provide additional data for assessment of project effectiveness. In addition to analysis of MySpace grading rubric data, instructors may consider participation data as an indication of engagement. For example, peer feedback and interaction beyond the minimum requirements serve as indicators of student motivation and engagement. Qualitative analysis of reflective essays as well as comments posted to classmate project sites provides additional avenues of assessment.

To evaluate the student-learning benefits associated with the hybrid research laboratory, instructors may assess student attendance rates, participation rates, and successful task completion rates as evidence of pedagogical effectiveness. As students interact with peers online, quantitative and qualitative analysis of discussion board posts may also provide insight into student attitudes, engagement, and performance.

Motivating student engagement presents a long-standing problem for instructors. Engaged students are more likely to attend class, pay attention to lectures, participate in discussion, and carry their learning outside the classroom setting (Kuh, 2009). In an increasingly "plugged-in" society, parceling out student attention for course requirements may prove even more difficult. Further, there may be a disconnect between the traditional learning environment and how students routinely choose to use and gather information. Increasingly younger individuals are using technology to maintain connections, have social interactions, and present themselves to the world. Instructors can co-opt technology in ways that maintain and increase student engagement and participation by utilizing the very tools with which most students are already familiar. The MySpace assignment and Web-enhanced research labs provide two ways to successfully weave technology into instruction such that the technology enhances the learning experience.

References

Aragon, J. (2007). Technologies and pedagogy: How YouTubing, social networking, and other web sources complement the classroom. *Feminist Collections, 28,* 45.

Cain, J. (2008). Online social networking issues within academia and pharmacy education. *American Journal of Pharmacy Education, 72,* 1–7.

Considine, D., Horton, J., & Moorman, G. (2009). Teaching and reading the millennial generation through media literacy. *Journal of Adolescent & Adult Literacy, 52,* 471–481.

Elicker, J., O'Malley, A., & Williams, C. (2008). Does an interactive WebCT site help students learn? *Teaching of Psychology, 35,* 126–131.

Gainer, B. (2008). Using MySpace to build community in college. *Teaching Professor, 22,* 5.

Kim, H., & Davis, K. E. (2009). Toward a comprehensive theory of problematic Internet use: Evaluating the role of self-esteem, anxiety, flow, and the self-rated importance of Internet activities. *Computers in Human Behavior, 25,* 490–500.

Kuh, G. D. (2009). The National Survey of Student Engagement: Conceptual and empirical foundations. *New Directions for Institutional Research, 141*, 5–20.

Lenhart, A. (2009). Pew Internet Project data memo. Retrieved April 26, 2009, from http://www.pewinternet.org/topics/Social-Networking.aspx.

Ryser, L., Halseth, G., & Thien, D. (2009). Strategies and intervening factors influencing student social interaction and experiential learning in an interdisciplinary research team. *Research in Higher Education, 50*, 248–267.

Salinero, D., & Beardsley, C. (2009). Enhancing the academic experience: The library and campus engagement. *College and Research Libraries News, 70*, 150–152.

Selwyn, N. (2008). "Not necessarily a bad thing …": A study of online plagiarism amongst undergraduate students. *Assessment & Evaluation in Higher Education, 33*, 465–479.

13 A Practical Guide to Using YouTube in the Classroom

Mandy Cleveland

Incorporating video clips from YouTube into classroom lecture is a simple and interesting way to enhance student engagement and promote class discussion. Fortunately, YouTube has videos about a countless array of topics, which makes it easy to find one that applies to a lecture. Perhaps because so many videos are available, they can be overused. Videos should not be a substitute for classroom lecture or discussion; instead, video clips should be a supplement. When preparing lectures, I am careful to ask myself if the video expands on what I am teaching. If the video is nothing more than a funny or interesting diversion (even though it still might be related to my topic) I do not use it. In fact, I explain to my class why I am using a YouTube clip and what I expect to accomplish with it. In general, I incorporate YouTube clips into my teaching approximately once every 2 weeks, but as often as once a week may work.

The first goal of this chapter is to explain what YouTube is and how it can be incorporated into classroom lecture. Research has found that the reasons educators most commonly cite for not using online-based technology are a lack of training and the perception that incorporating technology is time-consuming (Vodanovich & Piotrowski, 2001). By providing explanation and instruction about the use of YouTube in the classroom, I hope to make educators more comfortable incorporating it. This chapter will also describe the potential benefits and limitations of using YouTube in the classroom, and finally I will provide educators with a list of helpful YouTube hints.

A Description of YouTube

YouTube is a Web site for the uploading, sharing, and viewing of videos coded in Adobe Flash format. It was founded in February 2005 and officially launched in December 2005 (YouTube, 2009). Less than one year later, it was purchased by Google, Inc. When YouTube was first created, the site experienced difficulty as a result of copyrighted material being posted by its users. In an effort to correct these problems, YouTube has created partnership agreements with many content providers, such as CBS, BBC, Universal Music Group, Sony Music Group, Warner Music Group, and the NBA (YouTube, 2009). YouTube reserves the right to pull any video that violates its terms of agreement, such as videos that contain copyrighted or offensive material. However, due to the extremely large volume of videos on YouTube, monitoring the content of all videos is difficult. Hundreds of thousands of videos are uploaded to YouTube each day, and hundreds of millions of videos are viewed each day (YouTube, 2009). With the proper equipment, anyone can create a video and upload to YouTube, as long as the video is shorter than 10 minutes.

YouTube Content

YouTube contains a wide variety of videos from many sources. Some of the videos are user-generated content, and some are from other sources. User-generated videos are those that are created and uploaded by registered users of YouTube. These types of videos are often filmed on webcams, cell-phone cameras, or handheld video cameras. User-generated videos include almost anything that someone felt the desire to place on the Internet; therefore, it is important to note that YouTube does have some regulations about what can be posted on the site. For example, nudity is not allowed; however, it often takes some time for this type of content to be removed after it is posted. Although many user-generated videos are unlikely to be useful for educational purposes, some are excellent. For example, some videos created for class projects by high school and college students are of very good quality and cover a wide variety of topics.

Videos on YouTube from outside sources include news programs, sit-coms, documentaries, music videos, comedy performances, and many other television shows. Almost any type of TV show can be found on YouTube. Because clips on YouTube cannot be longer than 10 minutes, longer videos are broken into segments, and these segments are often numbered to make them easier to locate.

Finally, YouTube contains many videos and video recreations of well-known psychological studies that used to be available only on bulky VHS tapes. For example, video of Stanley Milgram's study on obedience (Milgram, 1963), Solomon Asch's study on conformity (Asch, 1955), Albert Bandura's study of social learning (the Bobo Doll Study; Bandura, Ross, & Ross, 1961), and Philip Zimbardo's (Haney, Banks, & Zimbardo, 1973) Stanford prison study (or accurate recreations) can all be found on YouTube. Although specific Web addresses may change, a search with relevant terms usually locates classic studies. Incorporating these videos into YouTube allows instructors to expose their students to these important studies while using a modern form of media familiar to their students.

Why Use YouTube in the Classroom?

The main goal of teaching is to help students recall, understand, and apply course material. In pursuit of this goal, countless teaching methods have been used, and technology has continually been incorporated to create new, and ideally better, teaching techniques. Incorporating new technology into existing teaching techniques can help keep students more interested and engaged, perhaps improving their learning experience.

Cleveland (2008) surveyed undergraduate students' attitudes toward YouTube. YouTube videos were incorporated into a PowerPoint-based lecture, and students reported very favorable perceptions of the use of YouTube in the classroom. Ninety-four percent of the students surveyed indicated that they believed the incorporation of YouTube into the PowerPoint lecture either improved or somewhat improved their overall experience in the class (Cleveland, 2008). Seventy-three percent of students indicated that they believed it increased or somewhat increased their level of participation in class discussions. Almost 89% of students polled indicated that they believed it increased or somewhat increased their level of comprehension of the material being presented. Lastly, three quarters of the students indicated that they believed YouTube increased or somewhat increased their ability to recall the material that was being presented.

Using YouTube in the Classroom

With new videos posted daily, a virtually endless supply of videos is available on YouTube. To locate a relevant video, go to www.youtube.com and enter the search terms of interest. The process for searching for a video on YouTube is similar to searching through an Internet search engine such as Google. YouTube will provide suggested spellings as the search term is typed. After the search terms have been entered, a list of videos that match the terms will be presented. This list will sometimes be quite long, which can make it difficult to find the desired video. Just as with any other type of search, narrowing the search terms is often helpful. YouTube also provides some other ways to narrow a search, such as using the time the video was uploaded (i.e., today, this week, this month). To use this method of sorting, place the cursor over the word *uploaded* (located under the search box) and choose the appropriate time frame from the pull-down menu. This feature can be helpful when searching for videos of recent news stories. Videos can also be sorted by the number of people who have viewed them. This feature can be helpful in locating popular videos. To use this feature, place the curser over the words *Sort by: Relevance* (also located under the search box) and choose *view count* from the pull-down menu.

YouTube videos can also be located by doing a video search through a regular Internet search engine (e.g., Google, Yahoo!). The advantage to this type of search is that it will result in videos from video-streaming sites other than YouTube. Obviously, YouTube is not the only video-streaming site on the Internet; however, at this time it does seem to be the most comprehensive. In other words, some of the videos located on YouTube can be found on other video streaming sites, but almost all of the videos on other sites can be found on YouTube.

Incorporating Videos into PowerPoint Presentations

Video clips from YouTube can be incorporated directly into PowerPoint presentations by simply cutting and pasting the link to the desired video into a PowerPoint slide. Placing the video link into the PowerPoint ahead of time allows the instructor to go directly from a PowerPoint presentation to a video clip on YouTube. Advanced users can embed a Shockwave Flash object into the PowerPoint slide so the YouTube video will play in PowerPoint without having to view the video in a web browser. Because many colleges and universities require individuals to log on before accessing the Internet, it is helpful to make sure that you are logged on prior to beginning the lecture. This simple step saves time and makes the transition from PowerPoint to video seamless.

Including links to YouTube videos in PowerPoint presentations also allows students to view those videos on their own time if the PowerPoint presentation is posted (see Chapter 6 in this volume). This was not possible with more traditional ways of showing videos in class (e.g., DVDs, VHS tapes). Having the videos continually available is helpful to students who have missed class as well as students who are reviewing for exams.

YouTube Features

YouTube provides several advanced features that can be useful to instructors who use videos in the classroom. For example, YouTube allows users to create playlists (a group of favorite videos) that can be organized by course or topic. After a playlist is created, it can be shared with others. For example, colleagues who teach similar courses can share relevant videos with each other. Individual videos can also be e-mailed to others. Many (though not all) videos on YouTube can be downloaded and saved for future use.

Although a YouTube account is necessary to use the advanced features, no account is necessary to view videos. However, creating a YouTube account is easy and free. Signing up requires only an e-mail address, new password, postal code, date of birth, and gender. This process can be completed in about 2 minutes.

To create a playlist, simply click on +*Playlists* (located directly under the video screen) during or after watching a video. A pull-down menu will then appear, labeled *Add to Playlist*. This menu allows the current video to be added to an existing playlist (by clicking on the name of that playlist from the pull-down menu) or begin a new playlist (by clicking on *[New Playlist]* and typing in a new playlist name). Playlists are an easy way to organize videos, particularly when you have located many of interest to you.

To share a playlist, click on *Account*. Then click on *Playlists*. Next, select the desired playlist from the list of playlists at the left side of the screen. After the desired playlist is selected, click on *Share This Playlist*. Next, a small screen will pop up. Enter the e-mail address (or addresses) of the colleague with whom you would like to share the playlist and then click *Send*. A personal message about the playlist can also be included.

Downloading videos from YouTube is also very simple. When the cursor is placed over the upper right-hand corner of the video screen (when the video is not expanded), a download tab will appear if you have RealPlayer installed. Click on this tab to download the video. Other free downloading tools are available. Downloading allows instructors to save videos from YouTube and show them in environments where Internet access is not available or where the connection is not fast enough to show videos, although teachers should be aware of potential copyright issues.

Illustrative Examples for the Classroom

I have used many YouTube videos in the classroom and regularly search for relevant clips to update lectures. In this section, a few brief examples will be provided, including showing videos on health issues; sexual, racial, and cultural diversity; as well as political beliefs outside of the United States.

Health discussions often include the dangers of tobacco use and programs designed to prevent or discontinue tobacco use. During PowerPoint lectures on these topics, videos of current antismoking advertisements and videos of classic tobacco advertisements have a strong impact. Antismoking commercials can be viewed to promote discussion about the effectiveness of current programs. Classic tobacco advertisements can add an interesting perspective to the discussion because most students have never seen a commercial promoting the use of cigarettes (some of these older ads even have doctors endorsing a particular brand of cigarettes). Both types of videos can be found by searching YouTube for *antismoking advertisements* and *classic cigarette commercials*.

Clips of current news videos are also readily available on YouTube and can be used to demonstrate how a particular current event relates to issues such as sexism and racism. For example, media coverage of female political candidates can offer a powerful introduction to a discussion about sexism in current society. A similar approach can be taken to discuss racism; for instance, stories illustrating the continuing presence of racism in our society are readily available. Often, providing students with concrete current examples is much more powerful than reciting statistics about the current prevalence of various types of stereotyping and discrimination. Using search terms related to the specific news story or political candidate will easily locate these types of clips.

As another potential YouTube application, videos of advertisements from different countries illustrate cultural differences. For example, advisements for contraceptives from various countries can be viewed when discussing the different perspectives on sexuality held by various cultures.

Cultural and political differences are found in video clips posted by individuals in different countries. The recent protests of the Iranian election are an excellent example of this; during the protests, average citizens posted videos of their situation on YouTube. These videos could be used to discuss the relative freedoms that people experience in different countries and citizens' responses to their cultural/political climate.

Some Limitations of Using YouTube

As with any type of technology, YouTube has limitations. The sheer volume of videos on YouTube makes it difficult for inappropriate content to be removed immediately by the Web site. This lag time means that users of YouTube will sometimes inadvertently be exposed to inappropriate content. Similarly, YouTube offers videos similar to the one you have chosen. Even though you would not choose an inappropriate video, similar videos may contain offensive content. Even if the link to the desired video is placed into the PowerPoint presentation in advance, when the link is activated, the desired video will not be full screen; the instructor must click on an icon to make the video larger. In the time it takes to enlarge the video, the opening screen shot of similar videos will be visible on the right-hand corner of the screen. If, for example, the selected video is related to sexuality (this category can include documentaries as well as news stories and commercials), the related videos may be somewhat risqué. Obviously, high-school instructors may find this to be more of an issue than college instructors.

The open nature of YouTube also means that the same video often gets posted multiple times. Different postings of the same video are of varying levels of quality, and it can take some time to find the best-quality posting of the desired video. Sometimes even the best available video is not of very good quality. This low quality can be frustrating; however, because students are familiar with YouTube, they seem to be used to the occasional poor-quality video. In other words, even a less-than-perfect video is acceptable to most students and can still have educational value.

Two additional annoyances for some people are spelling errors and advertisements. Although YouTube does provide suggested spellings for search terms, it does not spell check the items that are posted. As a result, if the individual who posted the video you are looking for spelled words incorrectly, the video will be difficult to locate. The YouTube user must also put up with advertisements on the page. Because YouTube is free, advertisements fund the Web site. Although some people find the presence of ads annoying, the ads in no way interfere with the functioning of the site (i.e., they do not interrupt the videos).

The most frustrating limitation of YouTube is the fact the content is often removed or relocated on the Web site. This minor annoyance means that the links from last semester's PowerPoint presentation might not work this semester. I strongly recommend that instructors check old links to make sure that they are still active prior to giving a lecture or leading a class discussion where YouTube is used. Most of the time, the video can be found again. However, to avoid potential relocation problems, I recommend that instructors download and save all videos that they plan to use in the future (one of the decided benefits of the aforementioned playlists).

Beyond YouTube: Other Video-Sharing Web Sites

In addition to YouTube, other video-sharing sites are available on the Internet. If a video cannot be located on YouTube, simply conduct a Google search for the desired video. One relatively recent Web site called hulu.com provides a large number of full-length TV shows and movies. The site offers an improvement over the 10-minute YouTube clips. However, hulu.com does not, at present, seem to provide as wide a range of media as is available on YouTube. Due to the popularity of YouTube, additional sites likely will continue to emerge.

Table 13.1

Helpful Guidelines for Incorporating Film Clips into Classes

1. Be logged on to the Internet before class so there is no delay.
2. Choose only clips that expand on what is being taught in the class.
3. Do not overuse YouTube clips.
   - It is rarely useful to show more than one per class.
   - YouTube clips should not be shown during every class period.
4. Check links prior to class to make sure that they are still active.
5. Download clips that you think you will use later, but be mindful of copyright issues.
6. Use your YouTube account to share videos with colleagues.
7. Remember that like any other Web site, YouTube is continually being updated, so it is advisable to familiarize yourself with any changes made to the format of the site.

Summary

Teachers have long used video clips to illustrate concepts and engage students. YouTube and other video-sharing software offer a convenient way to bring brief videos into the classroom. Many students spend their spare time watching YouTube videos, which indicates that it is something that is familiar and well liked. Teachers can enhance the learning experience by embracing the technology that students have already chosen.

References

Asch, S. E., (1955). Opinions and social pressure. *Scientific American, 19,* 31–35.

Bandura, A., Ross, D., & Ross, S. (1961). Transmission of aggression through imitation of aggressive models. *Journal of Abnormal and Social Psychology, 63,* 575–582.

Cleveland, M. J. (2008, October). *Students' perceptions of the incorporation of YouTube into classroom lecture.* Paper presented at the Getting Connected: Best Practices in Technology-Enhanced Teaching and Learning Psychology Conference, Atlanta, GA.

D'Angelo, J. M., & Woosley, S. A. (2007). Technology in the classroom: Friend or foe. *Education, 127,* 462–470.

Haney, C., Banks, W. C., & Zimbardo, P. G. (1973). Interpersonal dynamics in a simulated prison. *International Journal of Criminology and Penology, 1,* 69–97.

Milgram, S. (1963). Behavioral study of obedience. *Journal of Abnormal and Social Psychology, 67,* 371–378.

YouTube Company History (2009). Retrieved April 15, 2009, from YouTube. Broadcast Yourself Web site: http://www.youtube.com/t/about

Vodanovich, S. J., & Piotrowski, C. (2001). Internet-based instruction: A national survey of psychology faculty. *Journal of Instructional Psychology, 28,* 253–255.

14 I Didn't Know I Could Do That

Using Web-Based Tools to Enhance Learning

Jorge Pérez and Kevin Hurysz

The World Wide Web provides ready access to many resources and tools that educators can leverage in the classroom. This chapter adopts a broad definition of online learning, and presents a host of Web-based resources and tools with which educators can engage students and enhance teaching and learning. We hope that educators in any discipline, working with students who have disparate capabilities, will have their interest piqued by these technologies and explore the links provided for more information and inspiration.

Online tools have been shown to engage students and enrich their educational experience. Implementation of technology in the classroom can have a positive influence, including increased student self-confidence and increased eagerness to learn (Kimble, 1999). There have been numerous books written to familiarize the educator with online instruction strategies. Richardson's (2008) *Blogs, Wikis, Podcasts, and Other Powerful Web Tools for Classrooms* and November's (2008) *Web Literacy for Educators* are two examples. Internet searches will reveal a wide array of ready-made resources that are free for the instructor to use in the classroom. A notable resource is the EDUCAUSE Learning Initiative's "7 things you should know about ..." series, available at http://www.educause.edu/Resources/Browse/ ELI7ThingsYouShouldKnow/33438, which summarizes online and offline technologies that can be used in the classroom. Additional technologies are regularly added to the database.

Young people today are already creating a wide variety of digital content recreationally, with web sites like Facebook, MySpace, and YouTube being prime repositories of their creativity. Preparing students for the working world entails more than content knowledge within their field of specialization. Once employed, some will be expected to use digital technologies to create a range of content—from documents, spreadsheets, and presentations to complex audio and video productions (Lippincott, 2007). The strategies presented here can be implemented in one of two ways: with either the instructor or the student as content creator.

A series of surveys conducted by the Pew Internet and American Life Project paint an interesting picture of user content creation on the World Wide Web. A survey by Lenhart, Horrigan, and Fallows (2003) found that 44% of adult Internet users had created content for the online world by building or posting to Web sites, creating blogs, and sharing files. Lenhart and Madden (2005) found that 57% of teens create content on the Internet—that is, these teens created a blog, created or worked on a personal Web page or a Web page for school, a friend, or an organization, shared original content such as artwork, photos, stories, or videos online, or remixed content found online into a new creation. An updated survey by Lenhart and Madden (2007) found that the proportion of teen content creators had grown to 64%.

Web-and-Flow Strategies

This section discusses *web-and-flow strategies* that entail different approaches to Web-based activities. The *topic hotlist*, the most basic instructional strategy, is ideally suited to novice Internet users. It is a collection of instructor-selected Web sites that serves to direct learner exploration in a particular area (March, 1999). The topic hotlist can be of any size and is usually offered as a list of hyperlinks given to the student to explore. A step beyond the topic hotlist is *scrapbooking*, where students visit Web sites and collect text and multimedia by cutting and pasting into a word processing or presentation program (Horton, 2000). Google offers an online scrapbooking tool at http://www.google.com/notebook. The *knowledge hunt*, sometimes called the scavenger or treasure hunt, leads the student to specific Web sites to answer factual questions drawn from the sites and written by the instructor.

Higher-level thinking can be promoted by posing an essential synthesis question at the conclusion of the hunt (Star, 1999). For example, a knowledge hunt about the planets and moons in our solar system might conclude with a question about which places in the solar system might support life and why.

March (1999) suggests other activities, including the *subject sampler*, in which a series of Web sites focused on a topic is presented and the student responds to the subject from a personal, affective perspective. In the *insight reflector*, Web sites are selected and presented to evoke an emotional response, and the student is prompted to engage in reflective writing. In the *concept builder*, higher-level thinking is encouraged by asking students to distill content found on several Web sites into new, cohesive concepts.

Dodge (1997) describes the *WebQuest* as an "inquiry-oriented activity in which most or all the information used by learners is drawn from the web." The Webquest.org (http://www.webquest.org) site has a large number of WebQuests available for free. WebQuests available on the site can be searched by curriculum and grade level. The WebQuest is made of a prescribed series of components that lead the learner to explore higher-level thinking, analysis, and problem-solving skills. The typical WebQuest has an introductory hook to capture the student's interest, an explanation of the task, a well-designed process through which the WebQuest is completed, an assessment rubric, the conclusion, and information for other instructors who might want to implement the WebQuest. Figure 14.1 shows screenshots from an example WebQuest on Johannes Kepler and his three laws of planetary motion.

Simulations

Simulations enable difficult-to-perform experiments to be conducted online and can be used to reinforce classroom concepts. Simulations, which permit identical experiments to be performed repetitively, are usually written in the Java programming language and can be used across a wide variety of operating system platforms. For example, ballistic motion is simulated at http://phet.colorado.edu/simulations/sims.php?sim=Projectile_Motion. In this simulation, a projectile can be launched at any angle or initial velocity and information about the launch obtained. The central limit theorem is simulated at http://www.stat.sc.edu/~west/javahtml/CLT.html, where one to five six-sided

Introduction

Johannes Kepler WebQuest

Toward the end of the 16th century, science in general and astronomy in particular were in a state of flux. New ideas were clashing with the cherished thoughts of Aristotle. One of these individuals with new ideas was a man named Johannes Kepler. Does the earth *circle* the sun? Why do the planets appear to do what they do the sky? Amongst other things, this Quest will yield the answers.

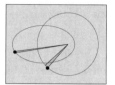

Two orbits with the same semi-major axis, focus and orbital period; one a circle with an eccentricity of 0.0; the other an ellipse with an accentricity of 0.8.

Image Source: NASA (Public domain)

Process

Johannes Kepler WebQuest

You will have only two 50 minute class periods to work on your poster, so use your time wisely and work efficiently.

In this quest, you and another one or two classmates–groups of 3 maximum–will be responsible for producing a one page mini-poster about Johannes Kepler, The page must be 8 1/2" x 11" (standard printer paper). This poster must:

• State the name "Johannes Kepler" and give a brief biosketch in words and pictures
• State Kepler's 1st law in words and a picture
• State Kepler's 2nd law in words and a picture
• State Kepler's 3rd law in words and an equation
• Fit on one side of a standard 8 1/2" x 11" piece of paper
• Feature proper citation of sources used
• Be something you understand. Don't put something into your poster if you don't know what it means.

While there is no minimum or maximum number of sources you must cite, if you choose Wikipedia as a source, you must have at least one additional corroborating source. For more information about citation, click "Resources" to the left.

It's hoped your poster will be aesthetically pleasing, but content is of paramount importance. You are free to format your poster however you wish–portrait or landscape, and arrangements on the poster is up to you. Use whatever software you like, Word, PowerPoint, Publisher, etc.

To get started, you should:

1. Choose one or two classmates to work with. Groups of 3 maximum.
2. Make sure you have read through the navigation links to the left. They will help you understand the goals and requirements of the Quest.
3. Designate roles. Someone might be a researcher, someone might be responsible for inputting information, someone might be responsible for design and formatting. You might consider using two computers if they are available.

Figure 14.1. Screenshots of a WebQuest on Johannes Kepler and his three laws of planetary motion. Above, the Introduction; below, the Process.

dice can be rolled 10,000 times with a single click of the mouse and the results shown in a histogram. There are online libraries dedicated to simulations. For example, the PhET project of the University of Colorado at http://phet.colorado.edu/index.php has simulations in physics, chemistry, biology, earth science, and mathematics.

Virtual field trips allow students to visit faraway or otherwise inaccessible locations without the time, expense, and inconvenience of travel. A good place to find resources is http://www.uen.org/utahlink/tours/. For an example, see the virtual tour of a violin-maker's shop at http://www.uen.org/utahlink/tours/tourFames.cgi?tour_id=13273.

Digital Photography and Video

Digital photography and video have become increasingly accessible to classroom use because of improvements in technology and affordability. Digital imaging can be used to document learning experiences. The images or video can then be incorporated into student work. Figure 14.2 shows digital photographs of everyday objects that contain elements of symmetry.

Many students today have a digital camera. Most students have a cell phone that incorporates a camera, and some cell phones even have video capability. Moreover, a number of compact, inexpensive video cameras are available. The Flip Mino and MinoHD video recorders (http://www.theflip.com/) are especially easy to use because they feature an integrated USB connection. Photographs and videos can be easily shared on the Web via a number of social networking sites. Flickr (http://www.flickr.com) is an online photo management and sharing tool. Student photographs can be quickly uploaded to these sites, and the sites can be searched for media that can be applied to student work. iREPORTS (http://www.cnn.com/video/) is a citizen media Web site to which students can upload brief videos that constitute news reports.

The images and videos found on Flickr and other Internet sources are subject to copyright and fair-use provisions of law. Creative Commons (http://creativecommons.org/) is a nonprofit organization that seeks to increase the amount of material "available to the public for free and legal sharing, use, repurposing, and remixing." Creative Commons is an excellent resource for material that can be used without copyright restrictions.

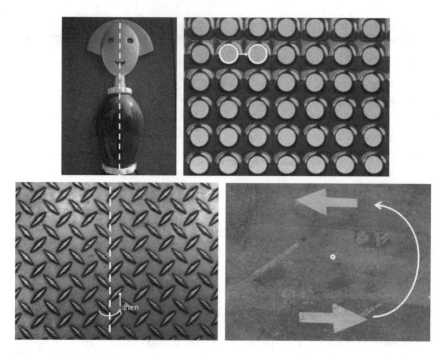

Figure 14.2. Digital photographs of everyday objects that exhibit elements of symmetry. Clockwise from upper left: reflection, translation, rotation, and glide reflection (a combination of reflection and translation).

Graphic Organizers

To focus on the connections between ideas, a graphic organizer—a tool used to create outlines that expand in all directions instead of linearly down a page—is useful for brainstorming or summarizing. For example, students in a biology class could begin with the main idea "animal" and create their own web of life by classifying a selection of animals or by researching their own list. Students can be directed to create a concept map from a single main idea or from an instructor-provided template designed to stimulate learning. The concept map shown in Figure 14.3 states Kepler's three laws of planetary motion in words. The concept map could be expanded by defining key terms such as "ellipse," "focus," and "period" or by using the laws to solve specific problems.

Software such as Inspiration (http://www.inspiration.com/Inspiration, education pricing, $69), which includes clip art and flexibility in the shape of

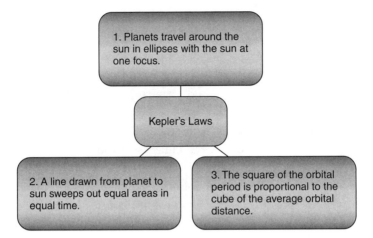

Figure 14.3. A simple concept map about Kepler's laws created using Bubbl.us (http://www.bubbl.us).

map components, can accomplish these tasks. Microsoft Office has some comparable functionality. There are also free online alternatives, such as Bubbl.us (http://www.bubbl.us), an intuitive Web application that allows users to create and collaborate on concept maps.

Wikis

"Wiki" is short for the Hawaiian *wiki-wiki,* which means "quick." Richardson (2008, p. 55) defines a wiki as "a web site where anyone can edit anything any time they want." Wikis are fertile ground for learning because the student can be made responsible for content creation. Wikispaces (http://www.wikispaces.com/) is a wiki hosting site that offers free and pay services. A wiki typically consists of a homepage containing links to content-rich pages. Options include the key to the wiki: "edit this page." The editing option allows users to create, delete, correct, or embed content. Any type of content can be posted to a wiki: written information, pictures, hyperlinks, and multimedia. Wikis can be set up in such a way that anyone can access and edit, or only those invited can access and edit. One way a wiki can be used in the classroom is in the collaborative writing and editing of an online class "textbook." Students can take the results of scrapbooking, digital photography, and video and create their own custom resource.

One of the most popular wikis, Wikipedia (http://www.wikipedia.com), is a tool that is well suited for instructional uses. In 2005, *Nature* carried out an expert-led, peer-reviewed, blind comparison of Wikipedia and the *Encyclopedia Britannica*. In the 42 entries evaluated, it was found that "the difference in accuracy was not significant: the average science entry in Wikipedia contained around four inaccuracies; Britannica, about 3" (Giles, 2005). Four serious errors were found in each encyclopedia. As such, Wikipedia is an area well suited to instructor exploration. As a teaching tool, instructors can have students write and post new articles, or critically review and edit the content of existing articles.

Blogs

A blog, short for "Web log," is a type of Web site for publishing of information that also permits asynchronous communication. Like wikis, blogs can be designed as learning environments through which electronic content can be posted. Students can post at any time, and posts can be updated with any frequency. The posts can then be searched, sorted, labeled, and archived. Blogging allows students to edit as much as necessary before posting, and even after they post. Anyone with little technical expertise can write a blog. Text can be cut-and-pasted into the publishing window and posted with one click. Microsoft Live Writer, (http://download.live.com/writer) a free desktop application, is a WYSIWYG (What You See Is What You Get) post editor that makes it easy to format and add rich multimedia.

An example of an effective classroom blogging technique is to use one for personal reflection on course material. Blogs may be set to allow commenting, which enables collaboration between classmates and interaction with the instructor. For the instructor, blogs have the advantage of providing a clear, chronological record of student progress over time that can be readily evaluated. Although blogs can be as formal as desired, they can be written conversationally, and permit students to use their own voice when they are writing about a topic.

Blogs can be hosted on a free or pay Web sites. Some of the most common are Blogger (http://www.blogger.com) and Wordpress (http://www.wordpress.com). These sites have different functionalities, outlined at http://pulsed.blogspot.com/2007/07/blogger-wordpress-chart.html. It is a good idea to have in mind what is to be accomplished with a blog before choosing one service over another.

RSS and Aggregators

RSS, or Real Simple Syndication, arose out of a difficulty in following blogs. Blog posts do not have to be made regularly, so somebody following a blog would have to visit the blog repeatedly to see if a new post had been made. As the reader follows more and more blogs, the task of finding new content increases in difficulty. By subscribing to a RSS feed for a blog, the follower can be alerted to new blog posts simply by launching a Web browser.

Many search engines exist that are specific to blogs, such as Technorati (http://www.technorati.com). By searching these sites, blogs with content relevant to the reader's interests can be discovered. The reader can then subscribe to the feed through an aggregator. Aggregators are applications that collect syndicated content on the Web and present it for easy viewing. Web sites like Bloglines (http://www.bloglines.com) and Google Reader (http://reader.google.com) take feeds chosen by the user and automatically update them.

Podcasts

Vincent (2009) describes podcasts as "a series of audio or video files on the Web that can be cataloged and automatically downloaded." Vincent's Web site at http://www.learninginhand.com has resources that help in the creation and distribution of podcasts. In its simplest sense, a podcast is a compressed audio file (usually an mp3 file) that is distributed using an RSS feed.

Plenty of podcasts are freely available. Similar to blogs, there are specific search engines that can be used to find podcasts. Learn Out Loud (http://www.learnoutloud.com/) is one example of a podcast search engine. Students can copy the address of a podcast into a podcasting application, such as Juice, freely available at http://juicereceiver.sourceforge.net/index.php. Podcast subjects are varied, from art history (http://feeds.feedburner.com/ArtHistoryPodcast) to zoology (http://bdown.astream.com/jzo_podcast_3.mp3). The free software iTunes (http://www.apple.com/itunes/) can also be used to search for, organize, and listen to podcasts. In the iTunes store under Podcasts, choose a subject area or search for podcasts, subscribe to those of interest, and the new episodes will download directly into iTunes each time it is launched. It is important to note that even though "pod" is part of the word "podcasting" and iTunes can be used for software, an iPod is not required. Only a computer capable of playing mp3 audio is necessary.

To produce a podcast, any computer equipped with a microphone can be used to record audio. The free audio recorder and editor Audacity (http://audacity.sourceforge.net/) can be used to produce the podcast, which can be submitted to the iTunes directory. Enhanced podcasts consisting of audio and images or video can also be created.

Screencasts

Screencasts are digital recordings of the computer video screen, described by Peterson (2007) as "recordings of a video of screen activities, including mouse movements and clicks." Screencasts rely on visual and audio cues and can also contain interactive features. They are quick to prepare and easy to update and change (Educause Connect, 2006). Screencasts are permanent and reusable. There are general collections of screencasts that can be searched (http://www.screencast.com) and subject specific sites (http://www.mathcasts.org) as well.

The screencast can cover course content, a particular problem, or a demonstration or can answer a student question. Sketching out the order of the presentation and preparing the narration can facilitate the screencasting process. Plan the screencast by storyboarding. While planning, identify software and hardware requirements. At a minimum, for hardware a desktop or laptop computer, a device to input your writing or drawing (e.g., Adesso CyberPad), and a microphone to record sound are required. Some tablet PCs come equipped with all of these devices. To enhance the screencast, additional equipment such as a digital still or video camera, a webcam, and appropriate memory cards and readers can be used. For software, Camtasia 6.0 (education pricing, $179) by TechSmith is a powerful and intuitive editing program. Jing from TechSmith (http://www.jingproject.com) is a free, easy-to-use alternative with less functionality.

Microsoft PowerPoint can be used to craft detailed backgrounds for screencasts. The Adesso CyberPad comes bundled with Power Presenter, software that in conjunction with PowerPoint allows writing to be captured by the computer. Recording and assembling the screencast can be done in takes, all at once, or written, filmed, and narrated separately, whichever is easiest for the situation. Editing can be accomplished in Camtasia and the screencast produced in Windows Media Format, iPod video, and a variety of other popular formats. The screencast can then be electronically delivered to the student. Figure 14.4 shows the end result of a 5-minute-long screencast on graphing the motion of two objects simultaneously.

Research has shown that students generally enjoy screencasts used to augment classroom learning. Pinder-Grover, Millunchick, and Bierwert (2008) used screencasts in a traditional Materials Science and Engineering class. Of 144 enrolled students, 72 responded to a term-end survey. A majority of the respondents viewed almost all the screencasts and found them helpful.

Instructors have also recorded entire lectures as screencasts. Winterbottom (2007) placed entire screencast lectures for a second-year university Environmental Science module in Earth and Landscape Evolution online

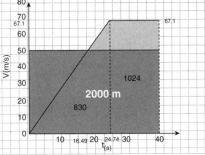

Roscoe is driving a Dodge Magnum custom-equipped with a police pursuit package that includes a HEMI engine with cold air induction and a Borla exhaust system. It is capable of accelerating uniformly from 0 to 100 mph (44.7 m/s) in 16.49 s and can continue this uniform acceleration up to its maximum speed of 150 mph (67.1 m/s). Will the Duke boys finally be caught? of course not...!

area of Δ = ½ bh

$\qquad$ (1/2)(24.74)(67.1) = 830m

area of $\square$ = bh
$\qquad$ (15.26)(67.1) = 1024m
$\qquad\qquad\qquad$ $\overline{\quad\quad 1854m}$

Figure 14.4. The end result of a 5-minute-long screencast on graphing the motion of two objects simultaneously.

using the WebCT platform. When asked if they liked having lectures delivered in this way, "85% of the students responded positively, while 8% were ambivalent, and 7% responded negatively. When asked if they would like more lectures delivered in this way, 76% responded that they would" (p. 7).

Google Apps

Google in particular deserves special mention for the free tools it has created that can be used to encourage online collaboration. A complete list of tools and their descriptions can be found at http://www.google.com/options/. An annotated list can be found in Table 14.1.

Table 14.1

A Selection of Free Tools Offered by Google that Can Be Used in Education

Google Tool	Description
Blogger	Blog hosting site
Books	Search books
Custom Search	Create your own search engine
Docs	Collaborate on documents, spreadsheets, presentations
Earth	Explore the Earth virtually
Groups	Create discussion groups
iGoogle	Personalize your Google homepage
Knol	Read expert-authored articles on topics
Notebook	Create an online scrapbook
Patents	Search U.S. patents
Picasa	Host pictures
Reader	Aggregator
Scholar	Search scholarly papers
Sites	Create a Web site or wiki and control who can edit it
Sky	Explore the night sky, the moon, and Mars virtually
Translate	View Web pages in or translate Web pages to other languages
Video	Share and view video

Teach Web 2.0

Advances in Web technologies that facilitate communication and interactivity are collectively referred to as Web 2.0. A community of educators and other interested parties is engaged in the ongoing process of collecting Web 2.0 applications from the Internet and evaluating them for how they can be used in educational settings. The Teach Web 2.0 wiki at (http://teachweb2.wiki-spaces.com/) is constantly updated with new tools. The self-stated goal of the site is to research Web 2.0 tools and social networking Web sites, to identify strengths, weaknesses, opportunities, and threats associated with these tools, and to brainstorm effective, appropriate educational applications of each tool (Teach Web 2.0, 2009).

Conclusion

There are numerous resources and tools on the World Wide Web that educators can use to engage students and enhance teaching. We provided examples of how educators can leverage a number of Web-based teaching tools. Some educators might not even be able to imagine teaching today *without* using the Web, if only to make readings available, interact with students, or deliver lectures asynchronously. Regardless of the degree to which educators incorporate Web-based tools, one might say that for most educators, teaching *sans* the Web is a thing of the past.

Suggested Readings

Educause Connect (2009). 7 things you should know … Retrieved May 8, 2009 from Educause Learning Initiative Web site: http://www.educause.edu/Resources/Browse/ELI7ThingsYouShouldKnow/33438

Khan, B. H. (2000). Discussion of resources and attributes of the Web for the creation of meaningful learning environments. *CyberPsychology & Behavior, 3*, 17–23.

Relan, B., & Gillami, A. (1997). Incorporating interactivity and multimedia into web-based instruction. In: B. H. Khan (ed.), Web-based instruction (pp. 231–237). Englewood Cliffs, NJ: Educational Technology Publications.

References

Dodge, B. (1997). Some thoughts about WebQuests. Retrieved May 8, 2009, from the WebQuest home page: http://webquest.sdsu.edu/about_webquests.html

Educause Connect (2006). 7 things you should know about screencasting. Retrieved March 19, 2009, from Educause Connect Web site: http://net.educause.edu/ir/library/pdf/ELI7012.pdf

Giles, J. (2005). Internet encyclopaedias go head to head. *Nature, 438*, 900–901.

Horton, W. (2000). *Designing Web-based training*. New York: John Wiley & Sons.

Kimble, C. (1999). The impact of technology on learning: Making sense of research. Aurora, CO: Mid-Continent Regional Educational Laboratory. (ERIC Document Reproduction Service Number ED450723)

Lenhart, A., Horrigan, J., & Fallows, D. (2004). *Content creation online*. Washington, DC: Pew Internet & American Life Project. Retrieved March 20, 2008, from http://www.pewinternet.org/~/media/Files/Reports/2004/PIP_Content_Creation_Report.pdf.pdf

Lenhart, A., & Madden, M.(2005). *Teen content creators and consumers*. Washington, DC: Pew Internet & American Life Project. Retrieved March 20, 2008, from http://www.pewinternet.org/~/media/Files/Reports/2005/PIP_Teens_Content_Creation.pdf.pdf

Lenhart, A., & Madden, M. (2007). *Teens and social media*. Washington, DC: Pew Internet & American Life Project. Retrieved March 20, 2008, from http://www.pewinternet.org/~/media/Files/Reports/2007/PIP_Teens_Social_Media_Final.pdf.pdf

Lippincott, J. (2007). Student content creators: Convergence of literacies. *EDUCAUSE Review, November/December*, 16–17.

March, T. (1999). The six Web-and-Flow activity formats. Retrieved May 8, 2009, from http://www.web-and-flow.com/help/formats.asp.

November, A. (2008). *Web literacy for educators*. Thousand Oaks, CA: Corwin Press.

Peterson, E. (2007). Incorporating screencasts in online teaching. Retrieved March 18, 2009, from http://www.irrodl.org/index.php/irrodl/article/viewArticle/495/935

Pinder-Grover, T., Millunchick, J., & Bierwert, C. (2008). Work in progress: Using screencasts to enhance student learning in a large lecture material science and engineering course. Retrieved March 19, 2009, from http://fie-conference.org/fie2008/papers/1362.pdf

Richardson, W. (2008). Blogs, wikis, podcasts, and other powerful web tools for classrooms. Thousand Oaks, CA: Corwin Press.

Star, L. (1999). Scavenger hunts: Searching for treasure on the Internet. Education World. Retrieved May 8, 2009, from http://www.education-world.com/a_curr/curr113.shtml.

Teach Web 2.0. (2009). Teach 2.0 web wiki. Retrieved May 13, 2009, from http://teachweb2.wikispaces.com/

Vincent, T. (2009, April). *Podcasting for teachers and students.* Retrieved May 13, 2009, from http://www.learninginhand.com/podcasting/Podcasting_Booklet.pdf

Winterbottom, S. (2007). Virtual lecturing: Delivering lectures using screencasting and podcasting technology. Retrieved March 31, 2009, from http://citeseerx.ist.psu.edu/viewdoc/download?doi=10.1.1.125.4869&rep=rep1&type=pdf

15 Think Fast

Using Web-Based Reaction Time Technology to

Promote Teaching about Racial Bias and Diversity

Kathryn A. Morris, Leslie Ashburn-Nardo, and Robert J. Padgett

"Is it a gun? Is it a knife? Is it a wallet? This is your life."

When singer/songwriter Bruce Springsteen (2001) first sang these lyrics on stage in New York City, he was using his popularity as a musician to raise consciousness about racial bias. His lyrics refer to a 1999 incident in which New York City police officers knocked on the door of Amadou Diallo, a Black immigrant from West Africa. As Diallo reached into his breast pocket, police officers shot him 41 times. The investigation later revealed that Diallo had no criminal record and the object he was reaching for was his wallet, not a gun.

The officers involved in this incident faced the same dilemma many police officers face: they have a split second to determine whether a suspect is armed and to respond accordingly. We know from decades of social cognition research (e.g., Sagar & Schofield, 1980) that Diallo's race likely played a role in the officers' interpretations of his ambiguous behavior (i.e., reaching in his breast pocket), and ultimately led the officers to guess that he was about to wield a weapon.

Although most people do not encounter dilemmas as consequential as those faced by police officers, people nonetheless encounter situations that require split-second decisions. Just as race may have played a role in the police officers' decision regarding how to approach Amadou Diallo, race also may influence split-second decisions people face in their daily lives. For example, a woman walking alone down a city street must quickly decide whether to cross to the other side when an unknown man approaches her; the race of that man may affect her decision unwittingly. Likewise, a student may have only a moment to decide whether to invite a classmate to join a study group; unbeknownst to the student, the classmate's race may be a factor.

Decisions that require people to "think fast" are particularly likely to be affected by implicit racial biases—biases that occur outside of conscious awareness. When given sufficient time, people involved in interracial interactions can consciously monitor their behavior toward someone of another race and, if they are so motivated, behave in an egalitarian manner. Under time pressure, however, people are likely to be influenced by their automatic biases (for a review, see Macrae & Bodenhausen, 2000). Thus, the police officers in the Diallo case, the woman being approached by an unknown man, and the student making a decision about a fellow classmate, all of whom must make a quick decision, may be influenced by implicit biases against Blacks. As a result, the police officers may have been more likely to fire at a Black suspect, the woman may be more likely to cross the street when a Black man approaches her, and the student may be less likely to invite a Black student to join the study group.

Although psychologists have done much to increase our understanding of implicit biases and their impact on behavior, they have devoted less attention to helping teachers convey information about such biases to students. Despite the fact that many individual faculty members endorse the value of a diverse academic environment (Simoni, Sexton-Radek, Yescavage, Richard, & Lundquist, 1999), addressing racial or other diversity issues in the classroom can be challenging (Kowalski, 2000). For example, when contemplating the inclusion of racial bias and diversity issues into their classes, teachers may anticipate experiencing personal or student discomfort upon leading instruction on such a highly charged subject, especially if they have not taught about diversity issues in the past. Teachers also may not feel personal responsibility for addressing diversity issues in their classrooms, particularly if they are not, themselves, "diverse" (e.g., a member of a racial, ethnic, gender, religious, or sexual minority group). In addition, faculty who teach courses where diversity issues do not fit naturally (e.g., research methods and statistics; but see Woolf & Hulsizer, 2007) may feel that it is not their job to discuss diversity issues in their classrooms, or they may find it difficult to do so. Finally, because racism is viewed more negatively and is more emotionally charged than sexism (Fiske & Stevens, 1993), teachers may be particularly concerned about initiating a classroom dialogue about race.

We propose that Web-based reaction time technology can be a viable avenue through which psychology teachers can provide meaningful instruction about and discussion of implicit racial biases and diversity in their classrooms—even in classes that do not directly focus on diversity issues. Specifically, we discuss two engaging reaction time demonstration tasks that utilize Web-based technology: the Implicit Association Test and the Police Officer's Dilemma demonstrations. In both of these tasks, the technology teaches students about content relevant to the courses in which they are used. In addition, because these tasks require students to make judgments about Black and White target persons and provide feedback about students' performance, they afford instructors who use them an opportunity to discuss the split-second decisions people make about members of racial minority groups and the real-life consequences of those decisions.

The Implicit Association Test

The Implicit Association Test (IAT; Greenwald, McGhee, & Schwartz, 1998) is a computerized dual categorization task in which participants use a standard keyboard to indicate category membership for two stimuli that are presented using a Web browser interface. In the Race IAT, for example, participants categorize faces as Black or White and also categorize words as Pleasant or Unpleasant. For some trials, the categories *Black* and *Pleasant* share a response key and the categories *White* and *Unpleasant* share a different response key. On remaining trials, the reverse pairings occur (i.e., *Black* and *Unpleasant* share a response key while *White* and *Pleasant* share a response key). The computer program records categorization response times and researchers use response latencies to infer implicit associations. To the extent that a given participant is faster to respond when Black and Unpleasant share a response key and White and Pleasant share a different response key relative to reverse pairings (i.e., Black and Pleasant; White and Unpleasant sharing response keys), researchers infer that the participant has an implicit preference for Whites relative to Blacks.

Although the IAT has been widely used by academic researchers in laboratory studies (for a review, see Greenwald, Poehlman, Uhlmann, & Banaji, 2009), it also has become available more broadly through the educational Web site Project Implicit (https://implicit.harvard.edu/implicit/). Any Web user may visit the site and complete one of the dozen or so IATs included on the site. Millions of individuals have visited the Web site (over 10 million since 1998; Greenwald, 2009), in part due to media attention from television coverage on Dateline NBC, The Discovery Channel, and CNN. Individual users are provided with detailed instructions prior to beginning one of the tests. Upon completion of a test, they receive individualized feedback indicating the extent to which their reaction time performance suggests that they have implicit biases. In the Race IAT, for example, participants are classified as having a strong, moderate, or weak automatic preference for Black people relative to White people; a strong, moderate, or weak automatic preference for White people relative to Black people; little to no automatic preference; or inconclusive results (too many errors to compute a result). Results are accompanied by a bar graph showing the frequency of IAT takers who score in each category. Thus, people who take the Race IAT demonstration test learn about their own degree of implicit racial bias and where they stand relative to the rest of the IAT-taking population.

The public nature of the IAT demonstration site makes it ideal for psychology instructors because they can assign students to take the IAT demonstration either in class (if classrooms are appropriately equipped with computers) or outside of class. Instructors can then compile the students' results (e.g., tally up the number of students who showed evidence of automatic preference for White people relative to Black people) and present those aggregate results to the class, which can then lead to a discussion about implicit biases and diversity issues. For example, teachers may discuss with their students basic social cognitive issues, including the nature of implicit versus explicit cognition and the behaviors that implicit and explicit biases predict. Teachers can also use the IAT demonstration as a jumping-off point to address broader racial diversity issues, such as the role of implicit biases in daily interactions between Whites and Blacks, as well as overcoming implicit biases. Indeed, the majority of White students who take the Race IAT demonstration test likely have explicit egalitarian self-concepts (see Henry, 2008) but will learn that they have some degree of implicit bias against Blacks (as most Whites do; see Nosek, Banaji, & Greenwald, 2002). Instructors, therefore, can explain how disappointment in one's results on the IAT test can motivate students to do their best to overcome any implicit biases they may harbor (see Monteith, Voils, & Ashburn-Nardo, 2001).

Some instructors may feel hesitant to ask students to complete the Race IAT. These hesitancies may be fueled by recent criticisms of the IAT. Blanton and Jaccard (2006), for example, recently asserted (albeit based on anecdotal evidence) that classroom use of the IAT may result in undue distress among test-takers (e.g., if the feedback they receive is inconsistent with their [explicitly] egalitarian attitudes). Inspired by our own positive experiences using the IAT demonstration in class, but aware of Blanton and Jaccard's criticism, we (Morris & Ashburn-Nardo, 2010) tested the extent to which an IAT assignment results in positive and negative affective reactions, both immediately after completing the IAT and later on. We also measured students' perceptions of their own and others' implicit biases and their understanding of implicit social cognitive concepts.

In our study, students from two different institutions that draw from very different student populations completed a pre-test at the beginning of the semester in social psychology courses. In this pre-test, students indicated their perceptions of their own and others' implicit biases against Blacks. Later in the semester, just before we began the section of the course on stereotyping and prejudice, we assigned the Race IAT demonstration test as an out-of-class assignment. We provided students with instructions on how to find and use the IAT demonstration Web site and asked them to complete an affect scale immediately after completing the test and receiving their results. We then spent the next several class periods lecturing about stereotyping and prejudice, and used the IAT demonstration and aggregated class results to facilitate classroom discussions. About one week after we finished this section of the course, we asked students to complete a post-test, in which they again reported their positive and negative affect regarding the IAT demonstration, completed the same items as in the pre-test to measure their perceptions of their own and others' implicit biases against Blacks and several items to test their understanding of implicit social cognition.

After taking the Race IAT, 86% percent of our students learned that they harbored some degree of implicit bias against Blacks. This percentage is comparable to that obtained in laboratory IAT studies with samples of White college students (e.g., Monteith et al., 2001). Furthermore, consistent with Blanton and Jaccard's (2006) concerns, our students did experience some negative affect immediately after receiving their results. However, they reported *more positive* than negative affect both immediately after receiving their IAT results and several weeks later, when reflecting on the exercise. In addition, at the post-test, students reported that they perceived themselves and others as having stronger implicit biases than they did during the pre-test. Finally, at the post-test, students had more knowledge of implicit processes than they had at the pre-test (though we cannot disentangle the effects of the IAT demonstration itself from the accompanying lecture material and classroom discussion).

Several aspects of these findings are worth noting. First, because we collected data from two institutions that draw from different student populations (small, private, residential university and large, public, commuter university), used different textbooks, did not standardize our lecture material, and have replicated our findings in subsequent semesters (replication data are not included in our 2010 study), our results are likely high in external validity. We argue that if instructors place the Race IAT demonstration in a broader educational context in which they discuss the meaning of the results (i.e., that having an implicit bias does not mean that you hate African Americans), then using the demonstration should not result in undue distress and students will learn from the experience. Second, because compunction (i.e., negative self-directed affect like guilt and self-criticism, which students experienced to some degree after receiving their IAT results) enhances motivation to control prejudice (Monteith, 1993; Monteith, Ashburn-Nardo, Voils, & Czopp, 2002), any negative affect students feel after taking the Race IAT may serve as a consciousness-raising experience that propels them to monitor future behaviors in mixed-race situations. Finally, because the IAT demonstration requires only a standard Web browser and Internet access, it is easy to incorporate as an assignment to complement classroom instruction.

The IAT is but one example of user-friendly, Web-based technology that can serve as a springboard for discussions about racial diversity in psychology courses. Another engaging, and arguably more realistic, Web-based demonstration, the Police Officer's Dilemma, can likewise be used to facilitate discussions about racial diversity. In the section below, we describe how we have used the Police Officer's Dilemma demonstration in a research methodology course not only to teach students about signal detection theory but also to create opportunities for the discussion of racial diversity issues.

The Police Officer's Dilemma

We have used a modified version of the Police Officer's Dilemma task (Correll, Park, Judd, & Wittenbrink, 2002) as a method for incorporating discussions of race and racial bias into our classroom teaching. In the Police Officer's Dilemma (POD) task, students use a standard Web browser to view a series of background images in which a target person appears in the foreground holding an object. In the POD, the student's task is to indicate, using one of two keys on the keyboard, whether the object in the target's hand is a gun or an innocuous object (e.g., a cell phone). Like the IAT, targets vary in terms of their race, but unlike the IAT, in the POD participants are not informed of this before beginning the task, nor are they asked to identify targets as Black or White. Participants in the POD are simply asked to identify quickly and accurately whether or not the target is holding a gun.

We have used the POD task as a laboratory exercise in a general research methods course when covering material on reaction time and signal detection methodologies. Because our primary goal for using this task was to enhance our instruction of signal detection methodology (Wickens, 2002) in a research methods course, our version of the POD (http://pod.butler.edu) differs from the version used by Correll et al. (2002) in at least two important ways. First, Correll et al. (2002) asked participants to press a key to indicate "shoot" or "don't shoot" at the target. Given our interest in teaching about traditional signal detection methodologies, we describe the task in terms of accurately distinguishing signal (i.e., gun) from noise (i.e., innocuous object), and thus instruct students to focus on the object in the target's hand and make a "it's a gun" (i.e., noise + signal trial) versus "it's not a gun" (i.e., noise only trial) decision. Second, Correll et al. (2002) structured their procedure to simulate a videogame by including a series of flashing background screens on every trial before a randomly selected background image (e.g., train station) remained on the screen followed by the target person in the foreground. To reduce the game-like feel of the task, we simplified the presentation by eliminating the flashing backgrounds on each trial and presented only a single randomly selected background image (e.g., the train station) before the target person appeared in the foreground.

Students who complete the demonstration receive individualized feedback concerning their hit and false alarm rates to the presence of a gun. The Web browser and backend server record both accuracy and speed for all students, allowing us to present the findings to the class. Unlike the IAT demonstration, the results from the POD demonstration can be analyzed and discussed completely free of any discussion of target race. Indeed, we begin by reporting reaction times, sensitivity, and response bias measures for only the "it's a gun" (i.e., noise + signal) versus "it's not a gun" (noise only) conditions. Based on combined data from several semesters and across three instructors, we (Padgett, Morris, & Dale, 2009) have found that students show clear sensitivity to the presence of the gun, have a generally lax criterion (i.e., when in doubt, students are more likely to say "it's a gun"), and have faster reaction times to signal (i.e., gun) trials than noise only (i.e., no gun) trials.

After presenting the data devoid of target race, we open the floor to student questions. Often, but not always, a student raises the issue of target race. On the occasions when no one asks about this issue, we ask questions that might lead students in this direction (e.g., "Did you notice anything else about the targets?"). Interestingly, some students inevitably comment that they never even noticed that targets varied in race and are surprised and intrigued by that information. Once students begin thinking about target race and how that might have affected their performance on the task, we present the aggregate results—reaction times, sensitivity, and response bias—including target race as a factor. Consistent with the results of Correll et al. (2002), typical reaction time results reveal that students are faster to identify that an object is a gun when the target is Black than when the target is White. We also typically find that students are both more sensitive to the presence of the gun when held by Black targets and have a more lax criterion (i.e., a greater tendency to say "it's a gun") when the target is Black.

Importantly, we argue that one of the key advantages to using this laboratory exercise, as opposed to a recognition memory task or other example of a signal detection methodology, is precisely because it leads easily to a discussion of race and racial bias in courses where such discussions rarely occur naturally. To this end, we conclude the demonstration with a discussion of real-world implications of the POD findings, including descriptions of research that suggest that actual police officers who train themselves using a similar demonstration can learn to overcome their biases (Plant, Peruche, & Butz, 2005).

We (Padgett et al., 2009) have assessed the POD demonstration by asking students to evaluate the demonstration on several dimensions (e.g., how interesting the exercise was, the extent to which it enhanced their understanding of signal detection concepts). Students rated the POD demonstration positively on every item on the evaluation scale. In an assessment of student learning of signal detection theory concepts, students were better at correctly answering a series of questions testing their knowledge of signal detection concepts after the POD demonstration relative to understanding before it. These findings suggest that the POD demonstration was an enjoyable and effective means of instructing students on signal detection methodologies.

Although we did not directly assess the utility of the POD demonstration for the purpose of facilitating instruction about diversity in the classroom, we suspect that one reason students evaluated the POD demonstration so positively is because it had real-world implications and made them think about how the targets' races affected their speed and accuracy. Given students' interest and enthusiasm about the impact of target race on student performance on the task, this is a plausible hypothesis. Even if the racial aspect of the POD demonstration did not lead to student learning and enjoyment of the task, the fact remains that incorporating the demonstration allowed instructors to engage students in a dialogue about race in a context where such a conversation was otherwise unlikely to occur. Also of note, because the POD produces aggregate data (rather than individualized data, like the IAT), students' individual performances are relatively anonymous. Thus, students avoid direct awareness of the extent to which target race affected their own performance. On one hand, this anonymity may reduce any negative reactions that might occur if students' performance is inconsistent with their explicit beliefs about Blacks. On the other hand, aggregate (as opposed to individualized) feedback on the POD demonstration may serve as less of a consciousness-raising experience for students who complete it. In the future, we intend to empirically investigate these issues.

Using Reaction Time Technology to Discuss Diversity

We describe two ways to utilize Web-based reaction time technologies to create opportunities for teachers to introduce discussions about race into their courses. The IAT and POD demonstrations are useful for a variety of reasons. First, they require only Web-based technology, which is familiar to both students and faculty, readily accessible, and easy to use in a variety of classes (even those where diversity discussions do not often spontaneously arise). Further, because students complete the demonstrations individually, the technology affords them a degree of privacy, which may be comforting to them when they receive performance feedback on tasks that provide insight into potential racial biases. Next, these demonstrations provide students with consciousness-raising experiences by informing them of the ways in which implicit racial biases affect their own and others' split-second decisions. Indeed, the fact that the demonstrations seamlessly weave course content and racial issues together allows students to become more aware of racial issues and their implications without diversity being the centerpiece of the discussion, which may in turn reduce backlash that students might experience (see Holladay & Quiñones, 2008) if they feel they are being "preached at" about diversity. Finally, these demonstrations are ideal for classroom use because they provide dual assessment opportunities: instructors can assess the demonstrations' impact on understanding of both classroom content and diversity issues.

Despite these benefits of the IAT and POD demonstrations, we include several cautions. First, instructors who use these demonstrations should be prepared to discuss basic diversity and social cognitive concepts, and to provide meaningful explanation of feedback students receive from the demonstrations. We have considered these demonstrations only in contexts where we, as instructors, felt comfortable discussing racial issues and explaining the implications of student performance on the IAT and POD tasks. Even though we have had very positive student reactions in our classes, we cannot recommend use in situations where teachers lack the knowledge or willingness to tackle these issues. (We encourage interested faculty to refer to several excellent resources for information on teaching about diversity: Gurung & Prieto, 2009; http;//teachpsych.org/diversity/index.php; http://understand-ingprejudice.org). Second, because students receive performance feedback from these two demonstrations, and the feedback they receive will likely suggest they have some degree of implicit racial bias, they may well experience some negative affect. However, our assessment of the IAT suggests more positive than negative affective reactions, and the instructor can provide context to channel any negative affect into positive action (i.e., strategies for reducing bias), further enhancing the consciousness-raising aspect of these demonstrations.

We have focused on two demonstrations to teach about *racial* diversity, but these demonstrations could easily be extended to address other forms of diversity. For example, the IAT demonstration site currently includes 12 different demonstration tests. We see no reason why instructors would have different results when addressing other forms of bias than the results we have shared here regarding race. An extension of the POD demonstration to other forms of bias would require a bit of programming work, but it could be done. For example, one could demonstrate anti-Hispanic bias, bias against darker- vs. lighter-skinned people, or a tendency to associate men more strongly than women with guns and violence. In addition, more subtle aspects of gender bias might be examined by having participants quickly identify the gender of a target person in sex-typed contexts (e.g., auto mechanic vs. school teacher).

We assessed the IAT in social psychology courses and the POD in research methods courses, but both tests could easily be integrated into a variety of other classes, including introductory, statistics, experimental, sensation and perception, and cognitive psychology courses. The demonstrations would likely have utility beyond the traditional psychology curriculum as well; we can easily imagine incorporating these demonstrations in appropriate sociology, business, and education courses, for example. We reiterate that instructors who utilize versions of these demonstrations that focus on diversity issues other than race, and those who integrate these demonstrations outside of psychology courses, should be willing and able to discuss the meaning of the results and their implications.

Conclusion

Diversity is a buzzword in today's academy, and many institutions adopt a comprehensive approach to diversity: admissions officers attempt to enhance the diversity of the student body; administrators attempt to enhance the diversity of the faculty and staff; and student life staffers provide co-curricular diversity training for students. Of all academic personnel, however, instructors have the unique opportunity to enhance classroom teaching with diversity content. While doing so may be challenging, we argue that Web-based reaction time technology, such as the Implicit Association Test and the Police Officer's Dilemma demonstrations, simultaneously enhance classroom instruction on course content and provide a springboard for classroom discussions about racial diversity. Indeed, both demonstrations are engaging, easy to use, and provide either individualized or aggregate results that offer students insight into implicit biases regarding Blacks. These demonstrations likely provide students with a consciousness-raising experience they can take with them beyond the classroom—to understand how implicit racial biases can affect us when we are forced to "think fast."

Author Note

We thank Joshua Correll for providing the photographs used in the Police Officer's Dilemma task.

References

Blanton, H., & Jaccard, J. (2006). Arbitrary metrics redux. *American Psychologist, 61,* 62–71.

Correll, J., Park, B., Judd, C., & Wittenbrink, B. (2002). The police officer's dilemma: Using ethnicity to disambiguate potentially threatening individuals. *Journal of Personality and Social Psychology, 83,* 1314–1329.

Fiske, S., & Stevens, L. (1993). What's so special about sex? Gender stereotyping and discrimination. In: S. Oskamp & M. Costanzo (eds.) *Gender issues in contemporary society* (pp. 173–196). Thousand Oaks, CA: Sage Publications, Inc.

Greenwald, A. (2009). Non-technical Summary of the meta-analysis of the IAT's predictive validity (appearing in the July 2009 issue of *Journal of Personality and Social Psychology*). Retrieved from http://faculty.washington.edu/agg/.

Greenwald, A., McGhee, D., & Schwartz, J. (1998). Measuring individual differences in implicit cognition: The Implicit Association Test. *Journal of Personality and Social Psychology, 74,* 1464–1480.

Greenwald, A. G., Poehlman, T. A., Uhlmann, E., & Banaji, M. R. (2009). Understanding and using the Implicit Association Test: III. Meta-analysis of predictive validity. *Journal of Personality and Social Psychology, 97,* 17–41.

Gurung, R. A. R., & Prieto, L. R. (eds). (2009). *Getting culture: Incorporating diversity across the curriculum.* Sterling, VA: Stylus.

Henry, P. J. (2008). College sophomores in the laboratory redux: Influences of a narrow data base on social psychology's view of the nature of prejudice. *Psychological Inquiry, 19,* 49–71.

Holladay, C., & Quiñones, M. (2008). The influence of training focus and trainer characteristics on diversity training effectiveness. *Academy of Management Learning & Education, 7,* 343–354.

Kowalski, R. (2000). Including gender, race, and ethnicity in psychology content courses. *Teaching of Psychology, 27,* 18–24.

Macrae, C. N., & Bodenhausen, G. V. (2000). Social cognition: Thinking categorically about others. *Annual Review of Psychology, 51,* 93–120.

Monteith, M. J. (1993). Self-regulation of prejudiced responses: Implications for progress in prejudice-reduction efforts. *Journal of Personality and Social Psychology, 65,* 469–485.

Monteith, M. J., Ashburn-Nardo, L., Voils, C. I., & Czopp, A. M. (2002). Putting the brakes on prejudice: On the development and operation of cues for control. *Journal of Personality and Social Psychology, 83,* 1029–1050.

Monteith, M., Voils, C., & Ashburn-Nardo, L. (2001). Taking a look underground: Detecting, interpreting, and reacting to implicit racial biases. *Social Cognition, 19,* 395–417.

Morris, K. A., & Ashburn-Nardo, L. (2010). The Implicit Association Test as a class assignment: student affective and attitudinal reactions. *Teaching of Psychology, 37*, 63–68.

Nosek, B. A., Banaji, M. R., & Greenwald, A. G. (2002). Harvesting implicit group attitudes and beliefs from a demonstration Web site. *Group Dynamics, 6*, 101–115.

Padgett, R. J., Morris, K. A., & Dale, R. H. I. (2009). *Is that a gun in your hand or are you just happy to be learning signal detection theory?* Manuscript in preparation.

Plant, E., Peruche, B., & Butz, D. (2005). Eliminating automatic racial bias: Making race non-diagnostic for responses to criminal suspects. *Journal of Experimental Social Psychology, 41*, 141–156.

Sagar, H. A., & Schofield, J. W. (1980). Racial and behavioral cues in black and white children's perceptions of ambiguously aggressive acts. *Journal of Personality and Social Psychology, 39*, 590–598.

Simoni, J. M., Sexton-Radek, K., Yescavage, K., Richard, H., & Lundquist, A. (1999). Teaching diversity: Experiences and recommendations of American Psychological Association Division 2 members. *Teaching of Psychology, 26*, 89–95.

Springsteen, B. (2001). American Skin (41 Shots) [Recorded by Bruce Springsteen & the E Street Band. On *Live In New York City* [CD]. New York: Columbia.

Wickens, T. D. (2002). *Elementary signal detection theory.* New York: Oxford University Press Inc.

Woolf, L. M., & Hulsizer, M. R. (2007). Understanding the mosaic of humanity through research methodology: Infusing diversity into research methods courses. In: D. S. Dunn, R. A. Smith, & B. C. Beins (eds.), *Best practices for teaching statistics and research methods in the behavioral sciences* (pp. 237–256). Mahwah, NJ: Erlbaum.

Technology: New Opportunities for Teaching

16 Online Tools to Promote Student Collaboration

Kevin J. Apple, Monica Reis-Bergan, Andrea H. Adams, and Grover Saunders

As a supplement to class instruction, faculty can ask students to use the Internet to work together, resulting in enhanced learning as well as social benefits. However, for students and faculty to take advantage of online collaborative tools, they need to be aware of them. In this chapter, we present potential technologies that might enhance student collaboration. As online tools continue to develop, instructors can take advantage of opportunities to connect student ideas in innovative ways.

Student Collaboration

Student collaboration can yield social and pedagogical benefits, whether collaboration is face to face (Barton, Van Duuren, & Haslam, 2007) or online (Cox & Cox, 2008). Social benefits include students building rapport with each other. Benson, Cohen, and Buskist (2005) concluded that when faculty members establish rapport with their classes, the students work harder and enjoy the course more. Similarly, we believe that student–student rapport is also important. When students have rapport with their classmates, they may be more willing to share their opinions, allowing the potential for collaboration. When working on a project, students are able to learn from each other.

For example, Lazonder (2005) reported that pairs of students collaborating together demonstrated stronger information-seeking skills than students working alone. Finally, from an instructor's perspective, collaborative assignments may reduce the amount of grading if instructors ask students to write papers in pairs.

Student collaboration can be either synchronous or asynchronous. For synchronous collaboration, students must find a common meeting time and then complete the assignment together. Finding a meeting time can be challenging for students; if students work part-time, have children, or commute from a different city, the available meeting times will be limited. For asynchronous collaboration, students need not schedule a common meeting time. Instead, students complete portions of the assignment on their own, ask other collaborators for feedback, and make corrections. However, a potential problem with asynchronous collaboration is that students may simply divide a task and combine completed sections with minimal contact, failing to take full advantage of the collaboration.

For both synchronous and asynchronous collaboration, social loafing (Latane, Williams, & Harkins, 1979) may be a problem; students may rely on other group members to complete the assignment. Conversely, students who have had negative experiences with groups may believe they need to work harder to counteract social loafing (Forrest & Miller, 2003). Group members realize that an instructor cannot easily discern who meaningfully contributed to the assignment and who did not (Meyers, 1997).

Emerging Technology: Synchronous and Asynchronous

Initially, instructors used the Internet solely for posting information. For example, an instructor could have posted an article about measuring prejudice with the Implicit Association Test (e.g., Greenwald, McGhee, & Schwartz, 1998). The Implicit Association Test assesses people's biases toward groups. Students could read about the test, but they could not interact with it online. As technology progressed, the Internet became more interactive and is now commonly called Web 2.0 (Web 1.0 refers to older versions of the Internet). Now an instructor can simply post a link to the Implicit Association Test (e.g., https://implicit.harvard.edu/implicit/), which allows students to interact with the Web page by taking the test and receiving a score. When creating student collaborative assignments, instructors should consider taking advantage of the interactivity of Web 2.0.

Traditionally, online student collaboration was asynchronous in nature (Hrastinski, 2008). However, with the technological advancements of Web 2.0, online collaboration can now be synchronous as well. In fact, Hrastinski (2008) pointed out that current technology blurs the line between synchronous and asynchronous, creating more of a continuum than a dichotomy. For example, e-mail can be considered either asynchronous or synchronous depending on how often users monitor their accounts.

Collaborating: Synchronous and Asynchronous

Web 1.0 presented many opportunities for students to share their work and ideas. For example, students could e-mail their written ideas to each other. After receiving work from their group members, students could use the Microsoft Word "track changes" feature to collaborate effectively with each other. The track-changes feature of Microsoft Word allows a user to make corrections on an electronic document without losing the original content. For example, a student using this feature is able to add comments to a document, cross out text, and add new text. Each editor's comments are shown in different colors, and the original author can click a button to accept or reject specific changes. This tool, coupled with e-mail, allows students to collaborate electronically.

However, this style of collaboration has disadvantages. The instructor is not easily able to discern which group members participated in the assignment and how much work each member contributed. Although the track-changes feature on Word will automatically create text in different colors when the text is edited on different computers, the text is identifiable to a particular student only if that student has personalized his or her copy of Word with a username, and it may be difficult for students using computer labs to personalize a copy of Word. An additional problem is that most students are not familiar with this Microsoft feature: in fall 2008, we asked 49 underclassmen about this tool, and only one student reported that he or she had used it. The remaining students reported that they had not used it ($n = 15$), or that they had no knowledge of the feature at all ($n = 33$). In addition, student groups using e-mail and track changes are challenged with keeping up with the various versions of the documents and combining all of the revisions into one final product. If students choose to edit sequentially (with each editor subsequently sending the document to the next editor), students must wait for their collaborator to finish a section before editing. This approach to student collaboration is consistent with Web 1.0 in that students are reacting to something sent via e-mail but are not interacting at the same time via the Internet.

As an alternative to track changes in Word, Google Docs is consistent with Web 2.0. With Google Docs, students are able to work together on one online document from separate locations. The changes one student makes automatically appear on another student's version of the text. If used synchronously, Google Docs may be less frustrating for students because they can ask and answer questions with immediate feedback (Hrastinski, 2008). Students using Google Docs can then share the document with other users of the program. Because the document is stored online, users can access the file wherever there is an Internet connection and Web browser. Another benefit of Google Docs is that the program automatically saves a new version of the document every 5 seconds. With this feature, users do not need to worry about losing changes made to the document. In addition, users can either revert to or review past versions of the text.

For the instructor of a course, Google Docs also has the capability of keeping track of which users made which changes. To take advantage of this feature, the instructor needs to have the students "share" the document with him or her. By using the revision-history feature, the instructor will see the text written by each user in a different color. Thus, an instructor will be able to verify that all students actually worked on the text. With this revision-history feature, the instructor can determine when the students began writing the assignment as well.

Disadvantages of Google Docs include the challenge of formatting the text in APA style, although the document can be downloaded into Microsoft Word for formatting when complete. In addition, students will need a password to access their document, and students may not wish to sign up for another account and remember yet another password for an assignment. Another disadvantage is that Google makes updates and changes often. Users may also be concerned about who actually owns the files stored on the web (Sydell, 2008). Finally, students' access to their files is dependent on Google and the Internet: if students lose Internet access, they will not be able to download their files. As a result of these disadvantages, some writers prefer to use track changes in Word. Although we are focusing on Word and Google Docs in this chapter, there are other word-processing programs for student collaboration. For a current comparison (as of September 2009) of Google Docs, Microsoft Word, and other word-processing programs, please see Table 16.1.

Table 16.1

Comparison of Word Processing Programs

	Google Docs	Microsoft Word	Zoho Writer	OpenOffice
Synchronous collaboration	• Yes	• No	• Yes	• No
Asynchronous collaboration	• Yes	• Yes	• Yes	• Yes
Online editing available	• Yes	• No	• Yes	• No
Saving files	• Online or desktop	• Desktop only	• Online or desktop	• Desktop only
Files can be saved as:	• Word, text, PDF, OpenOffice, HTML	• Word, text, HTML, XML, Works	• Word, text, PDF, HTML, OpenOffice, LaTex	• Word, text, PDF, OpenOffice, HTML, StarWriter, Unified Office Format, DocBook, AportisDoc (Palm), Pocket Word
Organization of revisions	• Easy	• Difficult	• Easy	• Difficult
Formatting text (APA style)	• Difficult	• Easy	• Easy	• Easy
Inserting equations	• Difficult	• Easy	• Easy	• Moderate difficulty
Cost of program	• Free	• Expensive	• Free	• Free
Automatic upgrade	• Yes	• No	• Yes	• No
Multiple versions in use	• No	• Yes	• No	• Yes

Experimental Comparison of Google Docs and Microsoft Word

Because students can collaborate with either the Microsoft Word track-changes feature or Google Docs, we chose to compare these programs experimentally. We investigated whether students collaborate differently with Google Docs compared with Microsoft Word. Further, we limited use of Google Docs to synchronous collaboration. According to Robert and Dennis (2005), the immediacy and richness of synchronous communication may facilitate the ability to communicate simple ideas but harm the ability to work on complex tasks. Synchronous collaboration facilitates easy tasks because users can get immediate feedback. This type of collaboration may be particularly useful for simple edits of a document and/or expanding ideas. Because both authors are making minor changes, neither author needs to spend a lot of cognitive resources to process the simple changes to the text. However, when students are collaborating synchronously on a difficult task, they are operating under a heavier cognitive load. While struggling to create their own text, they also have to react to their partners' text appearing on the screen; therefore, the quality of their writing may suffer.

To examine the impact of these different collaboration strategies, we conducted two studies. The first study focused on a relatively simple task of editing and expanding a prewritten essay. For this simple task, we believed that students collaborating synchronously would have an advantage. The second study focused on the more complicated task of creating an essay. For this complicated task, we believed that students collaborating asynchronously would have an advantage.

For the first study, editing a prewritten essay, we recruited 61 students who participated in our study for class credit. We asked dyads of students to collaborate to complete an essay about the importance of voting. (We conducted the study shortly before the 2008 Presidential election.) We randomly assigned each dyad to either the Microsoft Word or the Google Docs condition. The experimenter then handed each pair of students the prewritten essay and instructed teams to edit the first two paragraphs and write a concluding paragraph together. Before beginning the task, the experimenter briefly demonstrated how to use the assigned technology. Participants collaborated on the essay in separate rooms via the Internet using either Google Docs or Microsoft Word through e-mail. The students had 35 minutes to complete the task and all students were able to finish within the allotted time.

Students rated their reactions to the randomly assigned technology on 7-point scales, with higher numbers reflecting more favorable evaluations. Students in the Google Docs condition (M = 2.86, SD = 1.30) did not evaluate the program as being more difficult to use than students in the Microsoft Word condition (M = 2.72, SD = 1.28), $t(59)$=.43, p = .67. However, students assigned to Google Docs (M = 4.48, SD = 1.46) enjoyed the program significantly more than students assigned to Microsoft Word (M = 3.63, SD = 1.60), $t(59)$ = 2.18, p = .03. In addition, the students in the Google Docs condition wrote essays with significantly more words (M = 847.83, SD = 150.67), on average, than the Microsoft Word condition (M = 766.12, SD = 130.93), $t(59)$=2.27, p = .03. In summary, when completing a simple writing task, students reported that the Google Docs program was more enjoyable to use, and they wrote significantly longer essays.

For the second study, creating an essay, we recruited 36 students to participate for course credit. We used a method similar to Study 1 but created a more complex collaborative task: we asked students to write an entire essay about increasing the amount of time allotted for students to walk from one class to another on our large campus. Once again, we randomly assigned dyads of students to work on the task with either Microsoft Word track changes or Google Docs. We asked all students to complete the assignment within 20 minutes. (We discarded the data from two teams of students because one essay was dramatically shorter and the other was dramatically longer than the other essays. Both of the discarded essays were more than 2 standard deviations away from the mean length.)

Participants in the Google Docs condition (68%) were significantly more likely to have enough time to complete the task than the participants in the Microsoft-Word condition (31%), $\chi^2(1)$ = 4.39, p =.04. Perhaps the Google Docs participants finished the assignment quicker because they did not have to wait for a partner to finish his or her task—that is, writing synchronously was more efficient than writing asynchronously.

The total number of words written by Google Docs participants (M = 255.32, SD = 72.05) did not differ significantly from the number of words written by Microsoft Word participants (M = 215.92, SD = 64.39), $t(30)$ = 1.58, p = .12. However, the dyads in the Google Docs condition wrote significantly fewer sentences per paragraph (M = 4.46, SD = 2.11) than the dyads in the Microsoft Word condition (M = 7.28, SD = 3.31), $t(30)$ = 2.95, p = .01. Across the different conditions, participants wrote the same number of words, but they organized the number of sentences in each paragraph differently depending on the modality of collaboration. Based on this study, it is unclear whether one type of collaboration is better for difficult tasks.

Because these studies were completed in a laboratory instead of a classroom, we realize that our students probably did not put forth their full effort. If a similar assignment was for a grade, students may have worked harder. Based on these preliminary studies, we know that students are able to learn quickly how to use either of these editing programs. For the relatively simple task in Study 1, we found that dyads of students in the Google Docs condition wrote longer essays. For the relatively more complicated task in Study 2, we found that dyads of students in the Google Docs condition wrote fewer sentences per paragraph in their essays. Although we do not have definitive evidence that one type of collaboration is better for one type of task, we do have evidence that the different modalities affect writing output. As faculty members plan collaborative assignments, they may consider that the type of collaboration may have an impact on writing output. In future studies, researchers can investigate the effects of synchronous and asynchronous collaboration on graded assignments.

Word-Processing Recommendations

The main advantages we see in Google Docs is that the program is easy to use, files are saved online so students do not need to worry about losing copies, and the instructor can determine if all students worked on the assignment. Instructors can also monitor the progression of the assignment. For example, an instructor can check which groups have made substantial progress before the assignment is due. If a student group is not making sufficient progress, the professor can intervene. The instructor is also able to determine which students contributed early to the document and which students worked on the task immediately before the deadline. In addition, students are able to use Google Docs to collaborate synchronously or asynchronously. Some of the disadvantages of Google Docs include users having to open another account and remember a new password. In addition, it is difficult to format the text in Google Docs. Therefore, we would not recommend using the program for APA-style assignments, although students can easily download the final version of a Google Docs paper into Microsoft Word for formatting. Finally, it may be difficult for instructors to give accurate instructions on how to use the program because the program changes frequently.

In our own classes, we believe the advantages outweigh the disadvantages. If students already use Google for e-mail (Gmail), they can use the same account to access their Google Docs. Although Google's frequent changes may be frustrating, at least the program changes for everyone at the same time. With Microsoft Word, on the other hand, students may be working with different versions depending on the date of the program (e.g., Word 2003 versus Word 2007) or their computer's operating system (i.e., PC or Mac). We have used Google Docs for a variety of projects, including writing a research paper, creating questionnaires, and other writing assignments. Our students frequently tell us that they plan to use Google Docs for future group projects as well.

Our study focused on students collaborating on writing a paper. However, students can also collaborate in other ways. For example, students can collaborate on creating research ideas, composing a spreadsheet, or preparing for a presentation. In addition to word-processing documents, Google Docs, OpenOffice, Zoho, and Microsoft Office Live all offer tools that allow students to collaboratively create presentations and spreadsheets.

Collaborating with Other Online Tools

Wikis

In addition to using document editors, students can collaborate on an assignment by creating a wiki. A public wiki is a collection of Web pages that anyone can access and edit. A wiki can also be created so only selected people have access to it. Students are familiar with wikis; Lomas, Burke, and Page (2008) report that approximately 41% of undergraduates surveyed use wikis. Examples of wikis that are currently used for collaborative projects in education include Google Sites (http://sites.google.com), WetPaint (http://www.wetpaint.com/), and PBWorks (http://www.pbworks.com). The most popular wiki is the online encyclopedia Wikipedia.

Bernhardt (2009) used Wikipedia for a course assignment. Students in an upper-level social-psychology course either edited an entry on Wikipedia or created a new entry related to the course. Bernhardt's students felt additional pressure to put forth their best effort because the final version of the assignment was going to be posted online for anyone to read. Nine months after the students posted their assignment, Bernhardt checked the number of edits others made to his students' assignments. He reported that his students' articles had fewer edits than other Wikipedia articles, suggesting that his students' papers were fairly accurate. Although Bernhardt asked students to work individually on this assignment, we believe it could be modified to allow a group of students to create a Wikipedia entry together. Students may believe their effort on such an assignment is more worthwhile because their final product is being made available to others.

Blogs and Twitter

A blog is another option for student collaboration. The term *blog* is an abbreviation of Web log. Students can use a blog to post their thoughts on a class-relevant topic. Other classmates can then read the blog and post their reactions. Blogs can allow conversations to continue outside of class. For example, the second author uses blogs in an upper-level psychology course to discuss relevant topics. A second application might involve students blogging about potential research ideas. Students can create blogs with http://www.wordpress.com and http://www.blogger.com. Students who use Google for e-mail (Gmail) or Google Docs can use their Google password to access blogger.com. Although some students are intimidated about creating a blog, most learn how to blog with minimal instructor assistance. Similar to a wiki, a blog can be created so only select people have access.

Twitter is basically a mini-blog. With twitter, the posted entries must be 140 characters or fewer. Users may read the postings from either a Web page or their cell phone. Although students can use Twitter to share ideas about a project, we do not think it would be useful for in-depth assignments. Because of its focus on portability and immediacy, faculty members may use Twitter to remind students of assignments and due dates or let students know about a relevant item in the news.

Social Networking Web Sites: Facebook and MySpace

Facebook and MySpace are social networking sites students use to keep in touch with each other (Boyd & Ellison, 2007). Users are able to post pictures, list interests, and post notes and essays as well as leave comments to friends. Students can use social networking sites to find others with similar interests. (See Chapter 12 in this volume for additional information on social networking sites.) Because students use these sites frequently, Lomas, Burke, and

Page (2008) believe that collaborative assignments may be integrated. For example, a professor could set up a Facebook page and encourage students to post class-relevant materials to be reviewed by classmates. Although social networking sites could be useful for sharing ideas, brainstorming, or reflection, we do not recommend their use for in-depth collaborative projects. Because students use Facebook and MySpace as a social outlet, they may view its use for class instruction as an intrusion into their private lives.

Instant Messaging, Text Messaging, Video Chats, and Second Life

Additional options within the social realm offer more synchronous collaboration than is necessarily available through Facebook and MySpace. With instant messaging and text messaging, students can "chat" with each other electronically. Students type messages back and forth to each other and get instant replies. Students often use their cell phone for texting, and many of our students use the "chat" feature on Facebook, MySpace, or Gmail to communicate with each other. If a computer has a Web camera, students can have video chats with each other, allowing them to see and hear each other as they talk about their project. Video chats can be free if the students use programs such as Gmail or Skype. These messaging tools can be used in conjunction with other collaborative tools. For example, students working on a paper together from remote locations may use instant messaging or video chats to communicate while also using Google Docs.

Another option for synchronous collaboration includes students meeting in Second Life. Second Life is a virtual world in which students can communicate with each other using their avatars (a digital version of the user). For additional information on Second Life, please see Chapter 19 in this book.

Conclusion

Collaboration is an important skill for students during their college career as well as after they graduate. Regardless of career path, alumni who know how to collaborate effectively will have an advantage (Colbeck, Campbell, & Bjorklund, 2000). The best type of collaboration depends on the project (Hrastinski, 2008). For simple tasks, synchronous collaboration may be ideal; for more complicated tasks, asynchronous collaboration may be preferable

(Robert & Dennis, 2005). The myriad of software programs and web applications can facilitate both styles of collaboration.

In this chapter, we discussed current ways to collaborate online. Because technologies change rapidly, we are confident that there will be new ways to collaborate in the future. In fact, Microsoft recently announced yet another version of Microsoft Office. Instructors do not need to keep up with all of the latest technologies (see Chapter 20 in this book for additional information on emerging technologies); nor should instructors encourage online collaboration when in-person collaboration may be preferable. Rather, we recommend faculty members use the collaboration technologies that make sense for their assignments and their students. Because of the Internet, faculty members have more options for encouraging student collaboration. Finding the best tool for student collaboration may be challenging, but we believe the effort is worthwhile for both the students' education and the quality of the final product.

Acknowledgments

We thank Brian Koziol, Kelsey Cutchins, and Amanda Peterson for help with data collection, data entry, and data analyses. We also thank the James Madison University's Center for Instructional Technology (CIT). Without CIT, we would not have been able to complete this project.

References

Barton, A., Van Duuren, M., & Haslam, P. (2007). Perceived social benefits of voluntary student collaboration. *Psychology Learning and Teaching, 6*(1), 26–32.

Benson, T. A., Cohen, A. L., & Buskist, W. (2005). Rapport: Its relation to student attitudes and behaviors toward teachers and classes. *Teaching of Psychology, 32*(4), 237–239.

Bernhardt, P. C. (2009, June). *Engaging Wikipedia: Using students' contributions to Wikipedia in social psychology*. Paper presented at the Eastern Conference on the Teaching of Psychology.

Boyd, D. M., & Ellison, N. B. (2007). Social network sites: Definition, history, and scholarship. *Journal of Computer-Mediated Communication, 13*(1), 210–230. doi: 10.1111/j.1083-6101.2007.00393.x

Colbeck, C. L., Campbell, S. E., & Bjorklund, S. A. (2000). Grouping in the dark: What college students learn from group projects. *The Journal of Higher Education, 71*(1), 60–83.

Cox, B., & Cox, B. (2008). Developing interpersonal and group dynamics through asynchronous threaded discussions: The use of discussion board in collaborative learning. *Education, 128*(4), 553–565.

Forrest, K. D., & Miller, R. L. (2003). Not another group project: Why good teachers should care about bad group experiences. *Teaching of Psychology, 30*(3), 244–243.

Greenwald, A. G., McGhee, D. E., & Schwartz, J. L. K. (1998). Measuring individual differences in implicit cognition: The implicit association test. *Journal of Personality and Social Psychology, 74*(6), 1464–1480.

Hrastinski, S. (2008). Asynchronous and synchronous e-learning. *Educause Quarterly, 31*(4), 51–55.

Latane, B., Williams, K., & Harkins, S. (1979). Many hands make light the work: The causes and consequences of social loafing. *Journal of Personality and Social Psychology, 37*, 822–832.

Lazonder, A. (2005). Do two heads search better than one? Effects of student collaboration on web search behavior and search outcomes. *British Journal of Educational Technology, 36*, 465–475.

Lomas, C., Burke, M., & Page, C. L. (2008) Collaboration tools (ELI Paper 2: 2008). Retrieved on June 26, 2009 from Educause Learning Initiative: http://net.educause.edu/ir/library/pdf/ELI3020.pdf

Meyers, S. A. (1997). Increasing student participation and productivity in small-group activities for psychology classes. *Teaching of Psychology, 24*(2), 105–115.

Robert, L. P., & Dennis, A. R. (2005). Paradox of richness: A cognitive model of media choice. *IEEE Transactions of Professional Communication, 48*(1), 10–21.

Sydell, L. (2008). Computing in the cloud: Who owns your files? *All Things Considered.* Retrieved May 18, 2009, from http://www.npr.org/templates/story/story.php?storyId=93841182

17 To the Internet and Beyond

Surveying the Active Learning Universe

Beth R. Kirsner, Clayton L. Teem II, and Laura B. Underwood

Involving students in the design, construction, administration, analysis, and interpretation of results from surveys can increase student engagement with course material and may aid instructors in their quest to promote an environment friendly to active learning. Although students may easily design and implement traditional paper-and-pencil surveys and even analyze their data using high-speed computers, paper-and-pencil surveys require a huge time investment to gather and input even moderate amounts of data. This time investment often precludes the use of surveys as an instrument of student learning within the confines of a course lasting only one semester. The recent advent of online surveys shifts survey administration from paper and pencil to an environment that provides access to broader populations, increases the efficiency with which data can be collected, and eliminates the time investment and human errors associated with encoding data by hand. Hence, online surveys reduce the time from the start to the finish of a study dramatically, making a full integration of survey methodology in the classroom feasible.

The convenience, variety, accessibility, and the relatively brief time required to complete online surveys make it possible to incorporate a wide variety of survey-related activities into courses easily and inexpensively. This chapter describes a variety of ways that you can use online surveys to enhance the learning experience of your students. Although not all are appropriate to every course, most of you will find at least a few ideas that can enhance teaching and learning in every discipline.

Training Students to Use Online Survey Tools

Most online survey tools are relatively simple; using them, nearly anyone can set up a basic survey in just a few minutes. Designing effective survey items is more challenging, but excellent guidance is available from sources such as Schwarz, Groves, and Schuman (1998) and Dunn (2009, pp. 149–181). In this chapter, we use the term "items" to refer to questions that a respondent will see and answer. We use the term "question" to refer to a broader range of concepts, such as the question guiding the research. Designing effective survey items requires the student to think carefully and deeply about the question of interest, so developing this skill provides an active learning opportunity in virtually any course.

Requiring students to master the subtleties involved in writing appropriate survey items helps students develop critical thinking skills. To do this, you must first direct students to develop their own research topic or provide a specific research topic for them. Once developed, it is necessary to encourage the students to draft items that address their specific research topic to the exclusion of all other interesting research topics.

As students write each item, they require informed feedback about the construction of the item relative to the research topic. Fellow students, teaching assistants, or the professor might provide feedback. A professor can guide this feedback during a class devoted to basic principles of item design, applying those principles to items generated by the students. The Research Methods Knowledge Base (Trochim, 2006), a Web-based textbook covering most aspects of social science research methods, describes these principles well. After acquiring the basic principles, peers can use them to provide feedback in or out of the classroom.

Survey respondents provide what may be the most important feedback about the quality of the items. When items are piloted on a small sample, it usually becomes clear when those items fail to yield answers that address the specific research topic. When this happens, the professor or peers can guide the students back to specific items—asking the student to re-examine those items in light of the basic principles of item design and in light of the data the item produced. Students can then edit problematic items and add others to address the research topic more completely. If time is available, students then pilot the new item set or implement the survey with a full sample. Each cycle of feedback, piloting, and editing reinforces the iterative nature of science.

Students can learn item-writing skills by writing exam questions (items) covering classroom material and posting the items online for review by their peers. In addition, they can create their own online surveys, consisting of items examining mastery of course content, and post the links to those surveys for their classmates to access. Finally, the professor may select from among posted items, or items submitted in private, and include them in upcoming exams.

Requiring students to design and conduct survey research, or to generate exam items, provides opportunities to acquaint students with the item-writing process directly. Even when students are not involved in drafting items directly, however, they learn about online surveys and item design by completing surveys and class assessments online. Simply moving some of your existing materials to an online environment will familiarize students with online survey design, particularly when those materials take advantage of the full range of online-survey features. For example, instructors can demonstrate the advantages of online tools when conducting course evaluations by demonstrating various online-survey features, such as requiring responses to specific items, returning a message when the responses are not formatted properly, or using skip logic to proceed to or skip items based on earlier responses. Annotating the survey to explain these features encourages active learning among the students, whereas results from the survey provide item-quality feedback *and* useful (e.g., course evaluation) data to the instructor.

Assessing Students' Use of Online Survey Tools

Educators strive to ensure that students achieve course-specific learning outcomes. One such outcome is the set of skills involved in setting up a simple online survey. To assess achievement of this outcome, an instructor might provide survey items in a word-processing format and a description of how each item should appear in the online survey tool. Students could then demonstrate their skill by setting up the survey and providing a link to the final product. This could be done inside or outside of the classroom, with or without time constraints.

Assessing the quality of a student-constructed online survey is relatively easy; in contrast, it is more difficult to assess the quality of student-constructed items. The same techniques that you can use to teach students to write items, however, can be used to assess their item-writing skills. For instance, you could name a concept and ask students to create exam items that appropriately assess other students' understanding of that concept. For example, you could ask students to assess other students' understanding of the *benefits of random sampling*. Students would be expected to write multiple-choice items such as the following:

> What is the direction of the relationship between random sampling and generalizability?
> a. Random samples increase your ability to generalize to the population from which you sampled.
> b. Random samples reduce your ability to generalize to the population from which you sampled.
> c. Random sampling has nothing to do with the ability to generalize from your sample to the population from which you took the sample.

Grading such an item uses a three-step process. First, provide the students with a rubric that guides the construction of individual test items. Such a rubric should consist, mainly, of the general principles underlying test construction. This rubric includes basic principles guiding how to (1) select an important concept to test, (2) write a clear question stem whose answer could be anticipated before reading the answer choices, (3) write clear answer choices that can easily be distinguished from one another, (4) provide a single correct answer choice, and (5) use correct grammar, punctuation, and spelling. Second, grade the student's product based on the rubric. Third, require the student to rewrite each test item in light of the instructor's comments and then re-grade the final product.

Another means of assessing students' item-writing skills is to provide a survey item and examples of participants' responses to that item, and ask your students to edit the item so that it elicits a different set of responses that you specify. For example, I might provide the following item and sample answers:

Item: At what age did you first have sex?
Answers: 3, 4, 6, 7, 7, 9, 12, 14, 15, 18, 20, 21, 24

I might then ask students to reword the item to indicate the precise question they wanted participants to answer by operationalizing "having sex." For example, I would expect to see examples of appropriate revisions of the item such as:

1. At what age did you first engage in penile-vaginal intercourse (the insertion of a penis into a vagina) that was consensual (not against your will)?
2. There are many activities that people consider sexual, but not all of them lead people to say they "had sex." Name the activities you might engage in that would lead you to say "I had sex" afterward, and indicate the age at which you first engaged in each of those activities consensually (by choice).

Awarding an objective grade to this task is difficult if not impossible. Hence, we recommend the instructor provide dichotomous (improved/not improved) or trichotomous (greatly improved/somewhat improved/not improved) grading as feedback for this type of assessment.

After having taught students to identify and correct specific item-writing problems, you could give students examples of items that should be improved and ask the students to identify ways to improve them; alternatively you may want to instruct the students to rewrite the questions. For example, I might ask students to describe the problem with, and rewrite, the following items:

At what age did you first have sex? (The concept about which you are asking has not been operationalized clearly within the question. The revisions of this same item above would also be appropriate here.)

Do you agree with the new rules and will you abide by them? (The question is double-barreled, leading some respondents to produce opposite responses to different parts of the question. The question could be divided into two questions: Do you agree with the new rules? Will you abide by the new rules?)

How much do you support the new rules designed to improve everyone's outcomes? (The item hints at the response the researcher expects. Remove the words following "rules" in the original item.)

Because each one of the provided items violates principles that the instructor and students had previously entertained, it is appropriate to expect students to identify (and perhaps name) each principle properly. Moreover, it is appropriate to expect students to generate principled alternatives. Hence, this form of assessment is straightforward. Alternatively, the instructor may assess mastery of these principles using a matching format, which simplifies grading.

It is also possible to provide students with poorly written items, average items, and well-written items addressing the same concept and ask students to rank-order the quality of the items from best to worst. It is instructive to have students provide reasons for their rank order, and it is appropriate to afford the quality of these explanations considerable weight in grading.

You could provide students with a research question and ask them to write a set of survey items that help answer the research question. For example, I might provide the following research question and expect an answer such as:

How much of a role does fear of social ostracism play in students' unwillingness to "snitch" on other students by turning them in when they witness cheating?

Rate the following statements from −3 (strongly disagree) to +3 (strongly agree):

Students should not cheat.

I would like there to be less cheating in my classes.

It is everyone's responsibility, including my own, to help reduce cheating in class.

I am likely to do something about it if I detect another student cheating.

I would be concerned about the student finding out if I turned him in for cheating.

I care about fitting in with the other students in my classes.

As before, grading survey items involves a three-step process. First, the students receive a rubric that guides the construction of individual survey items *and* ways in which items may be pooled to address the research question. Such a rubric should address the (1) relevance of the items to the research question, (2) likelihood that the items will generate the expected responses, (3) appropriateness of the rating scale to the items generated, and (4) relations among the items that permit the items to work together to answer questions the items taken alone do not. Second, grade the student's product based on the rubric. Third, require the student to rewrite the pool of survey items in light of the instructor's comments and re-grade the final product.

Finally, you could extend the previous assessment technique by having students generate a specific research question based on a topic you provide, prior to generating survey items designed to address the question. For example, instead of providing the research question stated immediately above, the instructor might direct students to specify a research question on the topic of snitching on classmates who cheat. Grading such an assessment requires the instructor to assess the degree to which the research question (1) stays within the bounds of the topic assigned and (2) is answerable using survey methodology.

Using Online Survey Tools to Assess Changes in Students' Mastery of Course Content Across One or More Classes

In addition to using online surveys to facilitate student learning, online survey tools can gather data assessing students' baseline knowledge or mastery of course content. For example, online surveys are useful for administering *ungraded* pre-tests that identify concepts students have mastered before entering a course, uncover pre-existing misconceptions, and provide a baseline against which to measure eventual mastery of the course material.

Ungraded pre-tests have proven useful in a wide range of courses, including biology, chemistry, and physics (Marrs, Blake, & Gavrin, 2003), geosciences (Guertin, Zappe, & Kim, 2007), economics (Simkins & Maier, 2004), and statistics (Benedict & Anderton, 2004) as part of Just-in-Time Teaching (Novack, Patterson, Gavrin, & Christian, 1999). Just-in-Time Teaching requires students to respond to short-answer or multiple-choice questions before class, enabling instructors to make "just-in-time" adjustments to focus the lecture on poorly understood topics (Benedict & Anderton, 2004; Simkins & Maier, 2004).

Although online surveys can also be used to administer *graded* quizzes or tests (see Chapter 18 in this volume), they may not be ideal for this purpose. They often lack features available from online testing programs, such as the ability to limit the time allotted for taking an exam, or to determine the number of *correct* responses and compute a grade directly (contact the first author for examples of "grading" spreadsheets). Yet their useful features, such as graphical displays of the proportion of the class selecting each answer choice, may sometimes outweigh these drawbacks.

Using Online Surveys as Measures of Faculty Performance

Administrators often view measures of student satisfaction as one indicator of teaching effectiveness, and student input may be influential in the tenure and promotion process (Dunn, McCarthy, Baker, & Halonen, 2009). Most standard university or department evaluations do not elicit detailed feedback on the students' subjective sense of mastery of the course material or the use of and satisfaction with course tools such as online surveys. Instructors may wish to supplement standard course evaluations by eliciting personalized feedback measuring the impact of such teaching strategies on both course mastery and satisfaction. Online survey tools provide a convenient method to accomplish these goals. Examples of evaluation items designed to supplement standard evaluations may include:

- In your personal and professional life, how have you applied what you have learned about creating online surveys in this course? How can you do so in the future?
- How much more capable are you of setting up an online survey now than you were before taking this class?
- How much more capable are you of writing effective:
  o Survey items (enabling you to answer your research question)?
  o Assessment (e.g., exam) questions (enabling you to tell whether other students have mastered a concept)?

The second and third items can be posed as open-ended or using a scale ranging from 1 (*not at all*) to 7 (*much more capable*). These items should be designed to reflect *change* rather than absolute levels of mastery because students start and end at different levels.

Online surveys provide several useful ways to gather formative feedback throughout a semester. For example, you can set up an online suggestion box. This tool lets students provide feedback at will (though you may have to provide regular reminders of its availability). The online option may consist of nothing more than a comment box, or it can include specific questions to encourage students to provide feedback on topics of particular concern to you.

Many professors collect brief hard-copy responses to one or more open-ended questions posed during class. For example, the Minute Paper (Angelo & Cross, 1993) is a commonly used tool for collecting information about students' understanding of classroom material. Students typically write brief explanations of the most important point in that day's lecture or describe the "muddiest" point of the lecture. Using an online survey system is more efficient than traditional methods because responses can be compiled electronically in seconds, downloaded, and retained for future use with no need to use or store hundreds of sheets of paper.

Using Online Survey Tools to Promote Undergraduate Research

Group research projects can be valuable professional and intellectual learning experiences (e.g., Dunn, McCarthy, Baker, Halonen & Hill, 2007; Halonen, Bosack, Clay, & McCarthy, 2003). Professionally, employers increasingly demand that new employees demonstrate the ability to work well as part of a team (Adams, 2003; Braham, 1992; Wells, 2008). Intellectually, students and alumni report that undergraduate research experiences enhance their critical thinking, research, and communication skills. Moreover, those who conduct research as undergraduates describe greater satisfaction with their undergraduate education (Bauer & Bennett, 2003; Wayment & Dickson, 2008). Online surveys provide an opportunity to bring research experiences *and* experience with collaborative group projects to a large proportion of undergraduates by moving undergraduate research opportunities into the classroom.

We asked General Psychology students to create a survey, collect data, and analyze the results using QuestionPro (QuestionPro.com), which has a limited version available for free. Each member of a team of seven students served in a specific role: Team Leader (coordinates team efforts), Recorder (maintains team files and folders, handles note taking for team), Reporter (gives all oral responses and presentations for team), Monitor (responsible for teamwork area and timekeeper for team activities), Scribe (writes and/or synthesizes team paper), Surveyor (writes, posts, and maintains survey data collection), and Wildcard (acts as assistant to team leader and assumes role of any absent team member). The Leader, Recorder, Reporter, Monitor, and Wildcat roles were adopted from the University of Tennessee at Chattanooga (2002) Web site on cooperative learning concerning structured learning team group roles. We created the Scribe and Surveyor roles to serve both the technological needs of our survey project and give additional roles to a seven-member group.

We urged each team to train members in multiple roles to guard against the unavailability of any particular member. We emphasized that these were not groups but rather teams working toward a common goal that would reflect both their collective and individual efforts. Teams selected their own topics (subject to approval by the instructor; an alternative approach is for the instructor to provide a set of topics or topic areas from which students can choose), devised hypotheses, and wrote 10 to 20 survey items. Teams met in class for 15 to 20 minutes over several weeks, where they worked on survey items and examined relevant literature; most project work took place outside of class time.

Students discovered QuestionPro to be intuitive; they needed only 45 to 60 minutes to construct their surveys in class. Students responded to at least six surveys from other teams. Survey responses were automatically stored on the QuestionPro Web site. Teams then used both the descriptive analyses and graphical displays available in QuestionPro, or they downloaded, analyzed the data, and constructed their own displays using data analysis programs such as SPSS. They then incorporated the descriptive statistics and graphics into a required, scientific-style report.

We found that teams of five students are as effective as larger teams in conducting survey research, and in a pinch even a two- or three-student team could reasonably be expected to complete a survey project. Teams seem to do better with more frequent, but less lengthy, meetings throughout the term. Such an arrangement facilitates communication, structure, and timely completion of project tasks. Teams respond better with more structure imposed by the instructor (e.g., deadlines for completing each task). Periodic reporting of the team's progress (i.e., verbally and in writing) enhances record-keeping and reporting roles. It is also important to address student concerns about individual responsibility to the team by assigning both an individual and a group grade. Mid-semester peer evaluations show team members how their teammates perceive the quality of their efforts. Final peer evaluations can also be incorporated into the grading system to promote accountability.

Online survey systems can be particularly useful for exploring sensitive topics. For example, we used SurveyMonkey (SurveyMonkey.com) to conduct research in Human Sexuality and Social Psychology courses. Students in Human Sexuality designed and conducted a systematic replication of Binder, Kirsner, Wenner, and Jacobs (2002). Before conducting the study, each student completed ethics certification, as required by our Institutional Review Board (IRB). Students reviewed findings from the earlier study and developed a survey instrument to measure several related constructs. Outside of class, students entered the items into SurveyMonkey to illustrate how the measure would look to participants. Students spent 20 to 30 minutes in class each week discussing various aspects of the project, especially item choice and wording; outside of class, several students worked for 1 to 2 hours per week to revise items and research existing measures of additional constructs. Once satisfied with the majority of the items, the students completed the survey themselves, at which point they were surprised to find that the some of the items remained unclear. The students, in collaboration with the instructor, then edited existing items, added new items, and recruited survey respondents from among the students' friends, family members, and acquaintances. Students contacted potential participants directly and by posting invitations to participate on their social networking sites. In less than 1 week, more than 400 participants completed the survey. We obtained responses from people up to 78 years old and from as far away as the Middle East. Although some might attribute this to the nature of the survey (the ways in which people define what behaviors constitute sex), obtaining such a large and diverse sample in such a short time would not have been feasible without conducting the survey online.

The online survey tool permitted the students to explore survey results just 2 days after it began (over 100 responses had been received). Although the end of the semester precluded formal data analysis, the class obtained descriptive statistics, viewed the proportion of respondents who gave each response, and observed patterns in the variables. After the semester concluded, several students analyzed the data and presented the results at regional conferences. Many more students can now work with the data, generating further presentations and, perhaps, journal articles, because of the rich set of items the class generated. In the semesters since, several other Human Sexuality and Social Psychology classes have participated in the survey, compared their results to those obtained from the entire sample, and discussed any perceived differences in detail.

Learning from the experience with Human Sexuality, we integrated research into the fabric of the Social Psychology course, focusing on the theme of academic integrity and its relation to many topics in Social Psychology. Students selected three writing projects from among six available assignments, including (1) summarizing research articles, (2) writing survey items, (3) designing experiments, and (4) designing interventions to increase academic integrity (sample assignments are available upon request from the first author). Students completed surveys designed by the instructor to assess their attitudes toward cheating and plagiarism, as well as their past behaviors, both at the beginning and end of the semester. The students themselves contributed items to assess the effects of the course design on their attitudes and behaviors with respect to academic integrity.

As a final project, the class cooperatively created a survey that 90 students in our department's research participation program completed. Using SurveyMonkey, the class considered the ten topics they had worked on during the semester, voted to select their three favorites, edited the existing items related to these topics, and wrote new items to address gaps in coverage. During the final week of the semester, the students viewed some of the results within SurveyMonkey during class, and submitted suggestions for later analyses. Several students intend to work on further analyses in future semesters.

The Human Sexuality and Social Psychology projects demonstrate that students in content-based courses can gain practical experience designing and conducting research in content courses. In both examples, the entire class participated in the project design. A primary advantage of these class-based projects is the diversity of opinions and ideas about the study design. It is easy for a small group of researchers to overlook alternative ideas as they design a study, but this may be much less likely to occur with a large, diverse group of engaged students acting as a research team. Students in both classes pointed out and recommended solutions to potential problems that a smaller, more homogeneous group might have missed. Problematically, some students in a large research team disengage; we mitigated the problem by fully integrating the project into the course design. Although some students participated in class discussions more than others, everyone participated in the research through assignments involving the design of studies and interventions, and by writing and revising survey items.

Using Online Survey Tools to Enhance Classroom Teaching and Learning

Classroom response systems (see Chapter 9 in this volume) are a valuable tool because they can garner immediate student reactions; in a computer-equipped classroom, online survey tools can acquire data almost as easily and quickly. Unlike classroom response systems, instructors may also use online surveys to collect data between classes, and if the questions are sufficiently interesting, use those data to engage students (see, for example, Just-in-Time Teaching; Novack et al., 1999).

Results from online surveys can highlight classroom diversity (or lack thereof) by gathering and presenting data describing students' backgrounds, attitudes, or acquaintance with topics. In the aforementioned Human Sexuality class, for instance, we ask students to indicate, anonymously, how many of their friends, family members, or co-workers fit into various categories of sexual orientation or gender identity, have contracted specific sexually transmitted infections, or have engaged in various sexual behaviors. We then use those data, in the aggregate, to illustrate principles behind related topics as those topics occur during the semester.

Online surveys can be used to teach students about existing measures, such as personality tests. Provide the measure as an online survey and require students to complete it before discussing the measure in class. Depending on the nature of the measure, you might teach the students how to score their own responses, provide their scores to them individually, or present only aggregate scores to the class.

Selecting an Online Survey Program

Because there are so many online survey tools available, each with its own set of options, you must review a number of online survey tools to determine which ones suit the students' learning needs. After narrowing the list of online survey tools to those suitable for your students' needs, consider cost, use (number of surveys planned, number of respondents expected), availability of technical support, ease of use, anonymity, and types of items available.

Cost is typically a major institutional concern. Many online survey tools offer differential pricing based on customer type (e.g., academic, corporate, personal), the number of surveys or respondents, and term of contract. Some companies offer a free trial (e.g., SurveyGold) or a free version with limited features (e.g., SurveyMonkey, QuestionPro). Some versions limit the number of surveys you can create or the number of responses you can receive during a specified time. You may want to test-drive these free or limited versions before committing to any one tool. It is important to familiarize yourself with the tool during the trial period to ensure that it fits your students' needs.

Consider the tools your colleagues use. Some tools allow you to send a previously constructed survey to other account holders. This feature saves time by enabling others to edit a previously constructed survey or to use a survey in its entirety for their own purposes—a convenient feature when you or your colleagues use similar surveys. Moreover, sharing surveys in this way can promote cooperation and collegiality in a department or across a university.

Most of the commonly used tools have templates for creating items; knowing the types of items you will use and selecting a tool with appropriate templates simplifies the startup process. Many online survey tools permit you to create items from scratch and/or use customizable templates. You should be careful when reviewing these tools. Some do not permit full access to all the item types unless you purchase the most comprehensive plan, and the number of item templates varies somewhat across tools.

Access to technical support is an important consideration. Almost all of the major tools offer an online knowledge base with common questions and online tutorials. Paid versions of these tools also offer e-mail support. Some also offer phone support and technical support forums.

Most programs are easy to use *if you select from among the item formats provided*. Ensure that the online interface is easy to navigate, that it is easy to edit items, and that you can easily change most item types without recreating an item from scratch.

The ability to make surveys completely anonymous is indispensable. Normally, researchers do not collect information about IP addresses because those addresses identify the computer used to complete the survey. Institutional Review Boards, professional ethics, and the human rights of our participants usually require that data cannot be linked to an individual or to a particular computer. Moreover, many of the uses for online surveys, especially feedback forms or sensitive research, call for anonymity. Under some circumstances, however, recording IP addresses is central to the research; hence, the option to record them is essential. It is equally important that the survey tool make obvious which one of these options is active.

You may access comparison charts for many of the currently available tools online (Toledano, 2008; Van Bennekom, 2007), but these charts quickly become obsolete. Nonetheless, the selection principles described above will apply for some time to come.

Challenges in the Use of Online Surveys

Although there are advantages to conducting surveys online, doing so poses challenges, many delineated by an American Psychological Association advisory group (Kraut, Olson, Banaji, Bruckman, Cohen, & Couper, 2004). An advantage of designing and conducting research in the classroom is that students can recruit participants from among their personal contacts; however, as with all convenience samples, these participants may not adequately represent the population of interest. Moreover, the anonymity afforded by online surveys makes it difficult to know who is completing the surveys—even if participants provide personal information, it may misrepresent reality—and whether they meet your selection criteria. It is more likely that participants in online than in face-to-face surveys will fail to understand what they are consenting to before taking the survey, and that they will end participation before receiving the written debriefing or other explanatory materials, though both dangers can be mitigated (Kraut et al., 2004, pp. 16, 18–19). Online surveys have lower completion rates than those administered in person; this simultaneously decreases generalizability and may serve as an ethical advantage if lower completion rates reflect less social pressure to complete the survey.

Perhaps the greatest concern about student use of online surveys is that poor research may contaminate the participant pool (Kraut et al., 2004). The ease with which students can create and post surveys online heightens this concern. At the same time, teaching students to conduct research responsibly, and supervising them closely, is the best way to counter the possibility of poor-quality surveys decreasing the value of data from the online participant pool.

Conclusion

The activities described in this chapter span the universe of active learning. Using online survey tools, we can help students master course material by increasing engagement, motivation, and learning. Students can design and conduct research in just one semester; they can design a study, create appropriate items, collect and analyze data, and present the results. Online surveys can be used to assess what students already know, identify misunderstandings, and provide a measure of what they have learned. Finally, completed online surveys can provide formative and summative feedback.

The judicious use of online surveys can generate a graceful, interactive, and continuous student-centered interface between students and instructor. In addition, online survey tools permit the students to integrate classroom and real-world experience in meaningful ways.

Acknowledgements

The authors thank W. Jake Jacobs and Maureen McCarthy for helpful comments on an earlier draft of this chapter.

Recommended Readings

Couper, M. P. (2005). Technology trends in survey data collection. *Social Science Computer Review, 24*, 486–501.

Garson, G. D. (2008). *Survey research*. Retrieved April 26, 2009, from the Statnotes Web site: http://faculty.chass.ncsu.edu/garson/PA765/survey.htm

Schwarz, N., Groves, R. M., & Schuman, H. (1998). Survey methods. In: D. T. Gilbert, S. T. Fiske, & G. Lindzey (eds.), *Handbook of social psychology* (4th ed., Vol. 1, pp. 143–179). New York: McGraw-Hill.

References

Adams, S. G. (2003). Building successful student teams in the engineering classroom. *Journal of STEM Education: Innovations and Research, 4*(3/4), 1–6.

Angelo, T. A., & Cross, K. P. (1993). *Classroom assessment techniques: A handbook for college teachers*. San Francisco: Jossey-Bass.

Bauer, K. W., & Bennett, J. S. (2003). Alumni perceptions used to assess undergraduate research experience. *Journal of Higher Education, 74*, 210–230.

Benedict, J. O., & Anderton, J. B. (2004). Applying the just-in-time teaching approach to teaching statistics. *Teaching of Psychology, 31*, 197–199.

Binder, M., Kirsner, B. R., Wenner, C., & Jacobs, W. J., (2002, April). *Is "having sex" the same as "being sexual"?* Paper presented at the annual meeting of the Society of Behavioral Medicine, Washington, DC.

Braham, J. (1992). Employers demand new skills. *Machine Design, 64*(19), 42–47.

Dunn, D. S. (2009). *Research methods for social psychology.* Malden, MA: Wiley-Blackwell.

Dunn, D. S., McCarthy, M. A., Baker, S., & Halonen, J. S. (2011). *Using quality benchmarks for assessing and developing undergraduate programs.* San Francisco:Josey Bass.

Dunn, D. S., McCarthy, M. A., Baker, S., Halonen, J. S., & Hill, G. W. (2007). Quality benchmarks in undergraduate psychology programs. *American Psychologist, 62*, 650–670.

Guertin, L. A., Zappe, S. E., & Kim, H. (2007). Just-in-time teaching exercises to engage students in an introductory-level dinosaur course. *Journal of Science Education & Technology, 16*, 507–514.

Halonen, J. S., Bosack, T., Clay, S., & McCarthy, M. A. (2003). A rubric for learning, teaching, and assessing scientific inquiry in psychology. *Teaching of Psychology, 30*, 196–207.

Kraut, R., Olson, J., Banaji, M., Bruckman, A., Cohen, J., & Couper, M. (2004). Psychological research online: Report of Board of Scientific Affairs Advisory Group on the Conduct of Research on the Internet. *American Psychologist, 59*, 105–117.

Marrs, K. A., Blake, R. E., & Gavrin, A. D. (2003). Web-based warm up exercises in just-in-time teaching. *Journal of College Science Teaching, 33*, 42–47.

Novack, G. M., Patterson, E. T., Gavrin, A. D., & Christian, W. (1999) *Just-in-time teaching: Blending active learning with web technology.* Upper Saddle River, NJ: Prentice Hall.

Schwarz, N., Groves, R. M., & Schuman, H. (1998). Survey methods. In D. T. Gilbert, S. T. Fiske, & G. Lindzey (eds.), *Handbook of social psychology* (4th ed., Vol. 1, pp. 143–179). New York: McGraw-Hill.

Simkins, S., & Maier, M. (2004). Using just-in-time teaching techniques in the principles of economics course. *Social Science Computer Review, 22*, 444–456.

Toledano, Y. (2008). *Survey tools comparison chart.* Retrieved April 26, 2009, from the TechSoup.org Web site: https://cc.readytalk.com/cc/download/schedule/a74kijv001ke

Trochim, W. M. K. (2006). *Research methods knowledge base.* Retrieved April 26, 2009, from Web Center for Social Research Methods: http://www.socialresearch-methods.net/kb/

University of Tennessee at Chattanooga (2002). *Cooperative learning*. Retrieved from http://www.utc.edu/Administration/WalkerTeachingResourceCenter/Faculty Development/CooperativeLearning/index.html

Van Bennekom, F. (2007). *How to select a web survey tool*. Retrieved April 26, 2009, from the GreatBrook Web site: http://www.greatbrook.com/web_survey_tools.htm

Wayment, H. A., & Dickson, K. L. (2008). Increasing student participation in undergraduate research benefits students, faculty, and departments. *Teaching of Psychology, 35*, 194–197.

Wells, K. R. (2008). How to get an on-site interview with a top employer. *Black Collegian, 38*(2), 34–39.

18 Online Quizzes

Improving Reading Compliance and Student Learning

Lonnie R. Yandell and William N. Bailey

A recent advertisement for a textbook announced in bold letters: "Imagine what your lectures could be if your students read their textbook and understood the material ..."

How many times have you had strong indications from your students that they have not read the assigned readings? A lasting memory of the first author of this chapter as a graduate teaching assistant many years ago was an introductory psychology student at the beginning of the first class, in all seriousness, asking the professor, "What is the textbook for?"

In this chapter we will explore the issue of students' preparation for class and how Web-based testing can be used to improve reading compliance and student learning. After reviewing the evidence that students typically do not prepare for class by reading textbook assignments, we will provide the rationale for using quizzes to improve reading compliance and to facilitate learning. We will then argue that using out-of-class, online quizzing is an efficient and effective way to improve reading compliance. We will provide an example of how we have used online quizzing in a large introductory psychology class and the lessons we have learned using this methodology.

Reading Compliance

It is all too common for students to come to class not prepared to learn. Studies of reading compliance have shown that students typically do not come to class having read assigned material, with two thirds or more not reading assignments (Burchfield & Sappington, 2000; Connor-Greene, 2000; Sappington, Kinsey, & Munsayac, 2002). Similarly, Clump, Bauer, and Bradley (2004) found that less than one third of undergraduate psychology students read assigned textbook readings before class, and two thirds read the textbook immediately before major exams. Sikorski, Rich, Savill, Buskist, Drogan, and Davis (2002) reported that students admit to spending less than 3 hours a week reading textbooks for introductory courses and that purchasing and reading a textbook plays a minor role in how they prepare for exams. In fact, Boyd (2003) reported that from 10 to 25 percent of students do not even buy textbooks for a college course.

How important is it for students to read assigned material before class? Teachers tend to put varying amounts of value on the importance of reading a textbook for a class. Some tend to downplay the importance, with something along the lines of "Reading the textbook may help you understand my lectures, but it is probably not essential" (for example, see Lord, 2007). At the other end of the spectrum is the teacher who highly values text readings, with statements such as "Test content will come mostly, if not entirely, from the textbook, and much of the material on the test will not be covered in class." There are arguably good reasons for each of these approaches. Because reading a textbook is one of the most frequent assignments in college classes, it is safe to assume most teachers view it as very important. In a class like Introduction to Psychology, where students are relatively naïve about the subject matter and often do not have good study habits, it seems essential that they be motivated to read the textbook regularly, particularly because many college courses are organized around a textbook (Sikorski et al., 2002).

Given that we acknowledge that students should read textbook assignments (or any assigned reading, for that matter) and that we, as faculty, have some responsibility to encourage this practice, what are some methods we can use? Perhaps one of the most common methods is quizzing. Although authors have suggested other methods, such as graded long-answer questions based on assigned readings (Uskal & Eaton, 2005) and homework assignments (Ryan, 2006), quizzing to assess reading compliance is probably the most common method used and has a fair amount of research supporting it (see below). Quizzing research can be divided into (1) studies done before the advent of online information delivery and (2) those containing an online component, including classes that are delivered completely online and blended class delivery (classes with both online and in-class components).

In-Class Quizzing

Research on the use of in-class quizzing has varied greatly across studies. Quiz-delivery methods differ with regard to the frequency of quiz administration, from one per semester to daily (Connor-Greene, 2000; Wesp, 1986). Types of questions include essay questions (Connor-Greene, 2000), short-answer questions (Fernald, 2004; Ruscio, 2001), and multiple-choice questions (Azorlosa & Renner, 2006; Graham, 1999; Marchant, 2002; Wesp, 1986). Many of the quizzes were scheduled or announced (Azorlosa & Renner, 2006; Connor-Greene, 2000, Marchant, 2002; Wesp, 1986), but some were unannounced (Graham, 1999; Ruscio, 2001) or were determined by chance (Fernald, 2004) using a roll of the dice. Although all of the quizzes covered assigned readings, some did not count toward the final grade (Marchant, 2002); others accounted for 10 to 25 percent of the final grade (Azorlosa & Renner, 2006; Graham, 1999). Most of the quizzes were graded with delayed feedback, returning quiz results on the next class or later (Connor-Greene, 2000), but some had immediate feedback or a tutoring session that immediately followed the quiz (Wesp, 1986).

Early research on in-class quizzing revealed a variety of positive pedagogical effects of quizzing, such as increased attendance and higher grades (Fitch, Ducker, & Norton, 1951). More recently, positive effects include reduced student procrastination (Wesp, 1986), higher test scores (Graham, 1999), more punctual completion and deeper processing of assigned readings (Fernald, 2004), more thorough preparation for class discussion (Connor-Greene, 2000), increased reading completion rate (Marchant, 2002; Ruscio, 2001), better attendance, and reported improved studying and exam preparation (Azorlosa & Renner, 2006). Although not all studies have found universally positive effects of quizzing for reading assignments (e.g., Anderson, 1984), the majority of quizzing outcomes are positive.

Roediger and his colleagues (for a recent review, see Roediger & Karpicke, 2006) have argued that frequent testing in the classroom can boost educational achievement, often referred to as the "testing effect." They presented a large body of research indicating that testing not only measures knowledge but also changes it by improving retention of the tested knowledge. This testing effect has both direct and mediated effects on learning. The direct effects have been verified using free recall and paired-associate tests in controlled laboratory studies as well as using educationally relevant materials, such as essay, short-answer, and multiple-choice questions (Roediger & Karpicke, 2006). Some research has shown the testing effect applies to classroom settings as well as controlled laboratory settings (McDaniel, Roediger, & McDermott, 2007). Interestingly, frequent testing also has important mediated effects on learning. Mediated effects include encouraging students to study more and to be continuously engaged with the material, thus leading to more distributed learning. Finally, quizzing provides the student with feedback as to what knowledge has been acquired and what needs to be further studied.

Online Quizzing

More recently, with the increasing popularity of using the Internet to facilitate higher education, quizzing with an online component has been examined. Online quizzing typically has involved using a Web-based testing program or a course-delivery platform such as Blackboard (http://www.blackboard.com) to deliver a number of quizzes based on compulsory reading. Quizzes have been delivered on computers both in class (Daniel & Broida, 2004), and more commonly out of class (Brothen & Wambach, 2004; Johnson & Kiviniemi, 2009; Marcell, 2008; Utrel, Bahamonde, Mikedsky, Udry, & Vessely, 2006).

Marcell (2008) and Johnson and Kiviniemi (2009) recently used online quizzes to increase reading-related class participation and preparation and to improve exam performance, respectively. Each study posted regularly scheduled quizzes, with Marcell (2008) using timed, 5-item quizzes and Johnson and Kiviniemi (2009) using a 10-item, mastery-based format, which allowed for unlimited attempts but required all 10 questions to be correctly answered. Both studies relied on the Web program randomly selecting questions from a large bank of questions. When Marcell (2008) contrasted comparable but separate sections of the same course, students in the section with quizzes asked more reading-related questions and made more reading-related comments than did students in the section without quizzes. Johnson and Kiviniemi (2009) compared scores on exams that were preceded by quizzes with exams that were not preceded by quizzes in their class and found that students performed better on exams preceded by quizzes.

Utrel et al. (2006) gave students daily online quizzes to be taken prior to class time for half of a semester. They found increased class engagement (such as student questions in class) from the students for the half of the semester with online quizzes compared to the half of the semester with no online quizzes. They found no differences in attendance or exam performance and both positive and negative student perceptions of the effectiveness of the online quizzes.

Daniel and Broida (2004) provided students with either daily online quizzes, in-class quizzes on computers, or no quizzes. The quizzes consisted of primarily 5 to 10 multiple-choice questions from a larger bank of textbook publisher-provided questions or teacher-generated questions and were administered with a time limit. They found that online quizzes were effective in improving exam scores over students with no quiz, but only when instructors limited the amount of time students had to complete the online quizzes. Daniel and Broida (2004) found that when online quiz time is not limited, students have time to cheat on the quiz rather than read the text before quizzing. When given 24 hours to complete quizzes, students reported printing and sharing answers, looking up answers in their books, using online glossaries, and working in groups. When quiz time is limited, students must read the assignment first, facilitating actual learning. In addition, a Web program randomly chose questions from large test banks to reduce cheating.

Brothen and Wambach (2004) further explored the optimal time per question on online quizzes. They found that students who were given quizzes with 10 multiple-choice questions within a 15-minute time limit performed better on unit exams than student who took the same quizzes with no time limits. They suggest that time limits on online quizzes discourage the use of what they term "quiz-to-learn" strategies, defined by students using the quizzes to focus on correct answers found in the text rather than using the quizzes to test their acquired knowledge of the readings. Further consideration of the optimal time allowed for online quizzing seems warranted.

Online Solutions to In-Class Problems

Although in-class quizzing is clearly associated with positive student outcomes, some negative aspects have been noted. Some teachers object to the amount of class time quizzing takes, time that could be spent on lectures, discussions, or creative exercises. If teachers carry out a frequent quizzing schedule, a significant amount of class time will be used. In addition, frequent quizzing can be a burden to the teacher, requiring added time and effort in constructing and grading quizzes. Further, students may react with increased anxiety to frequent quizzing, particularly when quizzes are unannounced (Thorne, 2000). Lastly, some instructors may worry that quizzing is not effective for complex subject matter and may foster rote learning and boredom in students (Roediger & Karpicke, 2006).

An additional problem with frequent quizzing is related to a specific type of testing: multiple-choice tests. Multiple-choice tests are used frequently in higher education because many believe they provide a worthy measure of student learning (McKeachie, 1999). However, Roediger and Butler (2008) reported that because students are exposed to much incorrect information in the form of incorrect lures on multiple-choice questions, students may also learn incorrect information. Although the negative effects rarely overshadow the positive effects of testing on learning, there are ways to reduce the negative effects through feedback (Roediger & Butler, 2008).

The use of regular, online quizzing can minimize most of the negative aspects of in-class quizzing. Convenient course-management tools such as Blackboard can automate the process of creating, administering, grading, and providing feedback to students. Teachers can upload large, publisher-provided multiple-choice quiz banks into Blackboard. Blackboard then automatically can create quizzes with randomly selected items, administer the quizzes to the students on a set schedule, immediately grade the quizzes, and immediately indicate to students what questions were missed and what the correct answer should have been. This process requires a minimum amount of set-up time for the teacher and can serve a large number of students for multiple tests. Quizzing can take place outside of regular class time, and teachers can avoid spending valuable class time administering quizzes, and providing simple feedback to students, as well as time outside of class grading quizzes. Since the online quizzing can be administered on a regular, announced schedule that is controlled by the Blackboard program, students develop consistent expectations that can serve to reduce anxiety and increase regular, distributed learning. Roediger and Butler (2008) found that providing feedback soon after taking a quiz could reduce the negative effects of incorrect lures on multiple-choice items. Although Roediger and Butler (2008) used simple, factual information in their study, Marsh, Roediger, Bjork, and

Bjork (2007) found both positive and negative testing effects using complex, conceptual materials when no feedback was given. Marsh et al. (2007) suggested that feedback would reduce negative testing effects for conceptual material much as it has for factual material, although this conjecture must await empirical testing.

Our Experience with Pre-class Testing

Course Context

The typical introductory psychology class at Belmont University has an enrollment limited to about 24 students. However, the current authors are part of a three-person team and jointly instruct a single, large section of 96 students comprising four smaller class sections. Because of the rather large size of this combined class, we have made a special attempt to provide extra class structure and detailed information to facilitate communication, class participation, and student motivation. For example, in the required lab portion of the course, the large class is divided into four smaller lab classes that are further organized into smaller lab groups of three to five students each. This organizational structure complements the lab activities and exercises because most are designed to be group projects. Also, we use a variety of technology-based practices and activities, such as student response systems, PowerPoint, and Blackboard. We used the Blackboard course-management system for posting class materials (e.g., syllabus, study aids, grades) as well as to facilitate communication and provide pre-class quizzes outside of class meetings.

Special consideration was given to the role of pre-class quizzes. We hoped that pre-class quizzes would encourage and reward students for reading the assigned textbook material before discussing the information in class. It was anticipated that students who completed assigned readings before class would be more likely to participate in class discussions and better comprehend and remember the material. Consequently, we thought that as students benefited more from class discussion, they would earn higher test scores. Also, if students completed their pre-class readings, it would no longer be necessary to spend the majority of the class time just reviewing the text material. The instructor would be given greater flexibility when creating the classroom experience.

Structure of the Pre-Class Quiz

Each of the 10 pre-class quizzes comprised 15 multiple-choice questions. The quizzes were regularly spaced over the semester, with about one quiz per week of class. The quiz content was from the portion of the textbook to be covered that week. The Blackboard program had access to questions from the textbook publisher's large question bank (over 3,000 questions). For each individual quiz, the 15 questions were randomly chosen by Blackboard from the appropriate section of the question bank, with each section containing 176 to 603 questions. Students could take each pre-class quiz three times with different questions randomly selected for each attempt. The large number of questions and random selection virtually ensured that each quiz was different from every other quiz. We instituted a 20-minute time limit for each quiz version or quiz attempt. Only the highest score of three attempts for each pre-class quiz counted toward the final semester grade. The 10 pre-class quizzes counted a total of 10 percent toward the final grade, with each quiz contributing 1 percent toward the total.

Although pre-class quizzes could be taken as early as a student wished, there was a deadline for completing each quiz, after which no credit was awarded. All quiz attempts had to be completed no later than class time for the class session during which the assigned text material was discussed.

Problems with Computer-Assisted Pre-Class Quizzes

Our use of computer-assisted, pre-class quizzes resulted in a few unique issues and problems in the classroom. The Blackboard-based quizzes were typically easy to understand and allowed for quick learning of necessary technology skills. However, often there were small numbers of students who had problems taking online quizzes. Usually their concerns involved issues with their personal computers or browsers, maintaining proper Internet connections, or simply failing to follow the instructions for accessing and completing the online quizzes. In most cases these issues were remedied fairly easily with a quick review of necessary procedures with individual students.

A second concern was assessing the educational effectiveness of pre-class quizzes. It would have been difficult to require some students in a class to complete pre-class quizzes while not offering that opportunity to others. Having different requirements for different students within the same class would have been problematic for a number of reasons. Of course, another option would have been to compare exam performance in an experimental class receiving pre-class quizzes with a control class of the same topic and taught by the same instructor in which pre-class quizzes are not used, but we have not conducted that type of analysis. Three instructors, each teaching different topics at different times during the semester, have taught the course section in which we have used pre-class quizzes. Such a course structure has made any experimental analysis of pre-class quizzes quite difficult.

We have found that performance on the pre-class quizzes is positively correlated with performance on unit exams. Of course, this correlation could be explained by higher-achieving students performing better on both types of assessments.

Impact of Pre-Class Quizzes on Classes

Because we have little experimental or psychometric data for pre-class quizzing, we have relied primarily on anecdotal impressions of class performance and on student comments from end-of-semester class evaluations. In this limited context, the instructors, who average almost 27 years of teaching experience, reported students asking not only more questions but higher-quality questions, reflecting better command of the assigned material and perhaps deeper thought.

Class evaluations do not seem to provide any general student consensus on the benefits of pre-class quizzes. Student reactions to pre-class quizzes ranged from quite positive to very negative. Examples of comments supporting pre-class quizzes were:

- "The quizzes were a huge help."
- "I really appreciated that the professors did that for us; not only because it helped my grade but also because it helped in preparation for the tests."
- "The pre-class quizzes were very helpful in preparing for tests and for helping my grade."

Conversely, some students described their experiences with pre-class quizzes with as much conviction but in unflattering terms, such as the following:

- "Pre-class quizzes were not helpful; they were more frustrating than anything."
- "There was too much involvement for just a core class …"

Conclusions and Lessons Learned

Based on our experiences using pre-class quizzes and our review of the effects of testing on reading compliance, student engagement, and learning, we offer a number of lessons we have learned:

1. *Student compliance of assigned class reading is low.* Our experience, reports from other teachers, and numerous studies suggest that students need to be strongly motivated to complete assigned course readings in a consistent and effective manner.

2. *Regular testing on assigned readings can increase reading compliance.* Consistent testing may also serve to develop long-term, effective study habits, although we have no knowledge of direct tests of this type of learning generalization.

3. *Regular testing on readings may increase relevant classroom participation.* Evidence from one study as well as our personal experience suggests that students come to class better prepared to participate in class and participate at a higher level when they have completed reading assignments.

4. *Regular testing on assigned readings can improve student learning.* There is ample evidence that testing has direct effects on learning as well as secondary effects, such as increased study of relevant material and greater distributed learning.

5. *Online testing solves many problems involved with in-class testing.* Using online testing (e.g., through Blackboard) can greatly reduce the problems with creating, administering, and grading tests as well as improve the quality and timeliness of feedback to students than is often given by a teacher.

We believe that regular on-line testing of assigned readings can be an effective and efficient way for teachers to encourage the development of productive reading habits. In addition, we believe consistent online testing improves learning in the classroom because students come to class better prepared to participate in on-task discussions and other enriching activities. Although interesting textbooks and inspiring teachers can also motivate students to engage with relevant reading materials, we believe that providing tangible reinforcements for reading (or punishments for not reading) can help develop habits that will serve students' life-long learning.

References

Anderson, J. E. (1984). Frequency of quizzes in a behavioral sciencecourse: An attempt to increase medical student study behavior. *Teaching of Psychology, 11,* 34.

Azorlosa, J. L., & Renner, C.H. (2006). The effect of announced quizzes on exam performance. *Journal of Instructional Psychology, 33*(4), 278.

Boyd, D. (2003, June). *Using textbooks effectively: Getting students to read them.* Observer, (16, 6). Retrieved from http://www.psychologicalscience.org/teaching/tips/tips_0603.cfm.

Brothen, T., & Wambach, C. (2004). The value of time limits on Internet quizzes. *Teaching of Psychology, 31,* 62–64.

Burchfield, C. M., & Sappington, J. (2000). Compliance with required reading assignments. *Teaching of Psychology, 27,* 58–60.

Butler, A. C., & Roediger, H. L., III (2007). Testing improves long-term retention in a simulated classroom setting. *European Journal of Cognitive Psychology, 19,* 514–527. doi: 10.3758/MC.36.3.604

Clump, M. A., Bauer, H., & Bradley, C. (2004). The extent to which psychology students read textbooks: A multiple class analysis of reading across the psychology curriculum. *Journal of Instructional Psychology, 31,* 227–232.

Connor-Greene, P. A. (2000). Assessing and promoting student learning: Blurring the line between teaching and testing. *Teaching of Psychology, 27,* 84–88.

Daniel, D. B., & Broida, J. (2004). Using web-based quizzing to improve exam performance: Lessons learned. *Teaching of Psychology, 31*(3), 207–208.

Fernald, P. S. (2004). The Monte Carlo quiz: Encouraging punctual completion and deep processing of assigned reading. *College Teaching, 52*(3), 95–99.

Fitch, M. L., Drucker, A. J., & Norton, L. A. A. (1951). Frequent testing as a motivating factor in large lecture classes. *Journal of Educational Psychology, 42,* 1–20.

Graham, R. B. (1999). Unannounced quizzes raise test scores selectively for mid-range students. *Teaching of Psychology, 26,* 271–273.

Johnson, B. C., & Kiviniemi, M. T. (2009). The effect of online chapter quizzes on exam performance in an undergraduate social psychology course. *Teaching of Psychology, 36*(1), 33–37.

Lord, T. (2007). Please don't read the text before coming to lecture. *Journal of Science Teaching, 37*(1), 52–54.

Marcell, M. 2008. Effectiveness of regular online quizzing in increasing class participation and preparation. *International Journal for the Scholarship of Teaching and Learning, 2*(1), 1–9. Retrieved from http://www.georgiasouthern.edu/ijsotl

Marchant, G. T. (2002). Student reading of assigned articles: Will this be on the test? *Teaching of Psychology, 29,* 49–51.

Marsh, E. J., Roediger, H. L., III, Bjork, R. A., & Bjork, E. L. (2007). The memorial consequences of multiple-choice testing. *Psychonomic Bulletin and Review, 14,* 194–199.

McDaniel, M. A., Roediger, H. L. III, & McDermott, K. B. (2007). Generalizing test-enhanced learning from the laboratory to the classroom. *Psychonomic Bulletin and Review, 14*(2), 200–206.

McKeachie, W. J. (1999). *Teaching tips: Strategies, research, and theory for college and university teachers* (10th ed.). Boston: Houghton Mifflin.

Roediger, H. L. III, & Butler, A. C. (2008). Feedback enhances the positive effects and reduces the negative effects of multiple-choice testing. *Memory and Cognition, 36*(3), 604–616.

Roediger, H. L., III, & Karpicke, J. D. (2006). The power of testing memory: Basic research and implications for educational practice. *Perspectives on Psychological Science, 1,* 181–210.

Ruscio, J. (2001). Administering quizzes at random to increase students' reading. *Teaching of Psychology, 28,* 204–206.

Ryan, T. (2006). Motivating novice students to read their textbooks. *Journal of Instructional Psychology, 33*(2), 156–136.

Sappington, J., Kinsey, K., & Munsayac, K. (2002). Two studies of reading compliance among college students. *Teaching of Psychology, 29,* 272–274.

Sikorski, J. F., Rich, K., Saville, B. K., Buskist, W., Drogan, O., & Davis, S. F. (2002). Student use of introductory texts: Comparative survey findings from two universities. *Teaching of Psychology, 29*(4), 312–313.

Thorne, B.M. (2000). Extra credit exercise: A painless pop quiz. *Teaching of Psychology, 27,* 204–205.

Uskal, A. K., Eaton, J. (2005). Using questions to increase timely reading of assigned material. *Teaching of Psychology, 32*(2), 116–117.

Utrel, M. G., Bahamonde, R. E., Mikedsky, A. E., Udry, E. M., & Vessely, J. S. (2006). *On-line quizzing and its effect on student engagement and academic performance. Journal of Scholarship of Teaching and Learning, 6*(2), 84–92. Retrieved from http://www.georgiasouthern.edu/ijsotl

Wesp, R. (1986). Reducing procrastination through required course involvement. *Teaching of Psychology, 13,* 128–130.

19   Going Virtual

Virtual Worlds as Educational Tools

Suzanne C. Baker and Monica Reis-Bergan

O nline virtual worlds or "Multi-User Virtual Environments" (MUVEs) are online environments that can be used simultaneously by many people. The online environment may appear as a two-dimensional or three-dimensional space, often with structures such as virtual streets, buildings, parks, or other environmental features. Users of these virtual worlds create an "avatar," a character that represents them in this online space. Avatars can travel throughout the virtual environment and interact with one another using text chat, voice, or sometimes both, depending on the specific characteristics of the virtual world. Typically, users can also interact with objects in the virtual world; for example, they may be able to enter a building, or pick up objects and use them to accomplish a task. In fact, an important characteristic of virtual worlds is their interactive nature. Typically, many thousands of people are logged in simultaneously to a virtual world (numbers vary depending on the virtual world), and users are able to interact with one another in order to socialize, form friendships, and collaborate on tasks.

Virtual worlds share many similarities with Massively-Multiplayer Online Role-Playing Games (MMORPG; e.g., World of Warcraft, Everquest). In both virtual worlds and MMPORGs, users (avatars) can explore the environment, interact with one another, and work together to accomplish goals. However, games by their nature have a specified goal: the player is presented with a problem to solve or some task to accomplish (see Salen, 2008). Although it is possible to play games within a virtual world, virtual worlds are not games in and of themselves. In virtual worlds, there is no conflict to resolve, and no increasing "levels" to achieve. Users are free to explore the world as much or as little as they would like, and they can interact with other users or objects in the world to the extent that they choose.

In this chapter, we explore how these online virtual worlds can be used in teaching. We focus on Second Life (SL), which is currently the most popular virtual world in terms of its use by educators. SL is only one of many virtual worlds currently in existence. The primary activity in many virtual worlds is social interaction. Examples include There (http://www.there.com) and Kaneva (http://www.kaneva.com). Other virtual worlds center around specific activities or are directed toward certain age groups. For example, the popular virtual world Habbo (http://www.habbo.com), with over 11 million visitors per month as of April 2009 (Sulake Corporation Oy, 2009), is designed to appeal to teenagers, and game playing is a primary activity in addition to social interaction and exploring the virtual world. Whyville (http://www.whywille.net) is a virtual world for children that focuses on educational activities and games.

Second Life

SL was created in 2003 and is operated by Linden Lab. User statistics as of May 2009 indicate that over 1.4 million users had logged in to SL during the previous 60 days (http://secondlife.com/statistics/economy-data.php). Typically, over 500,000 users log in to SL during a given 7-day period. Several hundred universities currently have a presence of some kind in SL.

An important feature of SL is the ability of the users to create objects in the SL world. Using a fairly simple set of programming tools, users can construct objects, buildings, and entire environments to suit their needs. The vast majority of the content in SL, including everything from avatar clothing and basic objects such as furniture, to elaborate buildings, structures, and entire environments, was created by SL residents. The SL world is divided into square plots of virtual land ("sims"), and each of these plots is owned or leased by a resident or a group. Numerous universities (including our own, James Madison) have "virtual campuses" in SL, often consisting of a mix of buildings that replicate those on their "real-world" campuses, along with structures newly designed for the SL world. It is not necessary to own land in order to use SL; however, owning land provides users with a space to create their own customized environment, and to have a permanent presence and meeting location in SL. Land owners can also restrict access to their land so that only those with permission may enter. Details about purchasing land are available on the SL Web site (http://www.secondlife.com). Discounts for educational groups are often available.

Getting Started in Second Life

To start using SL, the user visits the SL Web site to download and install the program and begins by choosing an avatar. The SL program provides a set of standard avatars from which to choose. After choosing one of the standard avatars, beginning users ("residents") enter the SL world on Orientation Island, where they learn basic behaviors such as walking, flying, and interacting with objects. New residents also learn how to communicate with other avatars using the chat function and how to change the appearance of their avatars. In SL, virtually every characteristic of a resident's avatar can be modified. Gender, height, apparent weight, relative sizes of body parts, hair, eyes, and skin are all changeable. It is also possible to have an avatar that is not human. For example, users can choose an animal, a mythical creature, or even an inanimate object (e.g., a cardboard box). Users can create their own avatars, modify existing avatars, or acquire avatars in the SL world. A user can also change his or her avatar's appearance rapidly simply by using the mouse to drag a new avatar onto one's existing avatar. As we discuss below, this flexibility makes SL an interesting platform for examining issues related to self-presentation, and the role of appearance in behavior and social interactions (e.g., Boostrom, 2008; Yee & Bailenson, 2007). After users have mastered the basic skills of using SL, they are then free to leave Orientation Island and travel within the SL virtual world.

What do people do in SL? As we noted above, since SL is not a game, there are no tasks that the user is required to complete while in SL. Rather than a game, SL primarily functions as a space for social interaction. Users meet with friends and visit interesting locations in the SL world. In SL it is possible to attend performances by real-world musicians, go dancing at virtual clubs, visit art galleries and museums, explore virtual recreations of real-world cities (e.g., Dublin, Paris, Rome), and attend conferences, meetings, and classes.

Second Life and Teaching

Instructors can present course content in SL in several ways. For example, lectures or music performances can be delivered by streaming live audio into SL. PowerPoint slides and video can be posted, and these can remain available on the SL site so students can visit later and view or download the materials. This is typically enabled by setting up a video screen that students can click on to start the video or slide show. Text materials can be delivered via "notecards" created by cutting and pasting from Word. While in SL, students and faculty can communicate using voice, text chat (typing in their comments, which then appear on the screen), or both. Discussions that occur via text chat can be saved in a file, which can be reviewed later by the instructor or provided to students who were not able to attend the discussion. From within SL, users can send e-mail to residents who are not currently online; these messages are sent to their e-mail account or stored and delivered the next time the user logs in to SL.

Although virtual worlds are a relatively new technology, and SL has been available for only a few years, there are currently hundreds of educational institutions with a presence in SL, and several highly active education-oriented groups (see below). Instructors have begun examining how these tools can be used to engage students and provide learning opportunities (e.g., DeLucia, Francese, Passero, & Tortora, 2009; Gillen, 2009; Good, Howland, & Thackray, 2008; Jarman, Lim, & Carpenter, 2009; Jarman, Traphagen, & Mayrath, 2008; Warburton, 2009). For example, DeLucia et al. (2009) reported on the design of a virtual campus in SL. Good et al. (2008) had students design SL-based learning experiences as part of a course on interactive learning environments. Walker (2009) incorporated SL as a venue for role playing in an online counseling skills and techniques course. Students met in a virtual counseling facility in SL to practice counseling skills they were learning in the course.

Results of these early studies suggest that students find SL to be engaging and report that it enhances their experience of course content. For example, Jarman et al. (2008) incorporated a group project in SL into a graduate communication course. Students worked in collaboration with architects to design and build virtual environmentally friendly homes and to present them to the public at a virtual ribbon-cutting ceremony in SL. On end-of-semester evaluations, all the students reported that SL was enjoyable to use, that it increased their learning, and that it increased their engagement in the course.

Students also reported that they appreciated the capacity for creativity afforded by SL and the possibility of interacting with people around the globe (e.g. Cheal, 2009).

However, student reactions to SL are not uniformly positive. Students do not always find SL easy to use, and in some cases they may have difficulty seeing the relevance of the technology to course content. For example, the majority of students in Jarman et al.'s (2008) class found SL difficult to use, and only about half the students felt that the SL project was related to course content. Cheal (2009) and Herold (2009) also found that students responded negatively to SL when they did not see a connection between the use of the virtual worlds and learning objectives. While these studies provide important information, research on teaching and learning in SL is in its infancy, and it is still not clear how this technology can most effectively enhance learning.

As instructors of a variety of psychology courses, we chose to incorporate SL into our classes for several reasons. Our goals included increasing student engagement, providing learning options for students, and exploring psychological principles using SL as a platform. Below we provide examples of how we have used SL in several of our classes. Although SL was the specific virtual world we used in our classes, many of our experiences are relevant to other virtual worlds as well.

SL has obvious potential for use in online instruction. Student engagement is an important concern for teachers of online classes. Without a regular schedule of real-time, face-to-face interaction, some students may find it difficult to stay engaged in the course. When meeting face-to-face in the "real world" is not possible, virtual worlds may provide the next-best option. Interacting via a personal avatar in a virtual-world setting can elicit a sense of presence (a feeling of "being there") on the part of the user that can result in greater involvement in the task at hand (see DeLucia et al., 2009).

To provide opportunities for this type of interaction, one of us (Baker) has incorporated SL into online classes as a venue for holding office hours and meeting individually with students. Early in the class, students receive basic information about SL, such as how to create an avatar and travel around in the virtual world. After students have learned basic skills in SL, they notify the instructor, who then sends them additional information about things to do in SL and how to get to the location of office hours. Sometimes office hours are held at the JMU campus site, but students and faculty can also meet at a virtual coffee shop, park, or other site in SL. As in the real world, attendance at office hours is optional. Typically only a small number of students attend office hours, and office hours held the evening prior to a test have the best attendance; this also mirrors the real-world situation. One important advantage of SL office hours as compared to real-world office hours is that instructors and students can meet from home or from any location where they can log on to SL. Although few students attend office hours in SL, those who do typically rate the experience positively. On end-of-semester evaluations, the reason students most frequently give for not attending office hours is that they do not have questions about the course material. Once again, this is similar to student behavior in the real world.

The first author has also incorporated attendance at virtual lectures in SL as an extra-credit option for a face-to-face class in comparative psychology. In this case, students attended a guest lecture on manatee behavior and conservation given at the sim operated by the Nature Publishing Group, which publishes the journal *Nature*. Feedback from students on the positive and negative aspects of this experience indicated that many of them felt that moving around in the virtual world was awkward, and a small number of them had technical problems using SL. However, all of the students rated the activity overall as a positive experience. The students particularly liked the convenience of attending an event in SL. Students suggested that SL could be used as a venue for class meetings during times when the weather was bad or as an option for students who have difficulty scheduling time to be in a physical classroom. As an instructor, I appreciated the fact that SL provided an opportunity for students that they otherwise would not have had (in this case, to hear a lecture being given at a real-life venue in London).

The second author created an assignment for a Psychology of Personality course that linked the personality construct "openness to experience" with experiences in SL. One goal of the course is that students make connections between course material and out-of-class experiences. To that end, students were required to participate in community service and to write a paper and deliver a class presentation that linked course material to the culture and community in close proximity to the university. Through these assignments, students applied course concepts to a familiar real-world community. SL provided a mechanism for linking course material to a different community, a virtual one that was unlike the familiar surroundings of college life. The students were required to spend time in the unfamiliar SL environment in order to examine experientially their openness to experience.

Specifically, the assignment involved four parts. Part one was a summary paper on the construct of openness, along with a self-reflection component on aspects of the self that suggest the student's personal status on this construct. After this initial paper and assessment were completed, each student created an avatar and spent time in SL. The students recorded in a journal the amount of time they spent "in world," the locations they visited, and their reactions to the experience. Part three of the assignment involved a reflection paper analyzing their own reactions and behaviors in SL. Specifically, the students were asked to evaluate whether their experiences in SL matched their personal evaluation of their own openness to experience. In the final part of the assignment, students selected people they believed to be high and low in openness to experience and introduced them to SL. Students recorded their responses and whether these responses were consistent with the student's perceptions of the target's openness to experience.

On end-of-semester evaluations of the assignment and their SL experiences, most students did not indicate a desire to interact in SL on a regular basis. However, students enjoyed this assignment, and they indicated they appreciated the role of SL in accomplishing the learning objectives associated with the assignment.

In general, our experiences in using SL have been positive, as have the experiences of our students. Students often express initial awkward feelings and a sense of discomfort when learning to use the program and interact in the virtual world, and many of them do not express the desire to spend much time in SL outside of the time required for the assignment. However, student responses to assignments and experiences involving SL are typically positive, and students appreciate many of the characteristics of SL (e.g., convenience).

We plan to continue to explore the use of SL to meet our teaching goals. As we have learned, even some seemingly "negative" aspects of the SL experience (e.g., sense of awkwardness in a new environment) can sometimes be used to meet course objectives (e.g., examining openness to experience).

Second Life and Psychology

As our experiences indicate, in addition to its potential as a teaching and meeting space, SL provides researchers and instructors with a platform that can be used to explore psychological concepts. Comparisons of social interactions in the virtual world with "real-world" interactions offer one potential area of inquiry. Current studies suggest that some real-life social norms may carry over into virtual-world interactions (Yee, Bailenson, Urbanek, Chang, & Merget, 2007). To the extent that interactions in the virtual world are similar to real-world, face-to-face interactions, virtual worlds can be used for the study of social interactions and social behavior (Bainbridge, 2007). An advantage for research is that the virtual world enables relatively easy control of numerous variables that may affect social interaction (e.g., situational factors, presence of others). Environments can be quickly manipulated, as can the presence, appearance, and behavior of other individuals.

The role of physical appearance in social interaction and social perception can also be explored in SL. In SL, as we noted above, avatars can be highly customized and quickly changed. It is possible to change clothing, gender, skin color, size, and virtually every aspect of one's appearance (Figs. 19.1, 19.2, 19.3, and 19.4). Given this broad range of choices, how do users choose to present themselves in the virtual world? How do social interactions change based on the physical appearance of the avatars? Messinger, Ge, Stroulia, Lyons, Smirnov, and Bone (2008; https://journals.tdl.org/jvwr/article/view/352/263) examined how users represent themselves in SL. Most users in their study created an avatar that was similar to their real self

Figure 19.1. Reis-Bergan's avatar in SL.

Figure 19.2. One of the first author's avatars, at the James Madison University campus in SL.

Figure 19.3. In SL, it is possible to easily change appearance. Here, the first author visits a replica of the *HMS Beagle* in SL. Her avatar is the African grey parrot perched on the boat.

Figure 19.4. The first author, with a "boxbot" avatar.

but was significantly more attractive. Messinger et al. found that participants who created avatars that were more attractive than their real selves reported that they engaged in more extraverted, outgoing, risk-taking, and loud behavior in SL than they did in real life. Yee and Bailenson (2007) reported that virtual-world behavior is affected by avatar appearance. Participants in their study were given either attractive or unattractive avatars. The participants then interacted with confederates in a virtual-world setting using these avatars. Participants with attractive avatars self-disclosed more during the virtual world interaction, and they also stood closer to the confederates, than did those who were given the unattractive avatars.

Researchers have also begun to explore relationships, social groups, and communities in virtual-world environments (e.g., Steinkuhler & Williams, 2006). Research on online chat-based support groups indicates that these groups provide important benefits for participants (e.g., Haythornthwaite,

2007; Tanis, 2007; Wright, 2002). Are virtual-world support groups effective in similar ways? In addition to support groups, many social groups in SL may be organized around a theme, often involving role playing. How do these communities form, function, and operate? As yet, there appears to be little research on these topics, which means that both instructors and their students have the opportunity to advance knowledge in this new pedagogical arena.

Participating in virtual worlds can also provide students with opportunities to experience an unfamiliar culture. The virtual world has its own particular cultural practices (see Boellstorff, 2008; Boostrom, 2008). For example, Boostrom (2008) found that SL residents quickly learn norms about appropriate dress and ways of interacting with strangers. In addition, SL is host to communities of users from around the world. For example, students can visit French, Japanese, German, or Italian areas of SL. SL or other virtual-world environments may provide students with meaningful experiences of other cultures (see Diehl & Prins, 2008; O'Brien & Levy, 2008). These reports point to the possibilities for psychology instructors interested in using SL or other virtual worlds to provide cross-cultural experiences or collaborations for students.

Students interested in clinical psychology may be in interested in exploring the use of virtual worlds and virtual reality in therapy (Gorini, Fasano, Gaggioli, Vigna, & Riva, 2008; Josman, Reisberg, Weiss, Garcia-Palacios, & Hoffman, 2008). For example, Josman et al. (2008) examined the possibility of simulating a traumatic event in a virtual world in order to explore the possibilities of virtual-world–based treatments for post-traumatic stress disorder. Students interested in health psychology will find several virtual clinics in SL (see Boulos, Hetherington, & Wheeler, 2007). SL's Health Info Island currently features a Consumer Health Library, a Medical Library, a Health Information Outreach Research Lab, and information about numerous health issues.

With a bit of practice, instructors can even build their own learning environments. For example, a history of psychology instructor might construct a recreation of Pavlov's lab, or a psychology of learning instructor might build an "avatar-sized" working operant chamber. Either simulated setting would provide students with an interactive and thought-provoking experience that goes beyond the typical accounts provided in textbooks.

Tips, Hints, and Pointers for Using Second Life

Working, interacting, and exploring in a virtual world is an unfamiliar experience for many students. We offer a few tips to help the experience go smoothly. Baker, Wentz, and Woods (2009) and McVey (2008) also provide practical suggestions for using SL in classes.

1. *Develop clear learning objectives for your use of SL.* Students need to see some benefits from the investment of time they make in learning to use a virtual world. Clear learning objectives communicated to students, along with a clear explanation of how the technology helps to accomplish the learning goals, can play an important role in helping students deal with the learning time involved. In addition, students vary considerably in their openness to trying new technologies. Having clear learning objectives can help to convince students who might otherwise regard SL as a waste of time.

2. *Have a contingency plan.* No technology, from e-mail to PowerPoint to Second Life, is foolproof, and newer technologies such as virtual worlds may be subject to more than the typical number of technological glitches. Having a contingency plan for completion of an assignment or class activity in the event of technical difficulties, and clearly communicating that to students, is essential. In our experience, few things are more frustrating to students than being unable to complete a class assignment due to technological failure, especially when they have invested time and effort up front in learning to use the technology.

3. *Inform students about community standards in the virtual world.* Online communities, like face-to-face communities, expect certain behavior from participants, and individuals who violate community standards may be subject to penalties. In SL, the community standards are summarized as "The Big Six." Repeated violations of any of these six behavioral guidelines (intolerance, harassment, assault, indecency, disturbing the peace, and disclosing personal information about other residents) can result in expulsion from SL. Just as students may need some coaching prior to attending their first academic

conference, they may also need some guidance about appropriate behavior in an unfamiliar online setting.

4. *Discuss online security issues with students.* The SL virtual world plays host to residents from around the world. The free and open nature of the environment attracts a diverse group of users, some of whom may have questionable integrity. Students should be aware of safe practices when using this technology, just as they would when using other forms of social networking technology such as Facebook, MySpace, or public blogs. Students may need specific instruction about what to do if problems arise (e.g., how to leave an area or quickly log off SL if they are in an uncomfortable social interaction).

5. *Seek education-related resources for using SL.* Links on the SL Web site connect educators to multiple resources relevant to teaching in SL. These include the Second Life Eduscape Blog (Linden Lab's education blog; https://blogs.secondlife.com/ community/community/education), the Second Life Education blog (which focuses on K–20 education in SL; http://www. sl-educationblog.org/), and the Second Life Education Wiki (http://wiki.secondlife.com/wiki/Education). The Second Life Educator (SLED) List is a highly active discussion list for educators using SL. Information about subscribing to this electronic mailing list is available via the SL Web site. Resource books and "how-to" manuals (e.g., Mansfield, 2008) are available for help with performing tasks such as building and changing avatar appearance in SL. In addition, numerous educational groups exist in SL; joining one or more of these groups can quickly connect the new user with more experienced colleagues. In addition to resources specific to SL, information about virtual worlds in general can also provide helpful context. The Terra Nova weblog (http://terranova. blogs.com) is an excellent starting point.

6. *Collect data on the effectiveness of SL in achieving learning goals.* Incorporating virtual worlds in teaching is a recent endeavor. SL itself is only 8 years old, and many instructors who use SL have been doing so for only a short period. Whether virtual worlds such as SL are useful in teaching,

what types of content and skills can best be learned in a virtual-world platform, and which student populations respond best to learning in this way are all unanswered questions. Psychology instructors active in the scholarship of teaching and learning can contribute by providing data to help answer these questions.

Should You or Shouldn't You?

Should you consider using a virtual-world environment in teaching? As with any form of technology, there is no simple answer to this question. Instructors must weigh the benefits and costs of incorporating this technology into their teaching. A virtual world may or may not be the right tool for the job. Instructors need to consider an array of variables in choosing appropriate technology, including their learning goals, the characteristics of their students, and the capabilities and limitations of the technology.

In this chapter, we noted some of the potential uses of virtual worlds such as SL in teaching. SL offers instructors a new landscape for teaching, one in which they can create entirely new experiences and environments to engage students. The use of SL comes with downsides, however. The major cost associated with the use of SL is probably the time involved in creating an avatar and learning how to travel and interact in the virtual world. For some users, the time invested in getting comfortable using SL is well worth the cost; for others, this may not be the case. Other technologies (e.g., Web conferencing, instant messaging) enable many of the same types of interaction and collaboration as SL, so instructors need to carefully weigh the costs and benefits of using SL for themselves and their students.

Are SL and other virtual worlds "the next big thing" or just a passing fad? While we cannot answer this question definitively, we note that online virtual worlds directed at children are increasing in number. Although some of these virtual worlds primarily have an educational focus (e.g., Whyville), many of them center on play and social interaction. Examples include Webkinz (http://www.webkinz.com), Club Penguin (http://www.clubpenguin.com), and Free Realms (http://www.freerealms.com). In the next decade, students may arrive at their college classrooms having already participated in multiple virtual worlds. Instructors who can tap in to student experiences and interest in these technologies and use them in ways that promote learning will have a powerful tool at their disposal.

References

Bainbridge, W.S. (2007). The scientific research potential of virtual worlds. *Science, 317*, 472–476.

Baker, S. C., Wentz, R. K., & Woods, M. M. (2009). Using virtual worlds in education: Second Life as an educational tool. *Teaching of Psychology, 36,* 59–64.

Boellstorf, T. (2008). *Coming of age in Second Life: An anthropologist explores the virtually human.* Princeton, NJ: Princeton University Press.

Boostrom, R. (2008). The social construction of virtual reality and the stigmatized identity of the newbie. *Journal of Virtual Worlds Research, 1*(2), 1–19. Retrieved May 19, 2009, from https://journals.tdl.org/jvwr/article/view/302/269

Boulos, M. N. K, Hetherington, L., & Wheeler, S. (2007). Second Life: An overview of the potential of 3-D virtual worlds in medical and health education. *Health Information & Libraries Journal, 24,* 233–245.

Cheal, C. (2009). Student perceptions of a course taught in Second Life. *Innovate: Journal of Online Education, 5*(5). Retrieved July 27, 2009, from http://www.innovateonline.info/index.php?view=article&id=692

Diehl, W. C., & Prins, E. (2008). Unintended outcomes in Second Life: Intercultural literacy and cultural identity in a virtual world. *Language and Intercultural Communication, 8,* 101–118.

De Lucia, A., Francese, R., Passero, I., & Tortora, G. (2009). Development and evaluation of a virtual campus on Second Life: The case of SecondDMI. *Computers & Education, 52,* 220–233.

Gillen, J. (2009). Literary practices in Schome Park: A virtual literary ethnography. *Journal of Research in Reading, 32,* 57–74.

Good, J., Howland, K., & Thackray, L. (2008). Problem-based learning spanning real and virtual worlds: A case study in Second Life. *ALT-J, Research in Learning Technology, 16,* 163–172.

Gorini, A., Fasano, A.I., Gaggioli, A., Vigna, C., & Riva, G. (2008). A second life for telehealth: Prospects for the use of virtual online worlds in clinical psychology. *Annual Review of CyberTherapy and Telemedicine, 6,* 15–21.

Haythornthwaite, C. (2007). Social networks and online community. In: A. M. Joinson, K. Y. A. McKenna, T. Postmes, & U.-D. Reips (eds.), *The Oxford handbook of Internet psychology* (pp. 121–137). Oxford: Oxford University Press.

Herold, D. K. (2009). Virtual education: Teaching media studies in Second Life. *Journal of Virtual Worlds Research, 2*(1), 3–17. Retrieved July 27, 2009, from https://journals.tdl.org/jvwr/article/view/380/454

Jarman, L., Lim, K. Y. T., & Carpenter, B. S. (2009). Pedagogy, Education and Innovation in 3-D Virtual Worlds [Special issue]. *Journal of Virtual Worlds Research, 2*(1). Retrieved May 19, 2009, from http://www.jvwresearch.org/index.php?_cms=default,2,3

Jarman, L., Traphagan, T., & Mayrath, M. (2008). Understanding project-based learning in Second Life with a pedagogy, training, and assessment trio. *Educational Media International, 45,* 157–176.

Josman, N., Reisberg, A., Weiss, P. L., Garcia-Palacios, A., & Hoffman, H.G. (2008). BusWorld: An analog pilot test of a virtual environment designed to treat posttraumatic stress disorder originating from a terrorist suicide bomb attack. *CyberPsychology & Behavior, 11,* 775–777.

Mansfield, R. (2008). *How to do everything with Second Life.* New York: McGraw Hill.

McVey, M. H. (2008). Observations of expert communicators in immersive virtual worlds: Implications for synchronous discussion. *ALT-J, Research in Learning Technology, 16,* 173–180.

Messinger, P. R., Ge, X., Stroulia, E., Lyons, K., Smirnov, K., & Bone, M. (2008). On the relationship between my avatar and myself. *Journal of Virtual Worlds Research, 1*(2), 1–17. Retrieved May 19, 2009, from https://journals.tdl.org/jvwr/article/view/352/263

O'Brien, M. G., & Levy, R. M. (2008). Exploration through virtual reality: Encounters with the target culture. *Canadian Modern Language Review, 64,* 663–691.

Salen, K. (Ed.). (2008). *The ecology of games: Connecting youth, games, and learning.* Cambridge, MA: MIT Press.

Steinkuhler, C. A., & Williams, D. (2006). Where everybody knows your (screen) name: Online games as "third places." *Journal of Computer-Mediated Communication, 11,* 885–909.

Sulake Corporation Oy (2009). *Habbo–where else?* Retrieved May 18, 2009, from http://www.sulake.com/habbo/index.html?navi=2.1

Tanis, M. (2007). Online social support groups. In: A. M. Joinson, K. Y. A. McKenna, T. Postmes, & U.-D. Reips (eds.), *The Oxford handbook of Internet psychology* (pp. 139–153). Oxford: Oxford University Press.

Walker, V. L. (2009). 3D virtual learning in counselor education: Using Second Life in counselor skill development. *Journal of Virtual Worlds Research, 2*(1), 3–14. Retrieved July 27, 2009, from https://journals.tdl.org/jvwr/article/view/423/463

Warburton, S. (2009). Second Life in higher education: Assessing the potential for and the barriers to deploying virtual worlds in learning and teaching. *British Journal of Educational Technology, 40,* 414–426. DOI: 10.1111/j.1467-8535.2009.00952.x

Wright, K. (2002). Social support within an on-line cancer community: An assessment of emotional support, perceptions of advantages and disadvantages, and motives for using the community from a communication perspective. *Journal of Applied Communication Research, 30,* 195–209.

Yee, N., & Bailenson, J. (2007). The Proteus Effect: The effect of transformed self-representation on behavior. *Human Communication Research, 33,* 271–290.

Yee, N., Bailenson, J. N., Urbanek, M., Chang, F., & Merget, D. (2007). The unbearable likeness of being digital: The persistence of nonverbal social norms in online virtual environments. *CyberPsychology & Behavior, 10,* 115–121.

20 Emerging Technologies to Improve Teaching and Learning in a Digital World

Jeffrey R. Stowell

How might pedagogy change if existing technologies were suddenly unavailable? You might have already experienced this if the technology you planned to use in the classroom failed, and you suddenly realized how dependent you were on the technology. In this situation, you might have reverted to using technologies of the past, like the chalkboard or overhead projector (see Chapter 3). Undoubtedly, the appearance of new technology in the classroom has changed the way many instructors teach, but has it contributed to an improvement or an impairment in instruction? Is the power of technology making us better teachers or only giving us the appearance of such?

In Plato's *Phaedrus* (1925), Socrates used an Egyptian mythological tale to illustrate a concern that the invention of new technology (writing) would not improve our memory because we would rely on written letters to remember instead of the power of our minds. Today, teachers might blame the calculator or any other technology for making students mentally weak. Indeed, this skepticism persists today, as evidenced in a theoretical essay by Carr (2008) titled, "Is Google Making Us Stupid?" In this article, Carr suggested that relying on Google's power to provide easy access to desired information will cause us to become shallow thinkers and easily distractible because deep comprehension comes only during quiet, undistracted reading and reflection on long passages of text. On the other hand, there are those who acknowledge the drawbacks of new technology (i.e., distractibility) but consider the potential benefits to outweigh the disadvantages, as noted in Zimmer's article (2009), "How Google is Making Us Smarter." According to Zimmer, information on the Internet is merely an extension of our mind (see Clark & Chalmers, 1998) and tools like Google will facilitate a mind–machine connection between our thoughts and the Internet, making us smarter.

This chapter is devoted to the discussion of forward-looking implementation of technology to improve teaching and learning in our increasingly digital world. Although many of the practical applications are psychology-related, others readily will find applications within their own discipline. It is not possible to review every upcoming technology that could affect education, so the focus of this chapter is on technologies that are currently gaining momentum and those that are likely to have an impact on teaching and learning in the near future, as identified in recent Horizon Reports produced by the joint venture of The New Media Consortium and EDUCAUSE (Johnson, Levine, & Smith, 2008, 2009). Because some of these technologies are so new, there may be little empirical evidence of their effectiveness. In such cases, the potential impact on education is purely speculative but at the same time should stimulate ideas for further research.

When new technology appears, educators are faced with the decision to either reject the technology or adapt it to their purposes. The reaction of educators to new technology may be categorized along the following continuum of enthusiasm, as discussed by John and Wheeler (2008). One extreme end of the continuum is composed of the "new Luddites," named after the Luddites of the late 19th century, who attempted to prevent mechanical looms from replacing textile workers. The new Luddites are those who actively oppose or fear new technology, often noting potential catastrophes that could result, such as losing important information stored on a hard drive. Next on the continuum are the traditionalists, who passively resist educational technology and continue to rely on traditional pedagogical methods that require human interaction, such as the lecture method. Near the middle of the continuum are the pragmatists who support the judicious use of technology but are somewhat critical of its excess. Their view might be exemplified by the statement that technology is a good servant but a poor master (e.g., PowerPoint may control the design of a lecture more than the instructor does; see Chapter 6). Finally, on the other end of the continuum are the technology enthusiasts, who believe there is enormous potential in educational technology and are willing and able to master its complexities. Admittedly, the audience of this chapter will likely be technology enthusiasts, as they are most likely to express interest in new technologies and adapt them to education.

One of the overarching themes of this chapter is to emphasize that technology, despite its pitfalls, can be viewed as more than a "just a tool." Often, those who justify continued reliance on the traditional methods of pedagogy dismiss technology as "just a tool," or in other words something that merely makes student learning easier or more efficient, or it does the same thing as other existing tools but costs more. For example, having laser-guided power tools makes cutting or drilling more accurate, but these tools essentially do the same job as other saws and drills, with greater expense. Some technology is designed solely as a tool (e.g., disk defragmenters, anti-virus software, electronic grade books), but other technologies provide increased efficiency, as well as create new types of learning. In the forward to Resnick's book (1994, p. x), Papert stated that many people fail to "distinguish between tools (reasonably described as 'just tools') that improve their users' ability to do pre-existing jobs, and another kind of 'tool' that are more than 'just tools' because of their role in the creation of a job nobody thought to do, or nobody could have done, before." As I review selected educational technologies, I invite the reader to note the difference between tools that do existing jobs more efficiently versus those that offer new ways to enhance teaching and learning.

Current and Emerging Technologies

A relatively recent technology that provides new avenues for classroom interaction and assessment is classroom response systems (i.e., clickers). Clickers emerged as a way to collect immediate input from students in a way that provides more accurate feedback than relying on traditional hand raising (Stowell & Nelson, 2007). Some may criticize the technology as expensive, glorified "hand-raising," but the immediacy of feedback provides new ways of teaching. For example, in a course on controversial topics in psychology, I have students use clickers to provide ongoing visual feedback from the audience to the presenters during class debates, similar to visual representations of group opinions during televised political debates. In this reversal of roles, students are the ones getting immediate feedback about their performance.

One limitation of most clickers is that students are limited to a fixed number of choices (i.e., 0–9, or A–J). However, other possible uses of clickers are emerging as new polling applications allow open-ended responses from text-messaging devices like cell phones (see http://polleverywhere. com). With open-ended text responses, it can be difficult to summarize the incoming data in a meaningful way because an infinite variation of responses is possible. One way to summarize the results from an open-ended text poll is to create a word cloud, in which the font size of a word or phrase depends on the frequency of the words in the class's responses (i.e., frequently occurring words appear in larger font, while infrequent words are displayed in smaller font sizes). An iPhone application that receives students' text responses and creates word clouds viewable to the instructor or to the whole class is already being used at Abilene Christian University, where all incoming students receive an iPhone to use as a clicker, among other uses (Young, 2008).

Online Video

In December 2008, 150 million Americans viewed 14.3 billion videos online (comScore, 2009), which was up 13% from the previous month. Video cameras built into a variety of devices and free software for video production can make any teacher or student like a Hollywood producer. Online video sites such as Google video (http://video.google.com/) and YouTube (http://www. youtube.com/) offer instructors a growing library of instructional videos at their fingertips. Instructors may show educational videos in the classroom or as supplemental material outside of the classroom, where students view videos at their own convenience. Other sites are directly promoting educational content, such as iTunes U, where anyone can freely access nearly all of MIT's courses as audio or video files (http://web.mit.edu/itunesu/).

Podcasts

Do freely available recorded lectures facilitate learning? Do they make it too easy for students to skip class? Are recorded lectures an effective replacement for classroom lectures? Most of these questions have not been answered empirically. However, one recent study compared students who listened to a PowerPoint presentation in the classroom to another group of students who had access only to the audio recording (podcast) and video of the same lecture (McKinney, Dyck, & Luber, 2009). Students who had access to the media files performed significantly higher (nearly 10%) than the in-class lecture group on an exam. Furthermore, students in the podcast group who took additional notes on the podcast scored about 14% higher than students who only viewed or listened to the podcast. One weakness of the study was that the researchers did not randomly assign the participants to the different conditions, making it difficult to know if student characteristics accounted for the differences. However, one modest conclusion from this study is that mobile technology could affect learning for some students, if used in the proper context. At the very least, it does not appear to cause any harm. The benefits of podcasts, as pointed out by the same authors, is that most students listened to them more than once, at varying times of the day (mostly evenings), and could pause or rewind the lecture as they were listening to take notes (McKinney et al., 2009). Exposure to podcasts and vodcasts (video podcasts) might have similar effects as listening to an audio tape or viewing a lecture on television, but with the advantage of greater portability. For instructions on how to create your own podcast, visit http://www.apple.com/podcasting.

Digital Textbooks

What would you do if this chapter were available only in a digital format? Would you feel comfortable reading the text on a computer screen or an electronic text reader, such as Amazon's Kindle? With the advent of digitization of textbooks, instructors and students often have the choice of a printed or digital textbook (e-textbook). An e-textbook usually costs considerably less than the print version, but there are other potential advantages. For example, digitization of text allows greater ease of searching the content and allows individuals with sensory impairments to have access in alternative formats (e.g., larger text or audio files). Furthermore, e-textbooks can incorporate rich multimedia and can link to external resources, and authors can update the content more readily. Nevertheless, will these advantages lead to the replacement of the standard textbook carried around in students' backpacks? An increasing number of students are using digital textbooks, but the challenges of using e-textbooks include requiring access to a computer or digital text reader, increased ability to copy and paste plagiarized text, and unfavorable attitudes toward digital textbooks by faculty (Nelson, 2008).

What do students say about using e-textbooks? An in-depth analysis of written journal comments from graduate students who used electronic texts for the first 2 weeks of a social-work course revealed some interesting insights (Vernon, 2006). After requiring students to use an online electronic text for the first 2 weeks of class, Vernon allowed his students to continue accessing the material in their choice of format: electronic, print, or both for the next 6 weeks. A tally of the negative adjectives used to describe their computer reading sessions was greater than the tally of positive reactions during the first 2 weeks, but this trend reversed by the end of the study. Many students were not satisfied reading electronic text: 61% of the students switched to printing the electronic material after the first 2 weeks of class, while only 22% continued to rely solely on the electronic format. The rest reported using both approaches. Most (71%) of the students' written responses were negative regarding how well the electronic readings compared to reading a printed text. Some of the negative reactions included increased eye strain, headaches, and fatigue while reading online text, being distracted by incoming e-mail messages, not being able to highlight and take notes on the electronic text, waiting in line in a computer lab to print out the electronic text, and wanting to sit in a more comfortable environment than at a computer desk (Vernon, 2006).

Few studies have assessed the effect of digital textbooks on student learning, but one recent study determined that students do no better or worse with electronic texts, on average, than with printed textbooks (Shepperd, Grace, & Koch, 2008). Although the electronic text on CD was about half the cost of the printed text, 90% of the nearly 400 students in an introductory psychology class who participated in the study chose to use the printed text. Those who used the electronic text did not differ from the rest of the class in terms of background factors, except for being somewhat older. Of the 36 students in the sample who had used an electronic text in the past, none of them chose the electronic text for their psychology class. Students with the electronic text reported studying slightly fewer hours per week, but their course grades were not significantly different from the course grades of students using the printed text. Overall, students with electronic texts were neutral in their liking of the electronic text and were somewhat unfavorable on attitudes toward convenience and willingness to use the text in the future. The authors concluded that although electronic texts do not harm student learning, the potential benefits do not outweigh the present disadvantages (Shepperd et al., 2008). Considering that students, on average, read only about half of their assigned text anyway (Gurung & Martin, in press), getting students to use digital textbooks is currently an uphill battle.

Collaboration Webs

A collaboration web is a general term that refers to a network where individuals work together to create electronic materials. In a collaborative web, no longer is there a clear boundary between author and reader, as readers often become contributors to the work (e.g., blogs and wikis). Together, people connecting from anywhere in the world can use their collective knowledge to create documents, share information, and build knowledge. One of the most visible of these projects is Wikipedia. These collaborative projects may have millions of participants or only a few. In education, teachers can arrange for students to work together in groups or have all students participate in an ongoing class project. For example, in my psychology of learning class, I created a wiki to supplement the laboratory instructions in the "Sniffy the Virtual Rat" manual (Alloway, Wilson, Graham, & Krames, 2000). Together, students and I respond to other students' questions about common difficulties with the lab exercises. Over time, we are creating a small body of knowledge that can help current and future students complete the laboratory exercises, and reduce the number of redundant questions posed to the instructor. These collaborative tools, further described in Chapter 16, will continue to facilitate the development of quality resources for use within courses, departments, and beyond.

The Personal Web

In addition to the growing number of tools for collaboration, there are tools designed to help individuals find, filter, organize, and view electronic information found on the Internet. When Web users discover sources of information that interest them, they can customize the display of this information in their Web browser, home page, or other programs. For example, Pageflakes (http://www.pageflakes.com/), My Yahoo (http://my.yahoo.com/), iGoogle (http://www.google.com/ig), and other sites host personalized home pages, and users can select which "flakes," "widgets," or "gadgets," they want on their page, each of which pull content from other Web sites using Web feeds (Johnson et al., 2008). Thus, you do not have to visit different Web pages for your weather, sports, news, and e-mail because it is all on one page— your page. Add a gadget that displays a Web feed for current psychology news on your home page, and you don't have to search the Web for new information—it all comes to you.

How can the personal Web improve education? Once instructors find valuable Web resources, they can subscribe to Web feeds to receive current news and research related to their discipline. Furthermore, the personal Web makes posting content relatively easy with publishing tools such as Blogger.com, Twitter, and social networking sites such as Facebook and MySpace. Tools also exist to cross-post content published to more than one of these sites simultaneously (Johnson et al., 2009). Thus, faculty could create a single message (e.g., course announcement) that would be published to several sites at once, ensuring that more students are likely to get the announcement and, at the same time, allowing students the flexibility of getting course updates from the sites they most frequently visit.

Mobile Devices

Computing devices are becoming smaller and more portable. For example, in a 2008 EDUCAUSE survey of over 27,000 college students (Salaway, Caruso, & Nelson, 2008), 80.5% reported owning a laptop, up from 65.9% in 2006, while only 53.8% owned a desktop (some own both). Nearly every American college student owns a cell phone (Salaway, Caruso, & Nelson, 2007), and the number of Internet-capable phones is increasing rapidly. Whereas few college students in 2007 reported having cell phones with Internet access (13.9%), the 2008 report showed that 66.1% of college undergraduates owned phones with Internet access. In the future, students may favor Internet-capable mobile devices such as smart phones (e.g., iPhone, BlackBerry, and Treo) over laptops. The advantages of mobile devices compared to laptops include their smaller size, lower cost, and more widespread wireless access (e.g., 3G). However, many students with smart phones did not use the Internet feature, citing as reasons the small screens, high cost, and slow download speeds (Salaway et al., 2008).

Mobile devices, such as cell phones, are changing the way we access electronic information. With these devices, students can take notes or photographs and post them to a course blog. The note-taking and camera features would be particularly useful for field experiences such as museums, self-guided tours, and internship experiences. Incredibly, a person with a camera and an Internet-enabled cell phone can take a photograph of a product advertisement and send it to a Web site (http://snaptell.com/) that runs a detection algorithm to provide you with more information about what it is, consumer reviews, and places where you can buy it (Johnson et al., 2009).

Similarly, a mobile device can capture a snippet of ambient music recorded in the mall or elevator with the built-in microphone and send the audio clip to Shazam's Web site (http://www.shazam.com), which will send a return message with the name of the song and where it can be purchased. Shazam's tool might be useful for humanities and arts classes if a student is having difficulty identifying the name of a piece of artwork or the composer of a classical music piece.

Recent additions to mobile devices include a Global Positioning System (GPS) unit and built-in accelerometers that sense the position and motion of the device, similar to those found in the Nintendo Wii remote (see Chapter 11). These additions allow the user to interact with the world in new ways, such as in a virtual gaming environment. Hewlett Packard's *mscape* technology (http://www.hpl.hp.com/mediascapes/) offers a glimpse into the power of technology to blur the lines between real and virtual environments. In a video titled "Roku's Reward" on HP's Web site (http://tinyurl.com/3jwq4l), Roku uses his GPS-enabled device to find architectural patterns on city buildings; he earns points when he takes photos of them with his mobile device. As he enters certain geographical areas, his GPS location triggers events in the handheld game, such as oncoming virtual Indiana Jones-like rolling boulders. Other players in the game with their GPS devices appear on Roku's game screen as the players become geographically near each other, providing the opportunity to engage in virtual combat, resulting in only one winner who gets the virtual princess' kiss. This example also illustrates the potential of serious games (i.e., games with an educational purpose) to induce competition, challenge, and curiosity (Graesser, Chipman, & King, 2008).

In an educational application of *mscape* technology, users can take a 2-hour walk through Yosemite Valley, in which their GPS location triggers the delivery of multimedia information about that area of the park (i.e., a "mediascape"; http://www.mscapers.com/msin/ABA0000018). In another mediascape, visitors can re-enact a historically accurate escape of four prisoners from the Tower of London while avoiding being caught (http://www.mscapers.com/msin/ABA0000023). People do not actually have to be in the real geographical location to experience it. For example, Beecham (2006) developed a virtual moonwalk on a primary school's playing field, where students viewed their virtual position on a map of the Alphonsus Crater of the moon on their handheld device, while maintaining communication with mission control using two-way radios. Students felt like they had a much better understanding of how to complete necessary tasks on a moon mission without having to leave Earth.

What other possibilities are there for mediascapes? Imagine sending students down the hall of a real building that represents a mental institution on their mobile device screen. Entering a real classroom triggers a short video clip of a person who is experiencing symptoms of a mental disorder. The student must accurately diagnose the disorder to earn points and complete his or her psychiatric rounds in the virtual institution before the time is up.

Other more practical uses for mobile devices already exist. In addition to the polling features noted above, students can use cell phones for in-class experiments. For example, in an attempt to demonstrate how divided attention can cause a decrease in performance of two simultaneous tasks, I had a student talk on a cell phone while she performed another task (shooting baskets). Other examples of cell phones in psychology classes include demonstrating procedural learning of the phone's keyboard layout and discussing the role of cell phones in making first impressions.

Montclair State University in New Jersey is planning to require its over 17,000 students to have mobile devices compatible with MSU's mobile application suite, which is integrated with other university resources (Chapel, 2008). Through this cell-phone network, students receive text-message alerts regarding course notices posted in the Blackboard Learning System and safety notices related to weather and campus security. Students also have the option to enable the GPS feature in a medical emergency to notify campus police of their whereabouts and to provide first responders with critical medical-history data. Chapel (2008) also suggests that, in the future, students may use their cell phones as their student ID for residence-hall access, dining-hall charges, and commerce.

Using mobile devices for education, entertainment, and socializing epitomizes the phrase, "anytime, anywhere." Nearly two decades ago, Weiser suggested that "ubiquitous computers will help overcome the problem of information overload. There is more information available at our fingertips during a walk in the woods than in any computer system, yet people find a walk among trees relaxing and computers frustrating. Machines that fit the human environment, instead of forcing humans to enter theirs, will make using a computer as refreshing as taking a walk in the woods" (Weiser, 1991). Are we there yet?

Data Mashups

Data mashups are "powerful tools for navigating and visualizing datasets; understanding connections between different dimensions such as time, distance, and location; juxtaposing data from different sources to reveal new relationships; and other purposes" (Johnson et al., 2008, p. 20). For example, with Yahoo and Google's geocoding applications, it is becoming easier to map data geographically using ZIP code or other address information (see the Society for the Teaching of Psychology's interactive Google map showing the location of STP members at http://teachpsych.org/members/maps/map_dynamic.php). Geographical information can be extracted from anything tagged with geographical coordinates, including photos taken by GPS-enabled cameras. For example, Earthalbum.com takes geocoded information from photos published on Flickr.com and "mashes" it with a Google map to shows pictures taken in a specific geographical area when the user clicks on that area of the map. Some data mashups acquire the Internet user's computer network address, which is assigned by the Internet service provider to every computer on its network, to determine the approximate physical location of the computer. Areaface (http://www.areaface.com/twitter) geocodes network-address data and combines this with data from Twitter (a microblogging service used to publish short announcements; see Chapter 16) to map the location of Twitter users and display their profile picture with their most recent message ("tweet"). These results can be further filtered by searching for keywords in the "tweets." Instructors could use the resulting data to help teach critical thinking to students by having them formulate research hypotheses to test their explanations about how, for example, the age, sex, and race of "tweeters" in Akron, Ohio, are related to the views expressed in their "tweets" on health care reform. The idea of mashing geographical data with any other type of data opens endless opportunities to explore relationships between seemingly unconnected datasets.

One other example of a data mashup is Yahoo Pipes (http://pipes.yahoo.com/pipes/). Similar to what TiVo does with television show listings, users of Yahoo Pipes can select multiple RSS feeds (syndicated feeds that contain news or Web-site updates) and then filter, sort, and display the resulting output in a single RSS feed that contains only the desired output. For example, psychology instructors who subscribe to several RSS feeds of teaching-related Web sites and journals might only be interested in topics on statistics.

Yahoo Pipes would allow the mashing of multiple RSS feeds into one feed that contains items that have the word "statistics" in the title or description, truly producing a personal Web.

Collective Intelligence

Consider the collective knowledge of a society. First, there is the explicit collective knowledge found in libraries and Web sites like Wikipedia (http://www.wikipedia.com), written by thousands of people with current information about various topics. Second, there is society's implicit knowledge, revealed by analyzing the activities of many people over time (Johnson et al., 2008). For example, based on data from many people's prior searches on Google, the search engine will suggest a list of possible search terms as you type in the search box, as if it knows what you are trying to find. Likewise, Amazon.com seems to know what other products you would like to purchase when shopping on their Web site (Johnson et al., 2008).

What if the next time you logged on to Facebook (http://www.facebook.com), you were prompted with a list of people who might make good friends? This feature may not be so far-fetched if programs could analyze and establish implicit relationships based on a person's social graph, which is the tangible digital trail of your online social activities (Johnson et al., 2008). Your social graph is pieced together from the names of people in the carbon-copy field of e-mails, co-authors on published works, people at conferences you have attended, in tagged photographs of you with other people, and your comments on blogs. As online tools gather more information about our collaborative networks, this information might help facilitate new collaborations. Imagine working on a manuscript when suddenly your word processor begins to suggest the names of experts from a network of scholars who might serve as consultants or co-authors (Johnson et al., 2008). These technologies might seem on the distant horizon, but even now, tools such as Xobni (http://www.xobni.com/) will analyze e-mails for implicit social relationships, offering a taste of what the future may hold.

Collective intelligence of the explicit form may benefit students by drawing on the expertise of multiple authors to create shared resources (e.g., a wiki for Sniffy the Virtual Rat's laboratory exercises or a collaborative document with a comprehensive description of how neurons work). In the future, it may be possible to use implicit collective intelligence from students' social graphs when automatically assigning them roles in groups, such as selecting a frequent blogger to be the group's note-taker.

Challenges of Technology

Digital Divide

The digital divide refers to the difference between those who have access to technology and the skills to be proficient in using it and those who do not. The EDUCAUSE Center for Applied Research report (Salaway et al., 2008) suggests students have a wide range of comfort and skill in using technology. Unfortunately, technology use is unequal among various demographics, with half as many women considering themselves early adopters of technology (25.2%) compared to men (52.8%; Salaway et al., 2008). Although the gap in Internet use between Whites and other minority groups is shrinking, the most recent Pew Internet Survey (2008) on Internet use shows 77% of Whites use the Internet compared to 64% of Blacks and 58% of Hispanics. Gender and cultural differences in Internet use among student populations should be considered when assigning tasks that require technological competence. Instructors may consider pairing students who feel more competent with other students who feel less comfortable with new technology.

Academic Dishonesty

Technology affords new ways of cheating, such as using a cell phone to send or receive answers during a test. Although highly impractical, one extreme measure to prevent this form of cheating would be to magnetically shield the classroom, which would prevent wireless devices from working (Yaqoob, 2006). Based on more than a decade of research, the most important (and more practical) factor in deterring student cheating is establishing an institutional honor code that becomes part of the academic culture in which faculty establish and enforce clear policies on what is acceptable and what is not (McCabe, Trevino, & Butterfield, 2001).

Cost

Having the latest technology always comes at a cost. In addition to the financial cost, which may be prohibitive, there is also the cost of time, training, and support. In current economic conditions, technology may experience a Darwinian effect as the most cost-efficient technologies survive, while others do not. Bill Gates' statement in 2002 could just as easily apply to today's conditions: "Even though we're in an economic downturn, we're in an innovation upturn. I believe people are dramatically underestimating all the innovation going on in our industry, all the great products that are on the way, and the positive contribution that technology is making to our economy" (Gates, 2002, para. 2).

Ethics

Techno-enthusiastic instructors should be cautious of creating the "creepy treehouse" effect, which is "an institutionally controlled technology/tool that emulates or mimics pre-existing technologies or tools that may already be in use by the learners, or by learners' peer groups. Though such systems may be seen as innovative or problem-solving to the institution, they may repulse some users who see them as infringement on the sanctity of their peer groups, or as having the potential for institutional violations of their privacy, liberty, ownership, or creativity" (Stein, 2008, para. 3). One way to avoid the creepy treehouse effect is to make participation in these technology activities optional. Other ethical issues that may be encountered when using technology include determining intellectual property rights (e.g., authorship of wiki or other collaborative content) and copyright infringement (e.g., plagiarizing content posted on Web sites). Thus, institutions, faculty, and students who choose to adopt new instructional technologies should be aware of the potential limitations and ethical issues associated with their use (Millis et al., 2009).

Accessibility for Individuals with Disabilities

Although not always obvious to technology designers, new technologies must be accessible to those who have disabilities. In Illinois, a law was recently passed that requires employees of state institutions to make hardware and software, Web content, and multimedia content accessible to individuals with visual, auditory, or other impairments (see http://www.dhs.state.il.us/page.aspx?item=32765). Thus, faculty in Illinois who create Web pages or other electronically accessible content are required to meet these criteria, for example, by adding closed captioning to videos posted online. On a broader scale, all instructors should feel obligated to help reduce instead of enlarge the digital divide.

Assessment

A final challenge for instructors is the assessment of a technology's effectiveness. As recommended by Millis et al. (2009), instructors should base their decisions about the use of technology on empirical evidence. As is the case with many of the technologies described in this chapter, data on effectiveness are lacking. Therefore, early adopters of new technology should carry the burden of establishing empirical evidence, paying particular attention to how the technology interacts with instructor and student characteristics to create an optimal learning environment (Millis et al., 2009).

Conclusion

Technology is not going away. Some technologies, like electronic grade books or e-textbooks, help instructors and students do things more quickly or efficiently and are arguably "just tools." In contrast, other technologies, such as GPS-enabled mobile devices and data mashups, are more than tools. These technologies are changing the way instructors and students interact with each other and with their physical environment, creating avenues of instruction never before imagined. As new technologies emerge, research is needed to assess empirically the impact of the technology on common measures of program effectiveness, including student performance, satisfaction, and skills (Dunn, McCarthy, Baker, Halonen, & Hill, 2007). In the future, what visible role will technology have in the process of teaching and learning? "The most profound technologies are those that disappear. They weave themselves into the fabric of everyday life until they are indistinguishable from it" (Weiser, 1991, p. 94).

References

Alloway, T., Wilson, G., Graham, J., & Krames, L. (2000). *Sniffy the virtual rat, pro version*. USA: Wadsworth.

Beecham, A. (2006, November 26). *Project moonwalk*. Retrieved May 5, 2009, from http://www.createascape.org.uk/scrapbook/teachers/case_01.html

Carr, N. (2008, July/August). *Is Google making us stupid? The Atlantic, 301*. Retrieved May 4, 2009, from http://www.theatlantic.com/doc/200807/google

Chapel, E. (2008). Mobile technology: The foundation for an engaged and secure campus community. *Journal of Computing in Higher Education, 20,* 15–23.

Clark, A., & Chalmers, D. (1998). The extended mind. *Analysis, 58,* 7.

comScore. (2009, February 4). *U.S. Online video viewing surges 13 percent in record-setting December.* Retrieved May 4, 2009, from http://www.comscore.com/press/release.asp?press=2714

Dunn, D. S., McCarthy, M. A., Baker, S., Halonen, J. S., & Hill, G. W. I. V. (2007). Quality benchmarks in undergraduate psychology programs. *American Psychologist, 62,* 650–670.

Gates, B. (2002, Nov. 17). *Remarks by Bill Gates: Keynote, COMDEX fall 2002.* Retrieved May 5, 2009, from http://www.microsoft.com/presspass/exec/billg/speeches/2002/11-17comdex.aspx

Graesser, A. C., Chipman, P., & King, B. G. (2008). Computer-mediated technologies. In: J. M. Spector, M. D. Merrill, J. J. G. Merrienboer, & M. P. Driscoll (eds.), *Handbook of research on educational communications and technology* (3rd ed., pp. 211–224). London: Taylor & Francis.

Gurung, R. A. R., & Martin, R. (in press). Predicting textbook reading: The textbook assessment and usage scale. *Teaching of Psychology.*

John, P. D., & Wheeler, S. (2008). *The digital classroom: Harnessing technology for the future of learning and teaching.* New York: Routledge.

Johnson, L., Levine, A., & Smith, R. (2008). *The 2008 Horizon Report.* Austin, TX: The New Media Consortium. Retrieved from http://www.nmc.org/horizon.

Johnson, L., Levine, A., & Smith, R. (2009). *The 2009 Horizon Report.* Austin, TX: The New Media Consortium. Retrieved from http://www.nmc.org/horizon.

McCabe, D. L., Trevino, L. K., & Butterfield, K. D. (2001). Cheating in academic institutions: A decade of research. *Ethics & Behavior, 11,* 219–232. doi: 10.1207/S15327019EB1103_2

McKinney, D., Dyck, J. L., & Luber, E. S. (2009). iTunes university and the classroom: Can podcasts replace professors? *Computers & Education, 52,* 617–623. doi: 10.1016/j.compedu.2008.11.004

Millis, K., Baker, S., Blakemore, J., Connington, F., Harper, Y., Hung, W.-C., et al. (2009). Teaching and learning in a digital world. In: D. F. Halpern (ed.), *Undergraduate education in psychology: A blueprint for the future of the discipline.* Washington, DC: American Psychological Association.

Nelson, M. R. (2008). *Is higher education ready to switch to digital course materials? The Chronicle of Higher Education, 55,* A29–A29. Available at http://search.ebscohost.com/login.aspx?direct=true&db=aph&AN=35605268&site=ehost-live

Pew Internet & American Life Project. (2008, December). *Usage over time.* Retrieved May 5, 2009, from http://www.pewinternet.org/Static-Pages/Data-Tools/Download-Data/Trend-Data.aspx

Plato. (1925). Phaedrus (H. N. Fowler, Trans.). In: *Plato in twelve volumes* (Vol. 9). Cambridge, MA: Harvard University Press. Retrieved March 5, 2009, from http://www.perseus.tufts.edu/hopper/

Resnick, M. (1994). *Turtle, termites, and traffic jams.* Cambridge, MA: MIT Press.

Salaway, G., Caruso, J. B., & Nelson, M. R. (2007). The ECAR study of undergraduate students and information technology. Retrieved Aug. 5, 2009, from http://www.educause.edu/ecar

Salaway, G., Caruso, J. B., & Nelson, M. R. (2008). The ECAR study of undergraduate students and information technology. Retrieved May 5, 2009, from http://www.educause.edu/ecar

Shepperd, J. A., Grace, J. L., & Koch, E. J. (2008). Evaluating the electronic textbook: Is it time to dispense with the paper text? *Teaching of Psychology, 35*, 2–5. doi: 10.1080/00986280701818532

Stein, J. (2008, April 9). *Defining "creepy treehouse."* Retrieved May 5, 2009, from http://flexknowlogy.learningfield.org/2008/04/09/defining-creepy-tree-house/

Stowell, J. R., & Nelson, J. M. (2007). Benefits of electronic audience response systems on student participation, learning, and emotion. *Teaching of Psychology, 34*, 253–258. doi: 10.1080/00986280701700391

Vernon, R. F. (2006*). Teaching notes: Paper or pixels? An inquiry into how students adapt to online textbooks. Journal of Social Work Education, 42*, 417–427. Retrieved March 12, 2009, from http://search.ebscohost.com/login.aspx?direct=true&db=aph&AN=21216941&site=ehost-live

Weiser, M. (1991). The computer for the 21st century. *Scientific American, 265*, 94–104.

Yaqoob, T. (2006, September 24). *Exam halls could be insulated to stop mobile phone cheats.* Retrieved May 4, 2009, from http://www.dailymail.co.uk/news/article-406771/Exam-halls-insulated-stop-mobile-phone-cheats.html

Young, J. (2008, December 15). *Mobile college app: Turning iPhones into 'super-clickers' for classroom feedback. The Chronicle of Higher Education: Information Technology.* Retrieved May 4, 2009, from http://chronicle.com/wiredcampus/article/3518/mobile-college-app-turning-iphones-into-super-clickers-for-classroom-feedback

Zimmer, C. (2009, February). *How Google is making us smarter. Discover.* Retrieved May 4, 2009, from http://discovermagazine.com/2009/feb/15-how-google-is-making-us-smarter

Author Index

Subject Index

About the Editors

*D*ana *S. Dunn,* a social psychologist, is professor of psychology and direc-
tor of the Learning in Common Curriculum at Moravian College,
Bethlehem, PA. He received his PhD from the University of Virginia and his
BA in psychology from Carnegie Mellon University. A Fellow of the American
Psychological Association, Dunn served as President of the Society for the
Teaching of Psychology (STP) in 2010. Former Chair of Moravian's Department
of Psychology, Dunn writes frequently about his areas of research interest:
the teaching of psychology, social psychology, and rehabilitation psychol-
ogy. Dunn is the author of five previous books—*Research Methods for Social
Psychology, The Practical Researcher: A Student Guide to Conducting
Psychological Research, Statistics and Data Analysis for the Behavioral
Sciences, A Short Guide to Writing about Psychology,* and *Psychology Applied
to Modern Life* (with Wayne Weiten and Elizabeth Y. Hammer)—and the co-
editor of five others—*Measuring Up: Educational Assessment Challenges and
Practices for Psychology* (with Chandra M. Mehrotra and Jane S. Halonen),
Best Practices for Teaching Introduction to Psychology (with Stephen L.
Chew), *Best Practices for Teaching Statistics and Research Methods in the
Behavioral Sciences* (with Randolph Smith and Bernard C. Beins), *Teaching
Critical Thinking in Psychology: A Handbook of Best Practices* (with Jane S.
Halonen and Randolph Smith), and *Best Practices for Teaching Beginnings*

and Endings in the Psychology Major: Research, Cases, and Recommendations (with Bernard C. Beins, Maureen A. McCarthy, and G. William Hill, IV).

Janie H. Wilson, an experimental psychologist, is a professor of psychology at Georgia Southern University, where she has been teaching and conducting research for more than 15 years. Wilson earned her PhD at the University of South Carolina and her BS at the College of Charleston. Her research focuses on physiological and social questions; research projects recently transitioned from rats to humans. She also conducts research in teaching, particularly in the area of building rapport with students. One of her areas of specialization is teaching undergraduate statistics, for which she published a textbook, *Essential Statistics* (Pearson Prentice Hall). Wilson served as the STP's Program Chair for the American Psychological Association annual conference for 3 years, a position that entails creating a 4-day teaching-focused program for the convention. She currently enjoys working with STP as Program Director. Responsibilities include planning the annual Best Practices in Teaching Psychology conference series as well as an annual online conference to enhance teaching and learning.

James E. Freeman, an experimental psychologist, is a professor of psychology and director of undergraduate studies at the University of Virginia. He earned his AB degree at California State University–Long Beach and his PhD at Bowling Green State University. He primarily teaches research methods and statistics classes. Freeman has been a consultant to Educational Testing Service (ETS) for many years, as an AP Psychology reader, and served on three test development committees: AP Psychology, Graduate Record Exam (GRE)–Psychology, and Major Fields Test (MFT)–Psychology. He is a Fellow in the American Psychological Association and has had various positions of responsibility with the STP and with the Commission on Ethnic Minority Recruitment, Retention, and Training (CEMRRAT) in Psychology.

Jeffrey R. Stowell, a biological psychologist, is an associate professor at Eastern Illinois University in Charleston, IL. He earned his Master's degree in general psychology at Brigham Young University and his PhD in psychobiology at the Ohio State University, where he also did postdoctoral research on marital stress and wound healing. He conducts research on the psychological factors, particularly test anxiety and coping behaviors, that influence endocrine function and, secondly, the use of technology to increase student engagement and learning. He currently serves as the Internet Editor for the STP and has won several teaching awards, including the STP's Early Career Teaching Excellence Award.